Palestinian Ethnonationalism in Israel

NATIONAL AND ETHNIC CONFLICT
IN THE TWENTY-FIRST CENTURY

Brendan O'Leary, Series Editor

PALESTINIAN
ETHNONATIONALISM
IN ISRAEL

Oded Haklai

PENN

UNIVERSITY OF PENNSYLVANIA PRESS

PHILADELPHIA

Published by
University of Pennsylvania Press
Philadelphia, Pennsylvania 19104-4112
www.upenn.edu/pennpress

Printed in the United States of America
on acid-free paper
10 9 8 7 6 5 4 3 2 1

Library of Congress Cataloging-in-Publication Data
ISBN 978-0-8122-4347-5

For Na'ama, Maya, and Tom

Contents

A Note on Transliteration

There is no unanimity regarding the best approach to transliteration of Arabic. In this book, I sought to balance between academic conventions and accessibility to non-Arabic speakers. Diacritical marks for Hamzah and ʿAyn are used, except for where persons or organizations have a preferred spelling of their name in English or are commonly known by a different transliteration (thus, Adalah instead of ʿAdalah). Otherwise, when necessary to choose between readability and academic conventions, I preferred to err on the side of readability. Meticulous readers may find minor inconsistencies. I hope the choices made are worth the benefits that emerge from increasing accessibility.

Introduction

Palestinian ethnonational political activism in Israel has increased dramatically in recent decades. Since the early 1990s, numerous ethnically exclusive Palestinian Arab political parties and organizations have emerged, making ethnic claims on the state. These groups are demanding that the state recognize the Palestinian Arab Citizens of Israel (PAI) as an indigenous and national minority in Israel, that the exclusive Jewish identity of the state be replaced with a binational institutional framework, that there be power-sharing institutional arrangements, and that the PAI be granted extensive autonomy in a variety of cultural and social spheres. These demands, which had been only sporadically asserted in the past, have become the centerpiece of PAI political activism in the last two decades.

PAI politics have not always been overtly ethnonationalist. Until the 1970s, the PAI minority was described as quiescent.[1] In the 1970s and 1980s, the minority mobilized mostly through the Communist Party for social equality and integration into the state such that the Minorities at Risk Project (MAR) classified it as an *ethnoclass*—a category that reflects an inferior socioeconomic status—rather than as a national minority.[2] Although this minority's political expression of nationhood is not an event that occurred suddenly, it is only since the 1990s that ethnically exclusive PAI political and social organizations have been proliferating, increasingly mobilizing in the name of Palestinian nationalism in Israel, and making ethnonational demands on the state. What explains these transitions in the characteristics of PAI political activism?

The theoretical issues that arise from the transition in PAI mobilization strategies are not limited just to this case. Many disadvantaged ethnic minorities live in states dominated by majorities. Their mobilization strategies vary, as do the demands they make. Some groups demand the deethnicization of politics and public space, some embark on an ethnonationalist path, and some minority groups do not independently mobilize at all. In many cases, an ethnic group changes its political strategies and demands over time. Theoretically, we know surprisingly little about how such a process unfolds. What explains variations in the characteristics of minority political mobilization? How and why do the political paths followed by disadvantaged minorities change over time? What conditions are conducive to the emergence of minority ethnonational political activism in particular? By analyzing the transitions in PAI political activism, this book aims to generate theoretical insights into these questions.

In a nutshell, this book argues that transitions in the character and scope of PAI mobilization are largely a result of changes in the institutional structure of the Israeli state. Growing political fragmentation and state retreat from key areas in public life, coupled with continuous lack of state autonomy from the Jewish majority, has generated changes in minority mobilization and proved conducive to ethnonationalist minority political activism by multiple organizations claiming to speak on behalf of the minority. The changes in the institutional configuration were themselves a product of internal contestation within the dominant Jewish majority.

Conflict, Minority Political Organizations, and Demands

Multiethnic societies are by no means doomed to be plagued by strife. In many multiethnic societies around the world, ethnicity is not a politically salient factor, and diversity and cosmopolitanism are celebrated. At the same time, there can be no doubt that in many cases ethnic heterogeneity has been characterized by mistrust, intergroup antipathy, and ethnicity-based nationalism and seclusion, particularly in states that are controlled by a dominant ethnic group. Whatever the causes of ethnic conflict—and the vast literature on the topic is divided on this question[3]—one issue should be clear: when society is deeply divided, both majorities and minorities typically organize along ethnic lines and make ethnic claims.

Studies of ethnic politics tend to conflate ethnic groups with their political organizations. Ethnic minority groups (and majorities) never constitute similar actors that mobilize cohesively to advance a uniformly agreed-upon agenda. Rather, it is ethnically based organizations that engage in political activism and claim to speak on behalf of the minority. Thus, more often than not, what discussions of minority political mobilization and demands are really dealing with is the mobilization of ethnically based organizations that claim to represent the ethnic minority and advance its interests. This book focuses on ethnically based organizations as primary actors in minority political activism.

Societies that are deeply divided along ethnic lines typically produce ethnically exclusive organizations such as political parties[4] and nonparliamentary ethnic organizations that claim to represent group interests. Because it is these organizations that mobilize in the name of the minority, minority politics as a whole are defined not by mass sentiments but by the mobilization strategies and the types of demands made by minority group political organizations. It could conceivably be the case that masses belonging to a minority group will hold distinct ethnonational sentiments but, lacking political organizations, will not mobilize. In such a scenario, there is no minority ethnonational politics to speak of. Conversely, there could also be a situation in which a dominant political organization (or several leading organizations) will advance an ethnonationalist agenda in the absence of strong ethnonational sentiments among many individuals belonging to the minority group. Under these circumstances, the minority's main political path is defined as ethnonational. Thus, *minority political activism* refers to the activism of ethnically based organizations, *minority demands* refers to demands made by political organizations on behalf of the minority, and *minority ethnonationalism* refers to ethnonationalist claims made by leading organizations in the name of the minority.

Ethnically based organizations can vary along several important dimensions, including not only their ideology and the agenda they promote, but also their capabilities, their methods of mobilization, and their level of support among members of their ethnic group. Furthermore, the organizational structure of minority groups varies considerably from case to case and over time. In some cases, a single political organization dominates the minority's political activism and makes claims on its behalf (for example, the Movement for Rights and Freedom, MRF, representing the Turkish minority in Bulgaria). In other cases, a wide range of political organizations might arise to speak in the name of a single minority group (for example, the Coexistentia, the Hungarian Christian Democratic Movement, and the Hungarian Civic Party in Slovakia, before they merged into a single party in 1998). In some cases, disadvantaged minorities do not form significant political organizations at all (for example, Russian speakers in Estonia in the early 1990s).

The contours of minority organizational structure can have a profound effect on the path of minority political activism.

The Palestinian Arab Citizens of Israel

In 2006 and 2007, several leading Palestinian Arab organizations in Israel triggered a fiery public debate when they published a number of proposals and position papers that made national claims on behalf of the Palestinian Arab citizens of Israel. The Future Vision Documents, as they became known, demanded that the state recognize Palestinian refugees' claims to right of return to Israel, called for the abolition of the Jewish character of Israel, and proposed instead a new binational and power-sharing institutional arrangement alongside a Palestinian state in the West Bank and Gaza.[5] One leading advocacy group was reported to be considering proposing a single constitution for a "supranational regime in all of historic Palestine."[6] Prominent public figures from the Jewish majority, from the right and the left, responded with outrage.[7] Meanwhile, the head of the Shin Bet, Israel's security agency, sent a letter to one of the organizations involved, in which he reportedly warned that his agency has the authority to curtail political activities aimed against the Jewish character of the state and its foundational principles.[8]

Until the publication of the Future Vision Documents, changing relations between the state and the PAI, which constituted close to 20 percent of Israel's population in 2010, engendered relatively little public debate, because the attention of Israeli Jews and the international community at large has been focused on the conflict between Israel and the Palestinians in the West Bank and Gaza. Although not all politicians and observers have been oblivious to the rising tensions and expressions of PAI ethnonationalism, the overwhelming majority of policymakers have preferred to sidestep the question of Palestinian nationalism within Israel.[9] The vociferous demands made by this minority's leaders, however, constitute a call to stop ignoring the PAI's position as they view themselves as a significant component in the regional dispute.

If Palestinian ethnonationalist political activism in Israel is a relatively recent phenomenon, Palestinian marginalization is not. The Palestinian Arab citizens of Israel were a subordinate group from the onset. Israel was established in 1948 on the foundations of an array of prestate institutions constructed by the Zionist movement, which sought to create a national home for the Jewish nation in its perceived historic homeland. Under the reign of the British Mandatory state in Palestine, institutions were established in accordance with the values and objectives of the Jewish national movement. These goals included encouraging Jewish immigration, acquisition (or redemption) of land, the consolidation of a Jewish majority, and ultimately, the attainment of Jewish sovereignty. Prestate values, objectives, and dominant forces became embedded within the state when many of the Jewish community's institutions transformed into the state apparatus upon independence. Hence, although Israel's Declaration of Independence promised the PAI minority formal access to politics through the foundation of democratic procedures, the lack of state neutrality left this minority on the margins of the Jewish state.[10]

The establishment of Israel has been depicted by many scholars as a devastating event for the Palestine Arabs who found themselves inside the territory of the new Jewish state.[11] Having been led to believe by local leaders and by leaders of neighboring Arab states that the new Israeli state was *maz'umah* (make-believe/alleged) and ephemeral, they witnessed Arab governments in 1949 signing armistice agreements with Israel that would end the war, leaving approximately 156,000 Palestine Arabs residing within Israel and separated from their ethnic kin by the new borders. Over a very short period of time, they turned from a majority in the region into a minority within Israel. Not only were they isolated from the rest of the Arabs in the Middle East because of the Arab-Israeli conflict, but they were also left outside the social boundaries of the nation controlling the new state in which they resided. They did not share collective values or a historical memory with the dominant Jewish community, and they were differentiated from the Jewish majority culturally, linguistically, occupationally, and geographically. Whereas the Jewish majority spoke Hebrew, the PAI spoke Arabic. And whereas most of the Jewish community resided in urban areas and the Jewish economy was industrializing, the Arabs were mostly rural (although some lived in mixed cities). The Jewish majority greeted the new Jewish state with collective joy, but the PAI minority labeled Israel's birth *al-Nakba* (the catastrophe).

Despite being marginalized, the PAI did not immediately mobilize. From 1949 to the end of the 1960s, PAI involvement in Israeli politics was characterized by what Ian Lustick referred to as quiescence, whereby independent political activism rarely existed.[12] During this period, the PAI were generally co-opted by the ruling party, Mapa'i, the predecessor of the contemporary Labor Party. Attempts to organize separately from the Jewish political forces, when they did take place, were quashed by state authorities, which considered the PAI a security threat and subjected it to a military government until 1966.[13]

In the late 1960s and early 1970s, leaders of the PAI gradually began to independently mobilize, although not on an ethnically exclusive basis. With some exceptions, most of their political activity was dominated by the Communist Party, Rakah. It defined itself as a bi-national party and called for equal distribution of resources based on socialist principles instead of ethnic-national criteria, such that MAR identified the PAI as an ethnoclass rather than as an ethnonation or a national minority.[14] At this stage, political action sought mostly after an ethnically blind, civic public sphere coupled with a strong central state, both of which are compatible with a socialist vision. Rakah advocated the integration of the PAI into the redistributive central state, even though the party also called for the state to recognize the Arabs as a national minority and strong elements of national consciousness were gaining salience.[15]

Ethnonational politics have come to the forefront forcefully in the 1990s. The ethnonational turn has been reflected in several ways. First, "there has been a steady increase in the tendency to describe the collective identity of the Arab population as Palestinian," and to view this label as standing out against the civic identity.[16] Additionally, exclusively PAI parties, including ADP (Arab Democratic Party), Balad, and Ta'al, have emerged alongside numerous ethnicity-based civil society organizations.[17] The Islamic movement has also experienced a significant increase in popularity. These PAI political forces have been increasingly making demands for a distinct PAI public sphere and a constitutionally entrenched recognition of collective rights, basing their claims on the position that they ought to be recognized as a national and indigenous minority dispossessed by more recent settlers from Europe.[18] Unlike the communist ideology that sought to construct a unifying civic identity and espoused a penetrative central state with redistributive capacity, the ethnonational activists demand both state disentanglement from Jewish hegemony and state retreat from minority public space, where the PAI can build autonomous and exclusive minority national institutions with sole authority over issues pertaining to minority culture, education, and religious and social life.[19]

These are just general patterns, of course. Ethnonationalist political organizations existed prior to the 1990s, but they were on the political fringes. Likewise, contemporary activism is far from unidimensional despite the visible changes in the broader picture. Notwithstanding deviation from the general patterns, we cannot begin to understand and evaluate the politics of the PAI minority unless we see how their organizations and claims have changed over time.

The Argument in Brief

Much of the literature on the PAI stresses the grievances that arise from this minority's subordinate position.[20] According to grievance-based accounts, political, economic, and social inequality is the main reason for PAI mobilization and demands. To be sure, grievances are undoubtedly necessary for mobilization. Without grievances, there would be no reason for anyone to be politically active. Yet, the underlying causes of PAI grievances have remained relatively consistent since the 1950s, and this minority's position in Israel was certainly not better when it was quiescent in the 1950s and 1960s. Thus, grievances alone cannot explain variation over time in the character and scope of PAI political activism, nor the changing demands made by this minority's political organizations.

In contrast to grievance-based arguments, I argue that the increase in vociferous PAI ethnonational mobilization is a result of changes in the institutional structures of the Israeli state. Specifically, the fragmentation of political authority in Israel, coupled with the sustained lack of state autonomy from Jewish nationalism, have engendered conditions conducive to ethnonationalist minority political activism by multiple organizations claiming to speak on behalf of the minority. The Israeli state has seen the cohesion and extensiveness of its institutional infrastructure decline considerably over several decades, a transformation that increased the opportunities available for minority mobilization and encouraged multiple organizations to form. At the same time, the Jewish majority controlling the state has resisted demands to make the state more ethnically neutral, effectively rendering efforts to deethnicize public life futile.

It should be stressed that the changes in the state's institutional structure were themselves a product of social changes, primarily within the Jewish majority. Although the Jewish majority has retained high levels of support for maintaining Jewish ownership of the state, it has increasingly become internally fractured along other lines. The dominance of early state elites declined in the 1970s, and multiple Jewish-based organized forces have emerged, challenging each other for power and access to resources. Their ongoing contestation has led to the dispersion of authority and power away from the central government to other institutions and social organizations, including the judiciary, civil society, and private actors in the economy. Thus, the argument advanced in this book stresses the ongoing, dynamic, and mutually transformative state-society interaction.

This argument can be read in a different way: Changes in PAI political mobilization mirror changes in Israeli politics at large. Since Israel's independence, key dimensions of Israeli politics, economy, and society have liberalized, but the ethnic character of the state has not. Immediately after independence, there was a hegemonic political party, and the state performed many economic and social functions. Israel gradually transitioned to more competitive politics and a more liberalized economy and social activism. Multiple political parties and civil society organizations representing a wide spectrum of interests and internal groupings have emerged. Concurrent with these transitions, Israeli politics has become more divided and parochial. The rise of PAI political activism is part and parcel of this overarching transformation. As the boundaries of exclusion from the center of politics have remained impermeable to the minority, PAI parochialism has taken on a particularly ethnonationalist form.

A Brief Note on Changes in the International Environment

The focus on the interactive effect between state institutions and the actions of groups facing those institutions should not be interpreted as aiming to downplay the role of international factors. Clearly, any nuanced discussion of the factors that shape the dynamic of ethnic conflict must take changes in the international environment into account. Scholars have long emphasized the role of international organizations and norms in the politics of ethnic conflict and state-minority relations.[21] The evolution of international regimes has encouraged rule-motivated activity that affects relationships not only among states but also within states. Most notably, international treaties and declarations have introduced norms about how states—and by extension, dominant groups—have to treat minorities residing under their jurisdiction. Global and regional treaties and declarations calling for respectful and equal treatment of minorities include, but are not limited to, the International Covenant on Civil and Political Rights; the International Covenant on the Elimination of All Forms of Racial Discrimination; the Declaration on the Rights of Persons

Belonging to National or Ethnic, Religious and Linguistic Minorities; and the Declaration on the Rights of Indigenous Peoples. Although treaties and declarations of this sort are not judicially enforceable, in some circumstances—for example, when states wish to be integrated into regional or international organizations and regarded as advanced democracies—they can influence state behavior and provide openings for subordinate group mobilization.[22] In the words of Will Kymlicka, "States are increasingly monitored and judged for how well they comply with these norms, and failure to comply has resulted not only in criticism, but also, in some cases, in tangible consequences."[23]

However, changes in international norms and in the activities of international organizations have not affected all countries to the same degree. Some regimes have continued to repress ethnic opponents. In Syria, the Alawi minority regime continues to use coercive methods to curtail Sunni majority politicization, and in Burma, the military junta suppresses Shan and Karen opposition irrespective of international criticism. In Turkey, the central government continues to deny collective rights to the Kurds despite pressure from the European Union, and even though such pressure has contributed to the adoption of minority-friendly policies in other countries that sought accession to the EU.[24] Changes in the international environment undoubtedly play an important role, yet their impact on majority-minority politics is conditioned by state attributes and the preferences and resources of the dominant group within the state. Analysis of state-society relations must form the core of any comprehensive explanation. In this book, I do not ignore changes in the international environment; rather, I provide a systematic analysis of how such changes interact with the domestic politics of state-society relations.

Studying a "Unique Case"

Academics researching the Israeli-Palestinian conflict know that one will be hard pressed to find studies of political issues that stir so many passionate debates and that are animated by such intense normative controversies as those relating to Palestinian-Jewish relations. One example is the debate around the question of whether PAI transition from quiescence to political activism constitutes radicalization or "merely" politicization.[25] By now, this debate has run its course and is of little relevance. Whether ethnonational and Islamic political activism should be labeled radical is primarily a normative question that hinges on the analyst's personal position.

An additional loaded question is the label attached to the minority group. Israeli state officials have traditionally referred to the minority as Israeli Arabs. This label has been rejected by Arab elites because it is perceived to denote state superiority over minority identity. Public opinion surveys conducted over the years reveal that the minority itself holds diverse, multiple, and frequently changing views about the most appropriate collective label. Many attribute utmost significance to the Arab component of their identity. Some view themselves as Palestinians, indistinct from the Palestinians in the West Bank and Gaza, and hold that their national identity is primary to civic association with Israel.[26] To a large extent, self-identification labels reflect a changing social context and the social meaning of the label.[27] Some have argued that by adopting the language and labels of the ethnic groups under study, scholars are contributing to the reification of ethnic identities.[28] Notwithstanding these cautionary criticisms, I have chosen to use the encompassing label PAI because it is the label that comes closest to capturing all three national and civic dimensions of the minority's self-perception and social context. I use it interchangeably with Arab as shorthand. This choice, however, ought not to be read as endorsing the superiority of either ethno-communal or civic forms of association.

Finally, scholars have also been squabbling over whether the institutional arrangement that has been engendered by Israel's lack of state neutrality should be labeled *ethnic democracy*[29] or, alternatively, *ethnocracy*—a term that rejects the classification of Israel as democratic.[30] As Alan Dowty astutely observed, this dispute is more about labels than substance, as the scholars involved agree on the description of Israel's state institutions and on the actual substantive position of the non-Jewish minority in Israel.[31] Ruth Gavizon emphasized that, ultimately, underlying this debate are moral evaluations of Israel rather than deep conceptual or theoretical disagreements.[32]

The main problem involved in normatively motivated analyses of Israel and the PAI is that too often, the standards used to evaluate this case are not the same standards used to assess other cases and therefore undermine the credibility of the analyses. In order to offset this pitfall, it is of utmost importance that this case be studied through theoretical lenses used to study other instances of ethnic politics in deeply divided societies. Studies of Israel have often unduly treated Israel as an incomparable, unique case for which generally available theoretical claims and categories do not apply.[33] Concerns about state-minority and majority-minority relations, however, are of global relevance, and the lack of theoretical depth and comparative perspective hinders the ability to produce valid inferences. Theoretically informed analysis offers a measure of distance between the researcher and the subject of research. In this particular instance, theories of ethnic conflict, coupled with theories of state-society relations, can contribute to the explanation of changes in PAI political strategies by providing useful analytical tools that are employed to study similar phenomena in other parts of the world and ensure that this case is studied like any other case.

Studying the PAI in this way has an added benefit. Not only will it increase the potential for arriving at more credible conclusions, but it will also enhance the prospects of generating generalizable theoretical insights with relevance to other cases of deeply divided societies. Having shifted political leanings over the last sixty years, the case of the PAI provides a good opportunity for evaluating rival explanations for minority activism proposed by competing theories of ethnic conflict. Investigating the identical group in the same country at different points in time allows us to attain a relatively high degree of what King, Keohane, and Verba refer to as *unit homogeneity*.[34] A single case with diachronic variation provides more than one theoretically relevant observation, as is true for a synchronistic comparison of several different cases.[35] Although the general contexts and circumstances remain similar, the variation in outcome is largely explained by changes in particular conditions over time. Thus, this research approach enables us to examine whether the diachronic variation in minority behavior is accompanied by changes in what the rival theories identify as the explanatory variables.

Overview

Political organizations are the actors that mobilize in the name of ethnic groups. Existing institutional arrangements influence the modes of political activism, organizational structure, and political demands made by organized minority political actors. When institutional configurations change, so do the opportunities, incentive structures, and capabilities of disadvantaged minorities in ethnically dominated states. In Israel, increasing fragmentation among the dominant group led to institutional changes and liberalization in the political, social, and economic spheres that provided greater opportunities for ethnically exclusive minority political mobilization. At the same time, the ethnically exclusive character of the state has not changed, thus influencing the preferences of the mobilizing organizations.

Chapter 1 provides the theoretical foundations for the argument, develops the causal logic that was introduced in this chapter, and provides an illustrative application of the theoretical framework to the PAI case. Chapter 2, in the way of background, discusses the origins of the Jewish state and the process of Israel's state formation during the period of British rule in Palestine. It begins by providing a comparative lens for state formation. It then examines the institutional characteristics of the British Mandatory state, as well as Jewish and Arab group characteristics that explain why initial state attributes took the particular form that they did. On these foundations, Chapter 3 discusses the relative consistence in Israel's lack of state autonomy and PAI grievances over six decades, demonstrating why these factors alone cannot explain transitions in scope and character of PAI political activism.

Chapter 4 discusses the transition of PAI politics from quiescence to independent mobilization in the self-defined binational Communist Party. The discussion elaborates in detail the manifestation of PAI political organization and mobilization, and then proceeds to examine changing state attributes in order to demonstrate their effect on the political path of the PAI. Chapter 5 discusses the various contemporary forms and facets of PAI ethnonational politics. The chapter highlights changes in group demands and organizational structure, explaining how the new political actors that have emerged contributed to the consolidation of ethnonationalist political activism. Chapter 6 explains the state-society origins of the ethnonational turn. In order to make the analysis intelligible, I have attempted to organize the discussion along the lines of the framework's various constituents, even though they are interactive and the framework, in its attempt to capture transition, is necessarily dynamic. After examining preference transformation, the discussion proceeds to analyze changes in the institutional setting, most conspicuously state cohesion and state extensiveness, as well as the societal sources of these institutional changes, in order to demonstrate their effect on the consolidation of PAI ethnonational politics. The conclusion ties the empirical study to theory, highlighting the general lessons that can be drawn from the case. The book ends with a brief note on the policy implications of the analysis for majority-minority relations in Israel.

1

Transitions in Minority Political Activism, Grievances, and Institutional Configurations

The transformation of PAI political mobilization has been manifested in changing demands, as well as in the intensity and the channels through which the demands are made. During the first two decades of Israel's existence, the PAI were compliant. Throughout the 1970s and early 1980s, the Communist Party, which claimed to be biethnic and to advance an inclusive civic identity, was the primary channel for Arab mobilization in Israel. In recent decades, ethnically based political organizations have proliferated, making vociferous claims against the state in the name of minority nationalism.

Informed by social inequality and relative deprivation theories, many comparative and area studies analysts of minority political activism have stressed disparities, differential status, and minority grievances as the underlying cause behind ethnic mobilization.[1] These approaches have made considerable inroads into analyses of the PAI.[2] Changes in the demands presented by PAI organizations, however, have not been accompanied by changes in disparities and grievances. The unequal status of this minority and its negative sentiments toward its inferior status long preexisted the proliferation of ethnically based organizations that advance ethnically defined minority nationalism.

The transition that the PAI has undergone is largely a result of the institutional structure of the Israeli state. Profound changes in key domestic institutions in Israel, while other institutions have retained their defining characteristics, have produced an institutional configuration conducive to the politics of parochialism and minority ethnonationalist mobilization. On the one hand, Israel has always been characterized by a lack of state autonomy from the Jewish majority. Despite minority efforts to disentangle the state from Jewish domination, this trait has remained relatively stable. At the same time, the central government's capacity to coerce the minority into compliance has eroded considerably as a consequence of increasing institutional fragmentation and a substantial retreat of the state from many aspects of public life. These institutional changes themselves came about as a result of factionalism and internal contestation within the dominant Jewish majority.

Indeed, to a large extent Israeli politics, economy, and society have undergone a tremendous liberalization process since the 1980s, shifting the balance of power away from the central government and toward other institutions and organized social forces. At the same time, one key institutional characteristic has not liberalized: the formal ownership of the state by the Jewish majority. Israel is a state that lacks autonomy from the Jewish majority. It is the impact of these institutional contours that largely explains transitions in PAI politics.

State Autonomy

The term *state autonomy* has generally been used in political science in reference to the ability of the state to identify and pursue objectives beyond the demands and interests of organized social groups.[3] The extent of state autonomy is directly and negatively related to the ability of a dominant group to penetrate into the state apparatus and appropriate the state. State penetration enables the dominant group to influence state practices that affect ethnic power relations, status, and access to material and cultural resources from within the administrative apparatus. Extents of penetration range from a takeover of the state and its thorough subordination to group interests, to enclaves of support at some levels of the administration, to alliances with a handful of state officials in a single administrative office.[4]

Extensive penetration will frequently entail more than just having personnel and government officials of the dominant group occupying influential policy-making and policy implementation posts. It can also involve endowing the state with norms and ideologies that provide guideposts to state behavior that corresponds with group objectives—behavior that, in turn, legitimizes practices of uniethnic favoritism. Penetration, therefore, can influence the distribution of resources among communities and limit the ability of state institutions to formulate and pursue goals that are not simply reflective of the interests of the penetrating ethnic group.

At the extreme end of the continuum, penetration into the state is so deep that the penetrating ethnic group seizes control of the state and becomes so dominant that the state barely pursues goals beyond the group's demands and interests. In these situations the dominant group in effect, owns the state. The most extreme example is Apartheid South Africa, but there are many cases, like Malaysia, Thailand, Slovakia, Serbia, and Estonia where the extent of state autonomy from a dominant group has been very low as well. Conversely, in situations where the state remains insulated from ethnic forces and sustains or gains a large degree of autonomy, it can function as more of an arena for mediating and possibly accommodating communal relations, as, for example, in contemporary Canada. Most cases rest between these two polar ends, as the degree of state autonomy varies from state to state, but states are usually neither fully autonomous from dominant groups nor totally controlled by them.

The most important indicators of state autonomy are the ethnic identity of the head(s) of state and of the executive (and whether these positions are, formally or informally, reserved for a particular group), as well as the ethnic identity of the bulk of the personnel in the civil and military bureaucratic apparatuses.[5] It is when state officials are guided by a sense of mission on behalf of their group, and their position is dependent on serving the group, that state autonomy particularly decreases. The more one group has exclusive access to these positions of power, and the more government officials see themselves as representatives of their ethnic group, the more ethnocentric policies are to be expected. Conversely, when the governing echelon does not see itself as representing a privileged group, the possibility of resource distribution on the basis of nonethnic criteria is greater.

The norms and ideology embedded within the state also serve to indicate the degree of state autonomy. When societal values and norms that hold civic and cultural equality in high regard are ingrained in the state's ideological framework, more egalitarian practices are expected. Conversely, when the foundational principles of the state and its official ideology identify a core group whose interests the state is meant to serve, autonomy is low. The process of state formation is of paramount importance here, because during this process the foundational principles of the state set the platform for official state ideology, which then influences societal hierarchy and practices of distribution. As David Brown has observed, "In states with mono-ethnic national ideologies, the identity of the nation has come to be closely and explicitly associated with the values and attributes of the dominant cultural group in society."[6] Thus, the official values of the state serve to legitimize policies that favor the dominant group. The foundational principles and official ideology of the state, and the designation of formal languages, national holidays, and educational programs all provide guideposts for identifying to whom the state belongs.

Conspicuous examples of this kind of nonautonomous arrangements exist in practically all of the new states that were formed in Eastern Europe since 1991. Titular ethnic groups own all these states. To paraphrase Brubaker, they are "nationalizing" states that promote the interests of dominant majorities over minorities.[7] The lack of autonomy is manifested in the titular relationship between the majority group and the state, citizenship laws, language laws, and appointments in the state apparatus, among other things. For a long time, Estonia and Latvia made it extremely difficult for their large Russian minorities to obtain citizenship; Croatia forced out most of its Serbian population following a long and violent conflict; Slovakia, Romania, and most other new states adopted the language, culture, and symbols of the dominant majorities, even if sometimes offering scant protection of minority language. All of the new states ensured privileged dominant group access to the state apparatus.[8]

It is important to stress that autonomy is a dynamic variable. Its extent can change over time, frequently as a result of intergroup negotiation and contestation. Since the Quiet Revolution of the 1960s, for example, Canada has increasingly been shifting toward neutrality. Likewise, Romania and Macedonia have allowed increased minority access to politics.[9] Frequently, the activism of organizations that speak in the name of excluded minorities is implicitly focused on the issue of state autonomy.

In Israel the extent of state autonomy has remained relatively stable over the past six decades despite efforts made by PAI political organizations to change the situation. The lack of autonomy is manifested in the foundational principles of the state and its ideological and normative framework, as well as the societal identity of the personnel occupying high office in the central government and the bureaucracy. It translates into uniethnic favoritism in almost all policy areas. Israel's lack of state autonomy has grown out of the process of its state formation, an issue discussed in Chapter 2. The persistence of state autonomy and its implications for minority activism is the focus of Chapter 3.

Minority Demands and Ethnonationalism

It is only to be expected that most members of subordinate minorities in nonautonomous states will want to overcome their inferior position. Their responses differ between cases and over time: Russian speakers in Estonia did not organize and politicize for a very long time, Turks in Bulgaria mobilized primarily through a formally a-ethnic political party that called for deethnicization of public life, and Albanians in Macedonia fought a brief civil war to achieve a power-sharing arrangement. The experience of the PAI itself demonstrates vividly that a minority can react very differently to institutionalized disadvantage in different time periods.

Minority political activism is carried out by political organizations that form to speak in the group's name. The claims that organized leaders of ethnic minorities can make in the name of the minority vary a great deal. At one end of the spectrum, they can demand to de-ethnicize public life, essentially relegating ethnic identities to the private sphere. At the opposite end of the spectrum, ethnocentric organizations characteristically demand to privilege their group's ethnic identity in public life and to draw political boundaries around ethnicity.

Organizations that call for the deethnicization of public life typically demand that distribution of resources will be based on individual citizenship and social need rather than on ethnic criteria. They seek not only to make the state ethnically neutral, but also to make its policies ethnically blind. They may wish to retain their cultural identity but do not assign it political significance, thus allowing for political association on the basis of interests other than ethnic ones (and they are therefore more likely to organize on a multiethnic rather than an ethnically exclusive basis).[10] They accept the concept of a plural society in which the state is supposed to be neutral, such that all citizens, regardless of their background, are treated as individuals and have equal access to economic and political opportunities, although scholars doubt whether such neutrality can exist in practice.[11]

For parochial ethnically based organizations, on the other hand, politics revolves around substate communal identities, and these loyalties compete with, and in many cases override, civic attachments to the state. Political ethnically focused activism is characterized by demands for formal recognition of the minority as a separate community, coupled with transfer of political and social authority from the state to the ethnic community. Aspiring to make the communal boundaries—whether ethnic, linguistic, sectarian, or otherwise—congruent with political boundaries and the determining factor in distribution of resources, ethnically based organizations aim to disassociate the minority from other groups, either partially or altogether, by establishing ethnically exclusive social and political institutions.[12]

It should be noted that many hybrid options exist between these two ends, and that certain types of collective group rights can be seen as consistent with individual freedom and integration. Will Kymlicka, the influential Canadian scholar of multiculturalism, has long argued that granting collective group rights to a weaker minority can put it "on a more equal footing, by reducing the extent to which the smaller group is vulnerable to the larger."[13] In this context, ethnic differentiation as a basis for collective group rights can arguably facilitate the integration of individual members of the weaker minority group into the larger society, while also allowing them to preserve their cultural identity.

Minority nationalism, when pursued on an exclusive ethnic basis, constitutes one conspicuous form of ethnicity-centered mobilization. Although frequently associated with claims to statehood, minority nationalism can be manifested in other ways.[14] Rogers Brubaker has made the point that "minority nationalist stances characteristically involve a self-understanding in specifically 'national' rather than merely 'ethnic' terms, a demand for state recognition of their distinct ethnocultural nationality, and the assertion of certain collective, nationality-based cultural or political rights."[15] What defines minority ethnonationalism is that the claims are made on the basis of a distinct ethnically defined national identity. Moreover, such minority nationalism frequently occurs in states that are appropriated by an ethnically defined core nation, leaving the minority outside the national boundaries embodied by the state.

Recent PAI ethnonational mobilization fits neatly into this category. Israel was established as a Jewish state and has remained ethnonationally exclusive. PAI political organizations have been increasingly demanding formal recognition of the Palestinians in Israel as a national minority with collective group rights and a degree of autonomy to manage their own affairs. Therefore, although they are not demanding separate statehood, the mobilization of these organizations constitutes minority nationalism.

Such a manifestation of ethnonational political activism is not unique to the PAI. Organizations representing indigenous groups in Latin America, Canada, New Zealand, and Australia, as well as political organizations claiming to speak on behalf of "homeland minorities" in Central and Eastern Europe—such as Hungarian parties in Serbia, Romania, and Slovakia, or Albanians in Macedonia—make similar claims. They limit their national claims to formal recognition of the group as a national minority, coupled with collective rights and some degree of institutional autonomy in the political, social, economic, and cultural spheres.

Transitions

Transitions in minority claims and aspirations have taken place worldwide. In India, the self-determination movement of the Tamils in the 1950s and 1960s has disappeared from politics, and the Sikh secessionism of the 1980s also gave way to accommodation, but Muslim organizations in Kashmir turned to separatism in the 1990s.[16] In the Balkans, substate nationalism, which seemed to have subsided during Josip Tito's reign, reared its head again toward the end of the twentieth century. In the Middle East, the formation of the Kurdistan Workers Party (PKK) in Turkey accentuated ethnonationalist demands, while Alawi separatism in Syria gave way to integration and eventually political dominance.[17] In Western Europe, organized Republicans in Northern Ireland, who previously demanded reunification with Eire, have settled for a power-sharing arrangement with Unionists.[18]

Most studies of minority politics pay little attention to the question of transition. Furthermore, most accounts of minority political activism to date are derivatives of theories of ethnic conflict; as a result, they provide only a partial, usually static, picture of the phenomenon of minority political activism, typically at the point of conflict. Despite these shortcomings, these theories provide a useful starting point for evaluating causes of organized minority activism.

Grievances

Many scholars, observers, and activists point to inequalities and ensuing grievances as a primary cause of minority mobilization. Within the grievance-based approach, some look at social and economic inequalities, while others stress the social psychology dimension of collective sentiments of relative deprivations.[19]

Theories that view socioeconomic marginalization as the key explanatory variable have adopted Ted Robert Gurr's premise that "collective disadvantages are the root cause of ethnopolitical action."[20] Unequal distribution of resources and the material inequalities between the majority and minority groups in Israel have been a persistent undercurrent in the literature on the PAI, and there have been many informative studies that have documented unequal distribution of resources and discrimination in numerous spheres, including education, budgets of local authorities, and economic development.[21] Some of the scholarship on the PAI draws implicitly or explicitly on the inequality model, locating the origins of PAI politicization in socioeconomic disparities. From this perspective, the Jewish state has failed to provide economic growth, social equality, and full political rights to its Arab citizens. The PAI express their real-world grievances by turning to ethnonationalist politics and Islamism.

The inequality explanation is not wrong, but a comparative perspective demonstrates that it is insufficient. After testing a number of theories that deal with the relationship between economic grievances and conflict, Mark Lichbach found that no clear relationship exists. He concluded that "economic inequality may either have positive, negative, or no impact on dissent."[22] There have been many instances in which disadvantaged groups living under dire economic conditions have not mobilized; examples include the Armenians, the Baluchis in Iran, the Shi'ites in Iraq until the 1990s, the Roma people in Europe, and the Copts in Egypt. The case of the Copts is particularly enlightening, because the status of this group has deteriorated considerably from the days of the Monarchy. In Eastern Europe, too, the level of economic development has been found to not correspond with ethnonationalist mobilization.[23]

In Israel, too, no direct correlation exists—and therefore causation cannot be inferred—between the extent of real inequality, on the one hand, and the extent of politicization and the types of demands made by organizations of the disadvantaged minority on the other. At a time when politicization has taken a turn toward ethnonationalism, there have been changes for the better in many spheres, as As'ad Ghanem has noted, although discrimination and serious social gaps persist.[24] According to data from the Israel Central Bureau of Statistics, gaps in key indicators such as infant mortality rates, levels of education, and life expectancy have either narrowed or remained the same since the 1950s.[25] Arabs have increasingly joined the labor market; they benefit from more freedom of press, movement, and association than in the 1950s, 1960s, and 1970s; and a small number of Arab elites have been appointed into the senior level of the state apparatus, including the Supreme Court, Foreign Ministry, and Ministry of Interior.[26]

Another version of the inequality explanation focuses not on socioeconomic disparities but on political exclusion. According to this version, it is the lack of state autonomy that drives political action. Here, too, there is no correlation between transitions in political activism and the extent of state autonomy. The relative consistency of state autonomy over six decades is discussed in depth in Chapter 3. The chapter reveals that while exclusive Jewish ownership of the state has been a source of grief for the excluded PAI, the situation was not better when the minority was quiescent.

Ultimately, the inequality model can point to the source of grievance, but it alone does not provide an explanation for the evolution of PAI politics from quiescence in the 1950s to ethnonationalism advanced by numerous ethnically based organizations in the 2000s. What is required, therefore, is an explanation of the conditions under which inequality translates into political mobilization in general and ethnonational politics in particular.

The social psychology approach shifts the focus from objective material indicators of inequality to intergroup comparisons. Studies applying this approach have found that sentiments of collective injustice and deprivation can arise when members of a group perceive that their group has less than it deserves compared to other groups in its environment or even compared to previous experiences.[27] These studies argue that this perception occurs because humans have a basic need for self-esteem while self-evaluation relies heavily on comparisons of one's own attributes with those of others, regardless of whether the differences are real or imagined. The perceived status of a group influences the self-esteem of individual members of that group. The absolute value of the group's condition, although important, is less significant than the perception of the members of how their group stands relative to others. According to this approach, it is this perception that drives efforts to improve the status of the group.[28]

Several studies of the PAI draw explicitly or implicitly upon the social psychological model.[29] Noting that the PAI overwhelmingly view the Jewish majority as their reference group for self-evaluation, opinion surveys of the PAI population conducted from the late 1960s through to the 1990s consistently reveal widespread perceptions of relative deprivation.[30] For example, a 1967 survey, conducted by Yochanan Peres, found that between 50 and 60 percent of the Arabs in Israel felt they made less progress in various social and economic spheres than the Palestinians in the West Bank. Only 37 percent of respondents said they felt more at home in Israel than they would in an Arab country; the majority expressed preference for living in one of the neighboring Arab states.[31] A survey conducted by Sammy Smooha and published in 1989 found that a comparable rate of respondents, 35.7 percent, felt more at home in Israel than in an Arab state.[32] Similarly, a survey by Smooha in 1976, when the Communist Party was the dominant organization speaking on behalf of the minority, found that 64.3 percent of the PAI assessed their socioeconomic situation in comparison to Israeli Jews and that almost 61 percent found those gaps to be considerable (only about 20 percent assessed their socioeconomic development in comparison to Arabs in other countries or to Palestinians in the West Bank and Gaza).[33] A survey conducted by As'ad Ghanem and Sarah Ozacky-Lazar almost twenty years later found that a similar proportion of the PAI continued to believe that the socioeconomic gaps between the two communities were large,[34] even though according to several key social indicators the situation of the PAI was much better than that of their co-Arab nationals elsewhere in the Middle East.[35]

Thus, Arab sentiments of relative deprivation within Israel have always been widespread and undoubtedly fuel a desire for change. Ultimately, perceptions of deprivation and marginalization of equal intensity have preexisted the ethnonational turn and have not shifted considerably in conjunction with changes in minority political mobilization. Given that minority group perception of its status has remained relatively steady, additional factors are needed to explain the mechanisms that connect grievances with diverging forms of political activism.

Leaders

Indeed, prominent theorists of contentious politics and social movements have already recognized that "grievances alone cannot explain mobilization."[36] Some have argued that the transition from sentiments of deprivation to political activism is contingent upon a resourceful leadership apparatus that can serve as a mobilizing agent.[37] Leaders are necessary to organize and mobilize movements.

The precise role played by leaders in ethnonationalist mobilization has been the subject of intense debate in the scholarship on the politics of nationalism and ethnicity. Not all scholars agree that what motivates group leaders is a genuine commitment to the welfare of their group. Many scholars argue that elites work to politicize and ethnonationalize groups in order to advance their own narrow interests.[38] Self-interested elites, sometimes referred to as political entrepreneurs, can derive political and economic benefits from their status as community leaders and therefore deliberately work to increase the political salience of ethnicity.

Leadership-focused theories have made important inroads into the study of the PAI as scholars have examined the impact of leadership on group mobilization.[39] Directing attention to leadership styles and elite behavior is undoubtedly an important contribution of this approach, even if the premise of elite self-utility maximization is not accepted wholesale. Political organizations require leaders to form and guide them. Leaders are needed to formulate an agenda, decide on a course of action, provide direction, and articulate demands on behalf of the organization.

The theoretical formulations of elite-centric approaches, however, somewhat overstate the power of leaders. As political scientists have noted elsewhere, political outcomes are never a direct product of elite design.[40] In most cases, elites face social and political constraints that bind the political paths available to them. In Burundi, for example, the Tutsi elite found that its intention to depoliticize differentiated Tutsi and Hutu identities by molding an overarching Burundi identity in the early 1990s was overwhelmingly rejected by members of both the Tutsi and Hutu groups. Memories of ethnic hatred prevented the accommodationist program of the Tutsi elite from materializing.[41] Likewise, attempts by state elites in Turkey to impose a new identity on the Kurds resulted not in commonality but in a protracted conflict. In short, ethnic politics cannot be understood as the simple intended outcome of elite policies.

More significantly, the approach does not provide tools for explaining variation in elite preferences and transformation in the organizational structure and political demands of the minority. A description of PAI elite behavior alone does not explain *why* PAI leaders organized in a binational party, the Communist Party, and advanced a class-based ideology in the 1970s and why ethnically based political parties and NGOs have been proliferating and promoting an ethnonationalist agenda more recently.

Institutional Frameworks

In contrast to grievance-based approaches, leadership-focused theories, and other ethnic group-level theories, which have typically treated ethnic groups as if they were "acting on the state only from the outside,"[42] and inspired by renewed intellectual interest in the state in the field of comparative politics at large, students of ethnic politics began to "bring the state back in" to the analysis of ethnic conflict in the 1990s.[43] The state became the primary variable for explaining social change and ethnic politics. The resurgent literature on New Institutionalism in comparative politics provided the basic framework for integrating this new research agenda.[44] This shift was of tremendous significance to the evolution of ethnic politics studies, as the new approach provided an analytical framework for investigating the impact of previously overlooked variables such as institutional settings, state structures, and regime characteristics.[45]

Rogers Brubaker, whose work on nationalism in Eastern Europe has been at the forefront of this scholarly change of focus, has advanced the notion that ethnonations are not substantive entities, but a manufactured product of institutional characteristics. According to this view, institutional practices establish the parameters of self-identity. The origins of ethnonational political activism, therefore, are also to be found in institutions and state attributes, and they cannot be understood as an outcome of real group grievances or deep collective sentiments, given that groups are not real entities.[46]

Applied to the case of the PAI, the analytical framework advanced by Brubaker would suggest that members of the PAI group have only come to conceive of themselves as such and to mobilize because of the Israeli state structure, regime type, and government policies. The claim that institutional definitions constitute categories of identities is not utterly unreasonable in this case. In the pre-Israel period, the Arab-speaking population residing in British-governed Palestine was identified as the Palestine Arabs. In the aftermath of the establishment of Israel, their identity gained a new Israeli-civic dimension as they became Arab citizens of Israel, distinct from Palestine Arabs outside Israel. At the same time, the state was defined as a Jewish state, and its policies formally distinguished between Jews and Arabs, thus reinforcing the distinct communal identity of the Arabs as a minority in Israel.[47] The extension of Israeli rule to the West Bank and Gaza and the incorporation of a large Palestinian population that struggled for national self-determination heightened the Palestinian consciousness of the Arabs in Israel.[48] In short, changes in institutional boundaries influenced the minority.

This interpretation, however, has its limits. Most notably, it conceives of the state as socially separated and elevated from society, and of regime policies as devised in a social vacuum. And yet, state institutions are embedded in, and shaped by, a social context. The Israeli state took on a Jewish character precisely because it was constructed by a preexisting Jewish national movement. Distinct Jewish and Arab national movements in Palestine had existed in Palestine under British rule before the creation of the State of Israel. And when the British Mandatory government suggested building unified institutions for all residents of Palestine, their proposal was rejected outright by the Palestine Arab leadership.[49] To suggest that the state engendered distinct Jewish and Palestinian Arab identities in Israel, therefore, is to get things backward, even though state policies, once established, certainly reinforced differentiation and contributed to the ongoing reconstitution of the groups.

Other scholars within the New Institutionalist tradition of ethnic conflict studies have been less inclined to conceptualize institutions as a primarily constitutive variable. Instead, they view institutions as conduits for preferences and investigate the impact of institutional characteristics on the opportunities groups have for political action. For example, some have argued that the consolidation of state authority in France and the integration of a centralized republic following the French Revolution provided an institutional context that was less conducive to Basque ethnonational mobilization in France than the situation in Spain, where *fueros* (charters) had for centuries provided the Spanish Basques with relative autonomy and thus with more opportunities for mobilization during the nineteenth-century civil war. Unlike France, the Spanish state did not possess an extensive range of institutions over its territory, a circumstance that hindered its capacity to control the minority.[50]

The advantage of this more qualified version of the institution-centric perspective is that it can reveal the opportunities and incentive structures for mobilizing actors. Particular institutional configurations could provide opportunities for political action and encourage certain types of organizations to form. Some institutions are said to encourage centripetalism.[51] Conversely, certain institutional frameworks provide incentives for multiple ethnically based political parties to form, generating internal competition, which in turn often engenders an outbidding dynamic whereby each of the parties tries to build up its credentials as the one most loyal to the group and best suited to advance group interests.

State Cohesion and Extensiveness

Ultimately, we need to identify which particular institutional attributes are conducive to changes in minorities' reactions to lack of state autonomy. The key variables that explain changes in minority political organization and demands are *state extensiveness* and *cohesion*, qualities that affect the extent to which power is centralized in the hands of the central government. In a nutshell, the more extensive and cohesive the range of state institutions, the greater the capacity of the central government to establish hegemonic control in the territory under its jurisdiction, minimize dissent, and gain compliance from the minority. Conversely, in fragmented and narrow polities, power is more dispersed horizontally among various state agencies and vertically among state institutions and other groups in society. This dispersal of power provides more opportunities for minority organizations to form and to mount resistance.

State extensiveness refers to the variable range of social and territorial space occupied by the institutional infrastructure that constitutes the state. The range of institutions associated with a comprehensive state includes, among other things, armed law enforcement agencies, a military, a citizenship regime, a standardized education system, an elaborate and centralized bureaucracy, a comprehensive legal system, and a national communication system. Thus, when the state possesses a monopoly over the use of armed forces, the education system, and the communication systems, and its branches are able to reach all parts of society, its extensiveness is high. The more elaborate the range of state institutions, the more present they are across the territory; and the more they monopolize activity in their sphere of authority, the easier it will be for the central government to establish its hegemony, advance its preferences, and limit the opportunities for ethnic minorities to challenge that authority. On the other hand, powerful private actors in the economy, a robust civil society, independent parallel education and communication systems, and only limited presence of armed security forces can confine central government outreach and provide public space for ethnic minorities to establish political organizations that promote minority objectives.

State cohesion refers to the extent to which the polity in question behaves as an integrated and unified entity. Probing why state leaders have met with varying degrees of success in their attempts to control challengers to their authority, Joel Migdal has argued that not all states possess the same degree of cohesion.[52] A high degree of cohesion is vital for centralized control. The extent of cohesion will depend on the level of synchronization between the various arms of the state and among decision makers. When the integrated parts of a polity operate with a relatively high degree of harmony, the policy preferences of the central government can be more readily advanced. Conversely, uncoordinated state institutions and fragmented decision-making and implementation processes yield decentralization of power, thus hindering the ability of the central government to determine outcome even if state institutions are extensively present across the territory. To put it succinctly, decentralization engenders mechanisms that check regime capacity.

Thus, the variable range of combinations of state traits influences minority political strategies by setting constraints and providing opportunities for diverse forms of activism. In a nonautonomous state, a central government that gains the capacity to control societal challengers through an extensive and cohesive array of state institutions, most notably armed law-enforcement agencies, has better prospects of coercing minorities into submission.[53] Israel of the 1950s and 1960s is an example of a nonautonomous state, deeply penetrated by the Zionist movement, in which the Mapa'i-controlled government had the capacity to both redistribute resources favoring the dominant group and enforce its policies by controlling the disadvantaged minority through a military administration. Authoritarian regimes with extensive security apparatuses in Saddam Husayn's Iraq, Syria, Malaysia, and elsewhere have also exhibited repressive capacity to penalize challengers to the structures of ethnic domination.[54]

Conversely, the lower the degree of state extensiveness and cohesion, the less power is concentrated in the hands of the central government and the less capacity it possesses to control societal challengers. Under these conditions, there are more opportunities for minority organizations to form and mount bold and fierce contestation. When the state is controlled by a dominant group but the central government has difficulties containing the activism of the politically disadvantaged group, there are incentives for embarking on strident, if not violent, attempts to disentangle the state from the grasp of the ruling ethnic group and for ethnonationalist mobilization. Hutu rebellion against Tutsi control of the state in Burundi serves as a conspicuous example of a protracted violent minority campaign in a weak institutional setting.

In an ethnically dominated state, an institutional balance in which political fragmentation and state withdrawal from public space infringe on central government capacity to control the minority—but not to the extent that the dominant group is forced to renegotiate its dominant position, despite organized minority opposition—is conducive to the formation of minority political organizations that champion minority nationalism and make assertive ethnic demands on the state.

This is the story of Israel and its Palestinian Arab minority. A considerable decline in the degree of institutional cohesion and extensiveness, manifested in (among other things) the rise of niche clientele parties, the dispersion of authority from the central government and empowerment of the courts, the rise of civil society and changing state-society balance of power, and state retreat from the economy and the social sphere, have reduced the central government's capacity to control how the minority organizes. The electoral rules not only provide incentives for political parties to cater to particularistic interests rather than to form multiethnic alliances, but also encourage multiple parties to compete for the support of their niche clientele, thus generating an outbidding dynamic. Likewise, the retreat of the state from social spheres, combined with the empowerment of the court, have provided opportunities for multiple NGOs to form and to litigate on collective rights issues.

State-Society Relations

Minority political activism is largely influenced by institutional configurations. Transitions in the patterns of minority political activism entail institutional change. Understanding transitions in minority political activism, therefore, requires some understanding of institutional change.

In the field of comparative politics at large, institutional change has frequently been attributed to the actions of interested social actors.[55] Scholars such as Theda Skocpol, whose work alone and with Peter Evans and Dietrich Rueschmeyer is usually regarded as having pioneered state-centric theory,[56] studied the reciprocal effects of state and society.[57] Similarly, Migdal, Kohli, and Shue adopted a differentiated view of the state and insisted that state and society mutually shape one another through their ongoing interaction.[58] They labeled this dynamic *state-in-society*.

The institutionalist scholarship on ethnic politics has generally not shown much interest in understanding causes of institutional change or incorporating societal variables. The image of the state as a singular entity that is elevated from society and is capable of dictating outcome has by and large persisted. As a result, the reciprocal impact of ethnic groups and institutions has remained theoretically underdeveloped.

The explanation of transitions in PAI political activism requires going beyond the conventional, and somewhat sterile, institutionalist frameworks. Institutional structures affect and reflect. Not only do state attributes influence societal interactions and group behavior, but they are also shaped and transformed by societal forces. Understanding institutional configurations as an outcome of societal context helps to explain how institutional change can be conducive to transition in minority political activism.

According to the approach advanced here, the state is not elevated from society and is analyzed as a differentiated entity. A dynamic and mutually constitutive relationship exists between states and society.[59] Simply phrased, state institutions may very well have an important impact on ethnic communities; yet ethnically based and other organizations often play an important role in the initial process of state formation and act as agents of institutional change. State institutions undoubtedly play a central role in defining communal boundaries, determining access to resources and power, and shaping opportunities for societal action. At the same time, state institutions are subject to transformation as a result of societal pressures. The deliberate and nondeliberate actions of ethnic groups and other societal actors can modify and reconstitute the institutional setting. In many cases, state institutions are a product of conflicting interests and power struggles, and often a reflection of structures of domination. In divided societies, organized groups engage in negotiation and renegotiation of institutional structures that define boundaries of exclusion and determine distribution of power and resources in a way that advances their interests, increases their access to opportunities, and enables them to influence rule-making.[60]

To be sure, advancing the notion that state institutions are not elevated from society but are rather embedded within a societal context and communal power relations should not lead us to discard the constraining power of the state wholesale. A well-institutionalized state, even if nonautonomous, possesses what Michael Mann has termed *infrastructural power* in the form of a centralized organization, a regulated education system, expansive law enforcement agencies, a standardized judicial system, and other agencies that provide the state with vital influence on access and distribution of material and cultural resources in the territory under its jurisdiction, and with coercive means to enforce its rules, even if these rules are contested by rival ethnic groups.[61] It should not be forgotten that, as Migdal has argued, states, particularly younger ones, differ in their attributes and in their capabilities to implement their policy choices.[62] It is in this context that the degree of state cohesion and extensiveness matter.

How precisely society influences institutional frameworks in general is a debated question. Pioneering scholarship on this question in political economy posits that in the first place, institutions are humanly devised.[63] This claim brings us back to the question of state formation. Understanding how and why a state possesses certain characteristics—for example, lack of state autonomy—requires us to examine the process of state formation and the societal interactions and ethnic relations that existed before and during this process. This is the main theme of Chapter 2.

Once institutions are devised, organizations might pursue change in order to advance their interests, but, according to North, path dependence typically enables them to make only incremental changes.[64] Others have pointed out that critical junctures provide opportunities for excluded minorities to renegotiate the boundaries of social and political exclusion and achieve a more monumental institutional change.[65] Major changes are sometimes brought about violently. In Lebanon and Nigeria, for example, changes in levels of state autonomy from a dominant group, a decline in the extensiveness of the central state, and institutional fragmentation and decentralization have come about as a result of intergroup segmentation and violent contestations over power and authority. In both these countries, previously marginalized Muslim sects felt that the makeup of state institutions disadvantaged them, and they fought to renegotiate their positions.

In a state dominated by one ethnic group, institutional fragmentation can also arise from fractures within the dominant group. Even when the advantaged group is relatively unified in support of maintaining its privileged position, regime cohesion and extensiveness can be undermined when multiple internal actors challenge each other for political power. In the absence of an internal hegemonic subgroup within the privileged ethnic group, ongoing negotiations of governing institutional structures among rival actors affiliated with the dominant ethnic group mold the overarching structures of domination. Such negotiations therefore alter, if unintentionally, the constraints faced by the disadvantaged minority. Internal disputes between contesting subgroups can result in decentralization of state authority, whereby local levels of government gain more authority on local matters, the judiciary is empowered to act as an arbitrator, or civil society associations emerge.[66] Such transformations check the power of the central government and thus constrain its capacity to regulate minorities, changing in turn the opportunity structures faced by the minority.

When pinpointing the significance of opportunities, constraints, and organizations, it is important to avoid falling into the trap of depicting processes as inevitabilities and to resurrect the significance of leadership. Comparative research reveals that similar institutional conditions can yield variable outcomes. Several studies have noted instances in which institutional conditions conducive to political activism did not generate politicization, because of lack of resources or the absence of leadership with organizational skills who could take advantage of emerging opportunities and establish visible and effective political organizations.[67]

Thus, mobilization is contingent on mobilizing agent-leaders.[68] Strong, resourceful, and visionary leaders make the difference between activism and passivity. The formation of a successful political organization, gaining support, building alliances, transforming traditional political relationships, utilizing resources, and identifying (or creating) opportunities all hinge on the qualities of leadership. We should not presume that the institutional setting fully explains the choices of political agents. Institutional arrangements sometimes allow for flexible responses, providing political elites with space to politically maneuver and make choices. The vision and preferences of leaders matter for the outcome. Leaders with liberal, universalistic visions, such as Martin Luther King, Jr., may choose to mobilize for integration. Others, like Malcolm X, might prefer to follow the path of segregation and distance their group from the majority group. Obviously, outcomes are seldom precisely the result of leaders' intentions.[69] However, strong leaders are able to direct the path of minority political activism.

I postulate that leaders act rationally, in at least some minimal sense, and that the choices they make are at least moderately based on their evaluation of the environment in which they operate. This does not mean that I conceive of political elites as actors who are continuously engaged in devising grand strategies for ethnic empowerment. Few group leaders engage in careful, overt calculations of costs and benefits. Nor should it be expected that opportunities identified by outside observers would always be interpreted in the same way by those involved (indeed, it is not unusual for outsiders to point to opportunities missed by insiders). And yet, it is reasonable to assume that, by and large, leaders are goal oriented and will try to pursue a path they believe is feasible and will yield a desirable outcome. Goal-oriented leaders who initially demonstrate a preference toward a particular end may very well adapt their preferences through what Jon Elster has termed *adaptive preference formation*, if they detect that a previously desired goal is unattainable or if changes in the institutional environment make an alternative objective more accessible.[70]

It is important to keep in mind that multiple leadership actors frequently pursue multiple goals at any given moment, and they have to trade off different values and preferences against each other. Sometimes, leaders of political organizations who are engaged in interethnic politics are also simultaneously facing intragroup competition from other organizations for political power and the authority to represent their community in the conflict. This intragroup competition often engenders an outbidding race in which leaders try to demonstrate to potential followers that the organization that they head is the most loyal to group interests and is best suited to represent them.[71] The multiple dimensions of leaders' interaction, therefore, can sometimes result in instantaneous tactical decisions with little consideration of the eventual sequence of events, but these decisions do influence the overall outcome of minority political activism and demands.

An Illustrative Application
of the Theoretical Approach to the PAI Case

In the 1950s and 1960s, the PAI were relatively compliant. The Israeli state lacked autonomy from the Jewish national movement, which established Israel as a Jewish state with the purpose of serving the Jewish nation. Political authority was highly centralized in a relatively cohesive core, and the regime's outreach was extensive, enabling easy control of the minority. Until 1966, the PAI were subjected to a military regime that severely restricted their mobility and their ability to be politically active. The politics of Israel were dominated by the precursor of the Labor Party, the Mapa'i Party, which exercised vast control over the economy, social services, an elaborate bureaucracy, and the communication and education systems.[72] Mapa'i exploited PAI vulnerability following the 1947–1949 Arab-Israeli war, as well as its own capacity to mobilize state resources, to establish extensive patron-client networks with the PAI. The social organization of the Arab population around the extended family, the *hamula*, coupled with the absence of any significant challenge to Mapa'i's rule and of competing patrons, made it easier for Mapa'i to ensure compliance from those seeking access to opportunities that would alleviate their vulnerability. The social organization of the PAI also made it possible for the regime to fragment the PAI elite into factions that were unable to present a united front because of competition for patronage.

Independent minority mobilization took off in the late 1960s. Rakah, the Communist Party, was the primary mobilizing agent of the minority group, winning between one third and one half of the PAI vote in general elections in the 1970s and 1980s. Rakah—which rejected Zionism, espoused the establishment of a socialist regime in Israel, demanded egalitarian redistribution of resources, and advocated the integration of the PAI into the redistributive central state—was attractive to PAI voters.[73]

Conditions favorable to PAI independent mobilization were created by a combination of factors: shifts in state outreach, fragmentation of authority, and the beginning of an incremental trend of decentralization of power in Israeli politics, along with changes in the territorial boundaries of the state following the 1967 war and renewed contact with Palestinians in the West Bank and Gaza. First, the abolition of the Military Administration significantly reduced the state's coercive presence in Arab populated territories, thus limiting state capacity to control minority activism. Important changes in the patterns of authority were expressed by, among other things, the decline of Labor hegemony in the 1970s and the evolution of genuinely competitive politics, and the emergence of a more vibrant civil society. In addition, the increased independence of the electronic media provided opportunities for contestation over rule-making. Furthermore, the political significance of the hamula declined, and the role of intermediary patrons was undermined as a result of an enhanced modernization process. The accumulation of modernization, decline in Labor hegemony, and reduced PAI vulnerability following the demise of the Military Administration led to the collapse of the patron-client networks.

The Communist Party was the greatest beneficiary of these institutional and societal changes. It was the only anti-Zionist party that incorporated Arabs in its ranks and that was allowed to operate in the early days of the state (largely because until 1965, the party was dominated by Jews). The Communists largely benefited from being the only established political organization available to the PAI when political space became available for the PAI to mobilize, and their ideological vision determined the minority's political path.

The ethnonationalist phase has been enabled by the persistence of lack of state autonomy from the majority, combined with the accelerating decline in state extensiveness and cohesion and considerable liberalization in Israel. On the one hand, the PAI minority has grown increasingly frustrated by its continued marginalization and inability to integrate into Israel, such that sentiments of counter-rejection have arisen and an adaptive preference process of sorts has taken place.[74] On the other hand, the liberalization of important social, economic, and political institutions further weakened the central state and created opportunity space for bolder minority demands that challenge the ideological framework and foundational principles of the state.

Majority segmentation has played a major role in the dispersion of power away from the central government. Although Israel has always had a multiparty system, fragmentation became acute in the 1990s. The composition of the Israeli legislature, the Knesset, had changed considerably during the ensuing period, with the decline of the large ideologically based parties and the proliferation and growth of single-issue and parochial parties representing immigrants, retirees, secularists, settlers, and additional religious parties, as well as other interest groups. The number of PAI parties has also grown considerably. A new electoral system introduced before the 1996 elections has intensified the fragmentation of the political party system by providing incentives for small parties, including PAI parties, to appeal to parochial interests.[75] Moreover, the existence of multiple parties appealing to the same pool of voters has created internal competition that encouraged parties to harden their positions. At the same time, these patterns of political activism are consistent with the overall patterns of political organization and mobilization in Israel as a whole.

Moreover, segmentation has led to the empowerment of the judiciary vis-à-vis the legislature and the executive.[76] Whereas the Knesset has traditionally been the locus of authority, the 1990s saw authority disperse horizontally between state institutions, with the courts playing an increasingly central role in resolving societal and political disputes. The decline in the ability of the polarized legislature and executive to resolve contentious issues led many social groups to turn to the courts, and this development itself led to the refocusing of political mobilization in Israel. The access of subaltern groups—including women, reform and conservative Jews, and immigrant groups—to the courts has enabled the judiciary to bring to the forefront alternative values and practices that take into consideration the interests of marginalized groups. Arab NGOs have been able to utilize this avenue to challenge the regime's resource allocation policies and make demands on behalf of the PAI collective. On this front, too, the PAI method of political mobilization mirrors the overall patterns in Israel.

Vertical dispersion of authority was also consequential for limiting state outreach, with Jewish society increasingly becoming critical of top-down power relations and demanding more accountability and limitations to state intervention in social life. First, additional media reforms, along with the emergence of commercial electronic media and cable television, provided more avenues to contest central government practices. In addition, Jewish civil society associations began to emerge in the 1970s and solidified throughout the 1980s and 1990s with organizations like the Movement for the Quality of Government, the Israel Democracy Institute, the Association for Civil Rights in Israel, and many others scrutinizing government policies and working to limit the ability of the state to penetrate society and impose its preferences at will. Space carved out by these associations has provided opportunities for PAI associational activism that also demands limitations to state outreach.

State retreat from the economy and the privatization of state and quasi-state enterprises has been yet another very important prong of the dispersal of power.[77] As the state's redistributive capacity has been decreasing over the years, PAI access to social services has been reduced. Most significantly, the Islamists have been able to carve out space for an ethnically exclusive parallel sector that provides social and economic services in lieu of the state. Such exclusivist space, in turn, has facilitated the construction of parochial ties.

With state outreach far more limited and with a considerable decline in institutional cohesion, the central government's capacity to constrain minority organizations (or indeed many potent societal challengers) and set narrow boundaries for contestation has diminished appreciably.[78] Public space for minority assertion of ethnonational demands has grown in the parliamentary and nonparliamentary spheres. At the same time, PAI political organizations have themselves become agents of change. Promoting an ethnonational agenda, PAI leaders are raising communal awareness and contributing to the consolidation of the distinct national identity amongst members of the minority group. The more challenges PAI activism puts forth, and the more successful it is in its challenges, the less capable the regime is of controlling society and the more feasible future challenges become.

2

State Formation and the Creation
of National Boundaries

State characteristics that influence minority politics do not just appear. They are largely shaped by the societal context that exists during their creation. The period of state formation constitutes a juncture that sets the path for long-term relationships and practices. During the process of state-building, the institutional foundations of the state are established and the foundational principles provide the platform for official state ideology. Understanding how and why a state possesses certain relevant attributes, therefore, requires some understanding of the process of state formation and the societal interactions and ethnic relations that existed before and during this process.

Israel was formed as a Jewish people's state, with the Arab minority outside the boundaries of the national identity of the group that owned the state. At the same time, a small elite that led the process of state-building retained centralized control once the state was established. Thus, Israel's lack of state autonomy coupled with the centralization of authority in the hands of a small elite, which characterized the first decades of Israel's existence, have grown out of the process of state formation. This institutional configuration then proved conducive to minority political quiescence during the 1950s and 1960s. To understand how the Israeli state acquired the attributes that influenced minority political organizational structure, it is useful to briefly review the process of Israel's state formation and the societal interactions and ethnic relations that existed in the prestate period.

The phenomenon of state-building majorities that exclude minorities is relevant for other parts of the world and much can be learned from taking a comparative perspective. This chapter, in the way of background, briefly surveys the process of Israel's state formation and the evolution of communal relations during the prestate period and places this history in a comparative analytical context. The intent here is not to present new historical findings or a comprehensive discussion of the origins of the Israeli state. A comparative framework coupled with a minimal understanding of the historical background, is essential for grasping the constitution of the Israeli state, the means by which the state acquired its particular attributes, and the origins of majority-state-minority relations.

State Formation Through a Comparative Lens

Most of the written history on Israel's state formation has described this case in individual terms, emphasizing Israel's distinctiveness.[1] In contrast, I argue that many of the characteristics of Israel's state formation are very common in modern times. The process of modern state formation in most parts of the world has been premised on a specific relationship between state, national identity, and a dominant group. The state and the national identity that it embodies have generally been cast as an expression of that particular part of the population that played a decisive role in the process of state-building and came to dominate the state.

In many cases, the dominant group was titular: the group name was carried by the state. Examples from all over the world are ample and include Malay in Malaysia, Burman in Burma (Myanmar), Turk in Turkey, Russian in Russia, Serb in Serbia, Romanian in Romania, German in Germany, Irish in Ireland, and Tswana in Botswana. In other cases, the title of the state and the official national identity were not congruent with the name of a dominant segment of the population, but a dominant group nonetheless owned the state and determined its character and the national identity it embodied. This relationship translated into inbuilt, rather than tangential, lack of state autonomy from the dominant group, even if the link between dominant ethnic group identity and state identity was not made explicit. (Lack of autonomy, as discussed in the previous chapter, can be manifested in a variety of ways, including the social identity of the office holders in the civil bureaucracy and military and the commitment of these office holders to group superiority, as well as distribution of power and economic resources, official state language and symbols, and myths of origin and historical narrative.) The Indonesian state, for example, was practically constructed by Javanese elites as the state of the Javanese people, who have always dominated Indonesian politics, the government, and the security apparatus, and who used the instrument of state power to ensure the privileged status of their group.[2] The Chinese state, too, was effectively constructed as a Han state from the early days of the Ming dynasty in the fifteenth century.[3] In the Middle East, Iraq was officially formed as an Arab state (and implicitly at least, even more narrowly as a Sunni Arab dominated state), to the dismay of the Kurdish minority.[4] Iran, too, was essentially built as a Persian state. The Union of South Africa (later the Republic of South Africa) was most visibly a White's state, and so was Brazil, where property and literacy requirements prevented inhabitants of African descent from voting for a long time.[5] And in North America, the foundations of Canadian state formation were premised on loyalty to the British Crown, and it has only been with recent trends associated with multiculturalism that the boundaries of exclusion have become more permeable and allowed more access to previously marginalized groups.

Even in Western European countries that are now widely presumed to possess inclusive and liberal-civic, as opposed to ascriptive or ethnic, forms of nationalisms,[6] the process of state and nation building was exclusive and resulted in states that expressed the dominance of specific populations. Kaufmann and Haklai refer to these as *dominant ethnicities*.[7] Striking examples include the English in Britain, the Franks in France, and the Spanish in Spain. According to Anthony Marx, national identities in these three cases were constructed "by emergent states seeking to manage diversity by manipulating and reinforcing differences."[8] The social cohesion of the core group that came to constitute the nation was attained by demarcating narrow boundaries that excluded some internal constituents while enhancing loyalty and allegiance on the part of those included. For example, in seventeenth-century England, state laws banned Catholics from public office at a time when King Charles II, together with the Parliament, was trying to consolidate a central British state from the previously loose and decentralized polity. In early modern France, it was the Catholic Franks who provided the core, while the Protestant Huguenots were persecuted. The consolidation of central state power in Spain in the sixteenth century came after the Catholic population was unified against the Moors, Jews, and Protestants. Thus, in most parts of the world, ownership over the state and national identity by a particular part of the population, the dominant ethnicity, was inherent in the process of state building.

In the twentieth century in particular, the specific relationship between group and state gained the status of a formative norm for the creation of new states. The clearest expressions of this development were the principle of self-determination that American president Woodrow Wilson promoted as the key to a new and peaceful world order following World War I and Article 1 of the founding Charter of the United Nations (1945), which enshrined the right to self-determination as a fundamental international principle.[9] Numerous new states emerged in place of the collapsing Ottoman, Austro-Hungarian, and Russian empires, with the decline of European colonial powers throughout the 1940s, 1950s, and 1960s, and following the collapse of communism in the Balkans, Eastern Europe, and Eurasia. As in previous centuries, and backed by the increasingly definitive principle of national self-determination, the newly formed states were typically cast as expressing the national identity of a dominant part of the population.

Throughout the history of modern state formation, there has always been an intrinsic link between territorial boundaries of emergent states and the composition of the population inhabiting the territory.[10] The preferences of state builders about where the territorial borders of their state should lie were premised on dominant group presence in the territory (provided the status of the territory in question was variable in the minds of state builders). In many cases, dominant group population movement and settlement in outlying areas were correlated with changes in territorial sovereignty patterns, whether these population movements occurred by central government design or through voluntary migration in search of economic resources. This has been the case with Javanese settlers in remote areas of Indonesia. Likewise, from the sixteenth century, Han settlements in outlying areas "were almost always accompanied by the extension of the Chinese state: civil administration was organized in areas where the fiscal base was considered sufficiently stable, and garrisons were set up at strategic locations where military presence was deemed essential."[11] The demarcation of the territorial boundaries of the United States also depended on migration of white European settlers into the southwestern regions of Oklahoma, New Mexico, Texas, Arizona, and California. In the Philippines, the movement of settlers from Luzon to Mindanao was meant to consolidate the state's sovereignty in this region. This was also the case with the Moroccan state and its settlers in Western Sahara, and with the Russian-dominated Soviet state and Russian settlers in the Baltic and Caucasus regions.

Because groups were seldom neatly separated from one another, emergent states developed distinctive forms of relationships with minorities who were outside the sociological demarcation of the nation. In many cases, boundaries of exclusion transformed over time, providing previously excluded groups with increased access to public institutions.[12] This process has been particularly noticeable in several liberal and multicultural democracies in North American and European countries and in other parts of the world. However, coercive domination and marginalization were commonly practiced as well. In many cases, dominant groups, and by extension the new states they controlled, developed tension-laden relationships with minorities who were not a part of the state-building process. These minorities either did not receive citizenship rights at all or had differential types of citizenship (examples include blacks in South Africa until 1994, Chinese in Malaysia, Russian-speakers in Estonia, and blacks in Brazil), or they resisted assimilation and were therefore left on the margins of the national community (for example, Kurds in Turkey and Basques in Spain).

Furthermore, there were many cases in which subaltern minorities had transborder relations with populations in other states where they were dominant. Worldwide examples include Croats in Serbia; Serbs in Croatia; Albanians in Macedonia and Serbia; Chinese in Malaysia; Muslims in India; Tutsi and Hutu in Rwanda and Burundi; Russians in Latvia, Estonia, and other new republics of the former Soviet Union; Turks in Bulgaria and Cyprus prior to partition; and many others. In some cases, troubled relations developed between the dominant group in the emergent state and the state in which the co-nationals of the minority group were dominant. As a result, minorities were frequently suspected of being a fifth column.

Although frequently treated as anomalous, the case of Israel fits well into the commonly found pattern of state formation and subsequent majority-state-minority relations. The creation of Israel was premised on a distinctive relationship between the state and a particular part of the population—the Jewish population, which constructed its organizational infrastructure. As was the case in other emergent states, Israel was internationally recognized as a state for a particular national community (when the UN General Assembly adopted Resolution 181 on 29 November 1947, it agreed to partition Palestine into a *Jewish* and an *Arab* state: to each people a state. And the UN Security Council resolution that recommended Israel for membership in the UN followed Israel's Declaration of Independence, which defined Israel as a state of the Jewish people). As in many other cases of state-building, the demarcation of the territorial boundaries was intrinsically linked to group population presence on the territory. Like other cases, the process of state formation itself by the Jewish elites recognized the significance that settlement and population movement have on the eventual territorial boundaries of the state. And finally, as in other cases, a significant minority residing within the territorial boundaries of the emergent Jewish state found itself outside the boundaries of the national identity and had transborder affiliation with populations that had antagonistic relations with the newly formed Jewish state.

Jewish Institution Building

The Jewish national movement, known as the Zionist movement, emerged toward the end of the nineteenth century as an important movement that advocated Jewish national self-determination in the region of the Middle East that the Zionists identified as the ancient Jewish homeland, the historic Land of Israel. Although it is important to recognize that rising anti-Semitism in Europe and the need to physically protect Jews played a key role in motivating the creation of the World Zionist Organization (WZO),[13] which was officially established in 1897, it is also important to stress that the ideology advanced by Zionist elites in many respects resembled typical European nationalism, with its accent on the idea of an inherited and preexisting ethnic national identity of a community that should determine its own national institutions and govern itself.[14] Two notably distinctive characteristics that influenced the organizational infrastructure of the movement and the choices of its leadership were (a) the geographical dispersion of the Jewish population that was supposed to constitute the putative national community and (b) the fact that the vast majority of the population in question did not inhabit the territory that was identified as its homeland.

The process of institution building was guided by the motivation of the Zionist organization's elites to transform the dispersed population into a national community that resides in, and owns, the territory marked as its homeland.[15] Hence, two of the primary goals defined by the leadership were "the ingathering of the exiles" and "land redemption," which translated into great emphasis being placed on migration and land acquisition. The leaders of the Jewish national movement were ready to take advantage of the financial hardships experienced by Arab landowners and peasants at the time in order to purchase land and transfer it to the hands of the Jewish national movement.[16] To facilitate land acquisition, in 1901 the WZO established the Jewish National Fund (JNF), whose mandate was land purchase. It is worth stressing that to prevent the land from being further traded by profit-seeking individuals, the JNF operated according to a principle whereby land was never sold to individuals or groups. Instead, the acquired land was always granted on lease to Jewish settlers. It was defined as "the property of the people," which meant ownership by the national movement and de facto control by the leadership of the Zionist movement over its allocation and use.[17] Maintaining ownership of this scarce resource facilitated dependence on the leadership of the Zionist movement, enabling it to control much of the operations of the emergent settlements during periods of internal contestation.[18] Even Kibbutzim, the Jewish agricultural cooperative settlements where Jews worked and settled collectively, were only granted land by lease.

Throughout the prestate period, the movement's elites also recognized the significance of settlements in outlying areas for establishing ownership over the territory as well as preparing it for future mass migration.[19] The choice of location for Kibbutzim, for example, was largely driven by the logic of territorial expansion. As openly explained by an editorial in *Ha'olam*, the national movement's newspaper, the Kibbutzim provided an answer to the fears of individuals intimidated by settling individually in new and relatively remote places over which the Zionists wished to mark ownership.[20] Kibbutzim were often built on leased JNF-purchased land in outlying areas. Ultimately, the organizational infrastructure created for land acquisition, the significance of marking ownership over territory through population presence, and the principle of granting land by lease were passed on to the state.

Arguably the most important political and administrative organization to be established by the Jewish national movement in the prestate period was the Jewish Agency (JA), which was established in 1929.[21] This status largely stemmed from the JA being recognized by the British and the League of Nations as the legal representative of the Zionist movement and the Yishuv (Settlement), the emergent organized Jewish community in the prestate period.[22] The JA represented the Zionists before the British Mandatory administration, and practically all contacts between the British and the Zionist movement were done through the JA. By the 1930s, the executive of the JA was the chief decision-making body, and its chairman was the head of the Yishuv.

The JA was an overarching body responsible for coordinating the activities of the Jewish national movement. It established departments that in effect functioned as government ministries in key areas, most notably finance, diplomatic relations, immigration, education, labor, and trade and industry.[23] Thus, the JA also developed an extensive and autonomous education system that promoted the Hebrew language and a new Jewish-Israeli culture, goals that leading Zionists viewed from the onset as indispensable for spreading national sentiments.[24] No less significant, the JA was most active in facilitating immigration. The 1920s and 1930s saw inflows of hundreds of thousands of Jewish immigrants, primarily from Eastern and Central Europe, many of whom were driven out of their countries of domicile by the spreading anti-Semitism. The JA expanded its projects around the world to educate, encourage, and assist Jews in immigrating to Israel. Thus, whereas in 1882 only about .3 percent of world Jewry resided in Palestine—that is, 24,000 Jews, compared to approximately 470,000 Arabs—the proportion of the world's Jews living in the territory grew to 6 percent in 1948, the year Israel declared its independence.[25]

The activities of the JA were largely facilitated by the United Jewish Appeal (UJA), which was originally established in 1921 to raise money for the Jewish immigrants, their new settlements, and the Zionist movement as a whole. The UJA became the fund-raising arm of the JA. The emergent Jewish economy was not viable at the time, and without the coordinated financial support from the Jewish diaspora, the JA would not have been able to maintain its institutions and its support of mass immigration. Eventually, when the state was established, many of the Agency's administrative units transformed into state agencies and many of its officials became state officials. Most conspicuously, JA executive chairman David Ben-Gurion became Israel's first prime minister, and the head of the JA's political department, Moshe Sharett, became the first foreign minister.

Alongside the JA a local elected Jewish assembly was established, called Assefat Hanivcharim (Elected Assembly), which represented the Yishuv community only. The Assembly then elected the Vaad Leumi (National Council), an executive body of sorts. All members of the Jewish Yishuv, excluding those who renounced membership in the organized community, were eligible to vote for the Elected Assembly, and turnout was generally high, 56 to 70 percent of eligible voters. Considering that the elected body lacked significant execution power because it did not have territorial sovereignty and the JA possessed much of the practical authority, the high voter turnout signaled the emerging endorsement of the developing institutions by the local population.[26] Over the years, the realm of activity of the local institutions grew, as when the WZO transferred responsibility for the education system to the Vaad Leumi in 1932.[27]

A Proportional Representation electoral system was introduced and provided incentives for a large number of ideological groups to participate in the political process. Political parties with diverse worldviews were formed and took part in the elections: communist, socialist, liberal, and conservative; religious and secular; traditional and revolutionary.[28] The political parties, particularly those that consolidated in the 1930s, laid the foundations for political organization and mobilization for years to come, as well as the patterns of dominance in the Jewish institutions. Thus, in the 1931 elections that were held for the Elected Assembly, the Mapa'i Party (Land of Israel Workers' Party, the predecessor of the Labor Party), representing the unified forces of the Labor movement, received 22,336 votes—the equivalent of 46 percent—while its closest competitor, the more nationalist Revisionists (the precursor of the Likud Party), founded in 1925 by Vladimir Ze'ev Jabotinsky, received 20 percent. The non-Zionist Communist Party, which would become the major political party to attract Arab voters in the 1970s and 1980s, received only 506 votes, the equivalent of 1 percent and less than the minimum required for participation in the Assembly.[29] The results set the trend for the increasing concentration of power in the hands of the Labor movement, political dominance that would solidify and pass on to the state. At the same time, the principle of proportional representation would also pass on to the state and encourage participation and the formation of a multiparty system.

Yet another significant organization established during the era of British rule that would increase the capacity of the Yishuv leadership to protect its domain was the paramilitary organization called Haganah (Defense). The Haganah was established in 1920 to protect Jewish settlements in the face of growing physical aggression of Arab militants. Although the British government was officially responsible for internal security, the Jewish community faced growing challenges from Arab opponents to its attempts to create a Jewish "national home" in Palestine. Gradually the Haganah grew into the security apparatus of the Yishuv and came under the authority of the JA. Throughout the late 1930s and 1940s, it evolved into a national military body with an organized hierarchical structure: a chief of staff, a central command, and regional-divisional units. Somewhat inconsistently with the official British policy, the increasing scope of the Haganah's role was facilitated by the support of the British military commander, Captain Orde Charles Wingate, who strongly advocated the establishment of a Jewish army. When Israel was established, the Haganah provided the nucleus of the Israeli military, the Israel Defense Force (IDF).[30]

Probably the most significant organization to shape the economic landscape in the Yishuv was the Histadrut (General Federation of Workers in the Land of Israel), established in 1920 by the various left-of-center Jewish political parties as an overarching organization. Unlike a conventional trade union, the Histadrut did much more than simply represent employees; for example, it embarked on widespread entrepreneurial activities. The significance of the Histadrut was that it was active in sectors that were imperative for the development of the Jewish economy but were too risky to attract private investors.[31] The Histadrut's economic enterprises included, among other things, construction (Shikun Ovdim and Solel Boneh), banking (Bank Hapoalim, the Workers' Bank, which became Israel's second largest bank), food production (Tnuva, the largest supplier of fresh foods and agricultural products), insurance (Hasneh), newspapers (Davar), and many other manufacturing, commercial, and financial firms. Gradually, the Histadrut became the major employer in the Jewish economy. In 1939, its bureaucracy alone employed 2,500 people.[32] By the early 1940s, its manufacturing companies employed approximately 10 percent of all employees in the Yishuv manufacturing industries.[33] The Histadrut also provided social welfare services, most important, healthcare services and employment insurance. Many people were attracted to joining the Histadrut, primarily because of its network of social welfare services, and many relied on the Histadrut for their livelihood. Thus the Histadrut was a most powerful organization socially and economically. In 1930, of an estimated 170,000 Jews living in Mandatory Palestine, 30,000 were registered as Histadrut members.[34] By 1939, the Histadrut had 100,000 registered members (of almost 425,000 Jews that lived in Palestine).[35]

    In addition to providing the Jewish national movement with important means of building a Jewish economy, control of the Histadrut and its incredible resources translated into immense political power within the Jewish community. In the 1930s, the power holder in the Histadrut was the Mapa'i Party, formed in 1930 through a merger of a number of left-of-center political parties. The Histadrut's functionaries were by and large the same people that filled the ranks of the party. The party's leader, David Ben-Gurion, became the Histadrut's chair, and by 1935 he was chair of the JA executive and hence the leader of the whole Yishuv. The Histadrut leadership, headed by Ben-Gurion, managed to convince its colleagues in the JA that the Histadrut was imperative for the development of the Jewish society, hence securing its financial backing.[36] This situation resulted in staunch collaboration between the JA and the Histadrut and the fortification of Mapa'i as the dominant political party. If Mapa'i's initial dominance in the Yishuv was largely due to the relatively early arrival of its leaders and their organizational skills, the persistence of this dominance hinged on the party's control of the Histadrut and its incredible resources and on its leaders' ability to translate this control to political power in other Zionist institutions.[37]

It should not be inferred from this rather sketchy overview that the Jewish community was homogenous and had no internal contention. Internal dissent came from several directions, including the Revisionists, who took issue with what they saw as the cautious diplomatic approach of the mainstream leadership, and the religious establishment, which preexisted the new Yishuv, rejected the Zionist movement, and sought independent representation before the Mandatory regime.[38] Yet none of the challengers to the Yishuv's authority managed to undermine the Zionist institutions that laid the foundations of the Jewish state and that would ultimately yield a polity that would be nonautonomous from the Jewish national movement. One important reason for their success was the structure of the Mandatory state.

The Mandatory State

In 1920 the League of Nations granted Britain a Mandate to rule Palestine. Formally, this Mandate was to prepare the inhabitants of Palestine for self-rule. At the same time, the idea of national self-determination touted by the victors of the War, along with several diplomatic pledges, including what are known as the Balfour Declaration and the McMahon-Husayn Correspondence, created expectations on both the Jewish and Arab sides for attaining self-government.[39] Much has been written about Palestine under British rule and the complex intercommunal dynamic that emerged under the Mandatory government.[40] Rather than review all that has been written on the Mandatory government, it is important here to stress several of the institutional traits that were particularly important for facilitating the creation of a distinct Jewish domain that laid the foundations for a nonautonomous Israeli state.

The institutional setting established by the Mandatory administration facilitated the Zionist enterprise in two meaningful ways. First, the British authorities treated the Arab and Jewish populations as two distinct communities, dealt with them separately, and did not prepare or force joint Jewish-Arab self-rule, thus institutionalizing the bifurcation of the two populations. Although the British initially entertained ideas of building a unified polity, they very quickly recognized "the difficulty in reconciling Palestine Jews and Arabs."[41] Each community was allowed to build and operate its own separate internal institutions. In practice, the Arab and Jewish communities lived under the British administration as two distinct societies. It is not that the British had a grand design against binational engagement, but as Horowitz and Lissak observed, notwithstanding some exceptions, there was usually no need for direct Jewish-Arab cooperation, because for both sides it "was possible to conduct most of the political bargaining through the British Authorities in Jerusalem and London."[42]

Second, the Mandatory state was minimalist. It intervened very little in a limited number of areas, allowing considerable autonomy to each of the communities under its rule.[43] In effect, the institutional boundaries established by the British granted plenty of societal space for the leaders of the Jewish national movement to create a distinct public domain in which they were permitted to supply services, collect taxes, and make decisions about some social matters. This arrangement increased the dependence of the communities on the national organizations, something that was indispensable for the crystallization of authority of the Zionist institutions among the Jewish population in Palestine. Hence, although participation in the institutions built by the Zionists was voluntary and the institutions did not hold formal territorial sovereignty, these institutions did possess relatively significant authority over the increasing inflows of Jewish immigrants who arrived in the 1930s. These immigrants were generally middle class urbanites, who brought with them capital and professional skills that were indispensable for the development of the economy of the Jewish community and who, by and large, integrated into the existing structure created by their predecessors and accepted these institutions and their leaders as their legitimate representatives (notwithstanding the dissent by the Revisionists and others). Because of the minimalist character of the British government in Mandatory Palestine, the Jewish immigrants were largely dependent on the institutions of the Yishuv and the Histadrut for access to essential social and economic services, enabling the Yishuv leadership considerable power to set the rules in its public domain. Thus, the Yishuv had the capacity to, and did, tax the Jewish community to fund its institutions, such as its education system and the Haganah. The Histadrut collected membership fees to help finance its healthcare system and to provide social and unemployment insurance. That despite Mapa'i's dominance, the Yishuv established a relatively inclusive framework based on proportional representation in its institutions for almost all the significant factions, including religious Jews, was helpful for encouraging participation from diverse groups within the Jewish population. But ultimately the decisive factor was the ability of the strong leadership of the Yishuv to utilize the opportunities created by the British Mandatory state.

By the late 1930s, when the British approach toward the Zionist enterprise had changed because of the outbreak of the Arab Revolt in 1936, the institutional foundations of the Yishuv were already established enough to deal with the new challenges posed by the revolt and to operate outside the stricter rules that the British tried to impose. This was particularly evident in immigration, land acquisition, and security. The economic infrastructure, too, was strong enough to withstand the economic implications of the Arab Revolt.

Palestine Arab Mobilization and British Responses

The institutional framework of Mandatory Palestine established in effect two separate societies with separate opportunities for organizational infrastructure. The institutional premises that applied to the Zionists were also relevant to the Palestine Arabs. However, Arab leaders did not seriously engage in building an administrative organizational infrastructure, let alone elected institutions, that could serve as foundations for a future state in the same way the Zionists did.[44]

To be sure, by the early twentieth century, Arab nationalism was already taking root among urban Palestine Arab intellectuals who began to advocate the idea of an Arab state independent of colonial masters.[45] Zionist ambitions were creating anxiety, too, from a fairly early stage.[46] Although there were no public opinion surveys examining attitudes and self-identification among the Arab public during the prestate period, inferences can be made by examining Arab literature, reflecting the sentiments of the local intelligentsia, a stratum that is frequently seen as the vanguard of ethnic nationalism.[47] Much of the poetry written by notable Palestine Arabs in the prestate period, such as Sheikh 'Ali al-Rimawi, Iskander al-Khuri al-Beitjali, Ibrahim Tuqan, Ibrahim al-Dabbagh, Abd al-Rahim Mahmud, and Abd-al-Karim al-Karmi, expressed strong sentiments of Arab nationalism, on the one hand, with concerns over what the poets saw as Jewish penetration to Palestine under British auspices and the perceived threats of this trend to Arab national aspirations in Palestine.[48] The Arab nationalists demanded an Arab-controlled state over the entire territory and overwhelmingly refused to consider proposals for power sharing with Jews or any form of reduced sovereignty to accommodate Jewish national aspirations. And yet, Palestine Arab nationalism did not yield an alternative, or a separate, state formation process.

Palestine Arab society possessed several characteristics that were not conducive to national institution building. First, Arab society was far more localized and less cohesive than Jewish society. It was generally rural, with an economy based on self-sufficient agriculture. According to one source, about 70 percent of the Arab population in Palestine were dependent on agriculture for their livelihood in the late 1920s.[49] A Palestine government survey put the figure of rurally based Arabs in 1930 at around 75 percent, compared to about 17 percent of the Jewish population.[50] The Arab middle class, conversely, was very small and marginal. Primary loyalty was to the *hamula* (extended family). Second, there was long-standing internal rivalry between leading hamulas over leadership roles.[51] This factionalism had its roots in the Ottoman system of rule.[52] Large-scale organized collaboration between many clans and villages for the national cause required a strong and competent leadership that would overcome internal rivalries and build an institutional framework that could coordinate political efforts. According to Tamari, "since each leading family had a political power base in client villages or town quarters, it felt itself the equal of the others and bargained vigorously before forming alliances."[53] And even then, alliances shifted according to clan interests rather than ideology, even among those who were carrying the national banner.[54]

The starting position of the Palestine elites was already at a disadvantage. It was only after the fall of King Faysal of Syria and the new carving of territorial boundaries by the British and French following World War I that local leaders began to seriously conceive of Palestine as separate from Greater Syria and requiring separate political organization. Faysal's forced exile by the French in July 1920 left the Arab leadership in Palestine without organizational infrastructure.[55] The newly established political boundaries following World War I, separating Palestine from Syria and Transjordan, required a shift in strategy and vision. In this respect, the obstacles faced by Arab nationalists were greater than the ones faced by the Yishuv leadership and made it far more difficult for the former to utilize the opportunities created by the rules set by the British.

Fears of Jewish immigration, land purchases, and the materializing of Zionist institutions led to violent anti-Jewish riots in 1920–1921 and 1929.[56] When Jewish immigration nonetheless continued throughout the 1930s, and the Jewish population, which constituted only 4 percent of the entire population of the area in 1882, had grown through immigration to make up almost 30 percent of the population, local pressure by dispossessed peasants and workers finally forced the Palestinian leadership into a unified front.[57] The most conspicuous organizational aspect of the collaborative effort was the formation of the Arab Higher Committee (AHC) in 1936.[58]

The leadership role in the AHC was assumed by the hard-line Husayni-led faction of Jerusalem.[59] Having been appointed by the British as president of the newly created Supreme Muslim Council, Haj Amin al-Husayni came to control many resources through which he could provide patronage and secure his leadership role.[60] At the same time, the narrow basis of his authority impeded his ability to lead inclusive, national-scale mobilization. Several historians have stressed that the collaboration expressed in the national revolt of 1936 and the formation of the AHC came about only after the traditional leadership was hard pressed from below by dispossessed peasants and disillusioned marginalized groups who started to question their leadership's commitment to the national goal and economic well-being and drove the leadership into taking a more belligerent stance.[61] Notables who did not conform to the hard-line positions often became the target of internal Arab violence.[62] Under the leadership of Husayni's Al-Hizb al-Arabi al-Falastini (Palestine Arab Party), the AHC encompassed the six Arab factions.

The cooperation of 1936 enabled the Palestine Arab national movement to coordinate a widespread and often violent rebellion, lasting from 1936 to 1939, against the British, pose a serious challenge on a national scale, for the first time, and force the British to seriously revisit their policies on Jewish immigration and land acquisition. In 1939, the British government adopted the White Paper, severely confining Jewish immigration so that the Jewish component of the population would not exceed one third of the total population, while also vigorously regulating Zionist land purchases with the aim of terminating them altogether.[63] This significant shift in British policy reflected the ability of organized mobilization to influence the formal rules set by the British at a time when the latter were increasingly concerned with the prospects of war against Germany and its allies and needed to calm the situation.

The establishment of the Palestine Royal Commission, known as the Peel Commission, was also a response to organized unrest. After holding talks with leaders from both sides, the Commission reported that both national groups demanded a state in which their group would be sovereign.[64] As a result, the Commission proposed the first partition plan in 1937. The plan would have seen the emergence of a Jewish state on a part of the territory that included the Galilee and a narrow strip along the coast, alongside an Arab state on the bulk of the area. A narrow strip connecting Jerusalem and the coast of the Mediterranean Sea at Jaffa was to remain under British control.

The partition was to include population exchanges, so that each state would have as small a minority as possible.[65]

Realizing that under existing conditions, a Jewish state could be established on only a portion of the territory, Ben-Gurion, the leader of the Yishuv, accepted, albeit reluctantly, the partition plan.[66] Ultimately, a state that would belong to Jews and enable Jewish self-government was the highest priority for the head of the organized Jewish community. A similar logic led the AHC to reject the partition plan. Unlike the Zionists, the Palestinians had reason to believe that the Arabs of Palestine could maintain institutional hegemony in a state whose sovereignty encompassed the territory of all of Mandatory Palestine. According to the proposal the AHC presented to the Peel Commission, the existing Jewish population was to be granted civic and religious, but not national, rights in an Arab state, and questions such as future immigration would be determined by the Arab-dominated state.[67] The commission's report noted that this plan would have effectively surrendered any ability of the Jewish national movement to influence decision-making in the direction of increasing Jewish immigration and building a national home for the Jewish nation.[68] As a result of the AHC rejection, the plan of the Peel Commission was shelved.

Despite shifting policies on immigration and land acquisition, the British were unable to conciliate Palestine Arab volatile mobilization. At the same time, their new approach spurred widespread anti-British Jewish resistance from the mainstream Jewish Yishuv in the post-World War II years. Eventually, the British decided to terminate their Mandate and redirect the question of the future of Palestine to the United Nations. On 29 November 1947, the UN General Assembly passed Resolution 181, partitioning Mandatory Palestine into two states: a Jewish state and an Arab state.

Remaining consistet with the same principles that guided them when facing the plan of the Peel Commission, the Yishuv leadership accepted the partition plan and the AHC categorically rejected it. Part of the problem faced by the Palestinians at this point was that although the AHC was able to mobilize opposition, it did not act to build an effective administration to manage the affairs of a future Palestinian polity. The Supreme Muslim Council was the only national-scale institution that did try to provide some services on a wider scale.[69] It operated an education system and a religious judicial system. It also controlled the properties of the Muslim religious endowments (*Waqf*). However, its control was by no means as extensive as that of the Jewish institutions, had no popular or representative component, and proved insufficient for state formation. That the Arab state was never formed was at least in part a result of the absence of effective and expansive prestate military and civil administrative institutions that could lay the foundations for a future state. In addition, the leaders of the main hamulas fled to neighboring countries during the war that ensued. Instead, Jordan annexed the rest of the territory designated for the Arab state west of the Jordan River (the West Bank), and Egypt took control of the Gaza Strip, albeit without formally annexing it.

Conclusion

The war that accompanied the termination of the British Mandate and Israel's Declaration of Independence led to an enlargement of the territory under Israel's control, from approximately 5,200 square miles designated to it by the UN partition plan to 7,700 square miles.[70] A new demographic reality resulted from the war. An estimated 550,000 to 725,000 Arabs were displaced from the territory over which Israel took control.[71] Approximately 156,000 Palestinian Arabs found themselves living inside Israeli-governed territory.[72]

The Palestinians that remained within the territorial boundaries of the state were to face a new reality. The institutions of the new State of Israel, along with its leadership and its practices, were premised on the foundations of the organizational infrastructure of the Yishuv as they had evolved over more than three decades. They were to include, among other things, an effective administration, a security apparatus, the Histadrut labor union with its economic capacity and social services, political parties, the dominance of Mapa'i and its political leadership, a Zionist education system, a welfare system, a parliamentary system based on proportional representation electoral rules, and close and institutionalized ties with world Jewry. The foundations, according to Ze'ev Sternhell, "were so solid that the transition from the Yishuv to the state was hardly felt. The country was still ruled by the same people, with the same philosophy of government and the same principles of action."[73]

It was this new institutional framework that the Arabs left within the borders of the Jewish state were to face in subsequent decades. The process of state formation, which was directly connected to the majority-state-minority relations that ensued, yielded relations whereby the Arab minority was left outside the boundaries of the national identity embodied by the state. Furthermore, the minority was suspected of affiliation with those with whom the emergent state had troubled relations.

3

State Autonomy, Marginalization,
and Grievances

The process of state formation engendered ethnically based national boundaries that excluded the Arab residents. Inheriting the prestate institutional framework, the new Israeli state lacked autonomy from the Jewish national movement, which controlled its institutions. Lack of state autonomy was manifested in the ideological framework of the state and the societal identity of the officeholders at all levels of the bureaucracy and translated into uni-ethnic favoritism in almost all policy areas. On top of that, given the history of Jewish-Arab relations in the prestate period, the PAI minority was viewed with much suspicion.

Although the objective inequality yielded serious grievances, it did not engender independent political activism at first. In fact, even though the lack of state autonomy and its implications have remained relatively stable, and considerable minority grievances existed from the onset, it was only in the 1970s that the PAI began to mobilize seriously, and it has only been since the 1990s that ethnonationalist demands by multiple organizations have become the centerpiece of PAI activism. This variation indicates that PAI exclusion and grievances alone are insufficient for explaining the transition in minority political activism.

(Lack of) State Autonomy During the First Decades

It has been suggested that from its establishment the State of Israel set out, and managed, to gain a high level of autonomy from social forces.[1] In particular, scholars point to the statist ideology (*mamlachtiyut*) of Prime Minister Ben-Gurion who sought to transfer control of major organizations from independent social forces to the state. The prestate education systems, most of the land, and many major industries were nationalized. Likewise, the prestate paramilitary organizations were disbanded and were brought under the control of a unified state army.[2]

This understanding of state-society relations conflates state capacity with state autonomy. The newly established state was indeed powerful and had extensive capability to intervene in society, modify it, and check significant political activity outside its own institutional framework.[3] From the outset, the Israeli state exhibited high capacity relative to other new states to enforce its preferences, which included, among other things, forging a new Jewish society and creating solid lines of differentiation between the included and excluded populations.

Nonetheless, it is wrong to assume that because of its strengths, the State of Israel was ever an institution isolated from society, with its own independent interests and coherent goals. The Israeli state was never independent from the interests and support of the majority ethnonational group, and indeed the dominant political forces within it. Rather, the state was largely constituted by the Jewish national movement to serve the Jewish nation. Once established, it had significant impact on the character of society, but the underlying assumption that clear-cut boundaries between state and society were established is misguided. The social identity of the high officeholders has always been Jewish and the framework of the ideological values embedded in the state is that of Jewish nationalism.

To be sure, the Israeli regime that emerged following the establishment of the state was procedurally democratic, with elected officials, regular elections with universal adult suffrage, and a multiparty system.[4] Yet the reliance on the prestate organizational infrastructure and the embeddings of Zionist ideals in state institutions translated into a lack of state autonomy. Government ministries were essentially transformed from the JA administrative departments, and leading figures in the Agency were transferred to key positions in the state apparatus. Seven of the thirteen members of Israel's first government were from the JA executive.[5] Most notably, David Ben-Gurion, chairman of the executive, became the first prime minister; Moshe Shertok (Sharett), head of the political arm of the Agency, became the first foreign minister and Israel's second prime minister; and Eliezer Kaplan, treasurer of the JA, became Israel's minister of finance. Likewise, the armed forces and their organizational structure were established on the foundations of the Yishuv's paramilitary Haganah organization. Senior Haganah personnel—including Yaakov Dori (Israel's first chief of general staff), Yigal Yadin, Haim Laskov, Moshe Dayan, Yigal Alon, and Yitzhak Rabin—were transferred to the senior officer ranks of the Israeli military. In short, the leading personnel in the organizations of the Jewish national movement became senior officeholders in the civil and military bureaucracy of the new state as the Jewish national movement came to dominate state apparatus.

The JA was granted a special status, and its relationship with the state was formally codified in 1952 through the Special Status Law and a covenant signed by the two parties. On the basis of these documents, the state empowered the JA to act on its behalf in matters of immigration, absorption and settlement, public relations, fund-raising, Jewish identity and Zionist education in diaspora communities, and construction of agricultural settlements in Israel. The JA was also active in the Israeli economy. Among other things, it owned the country's largest bank, Bank Leumi, and the Raasco construction company, which was responsible for building dozens of settlements. The Agency also had significant partial ownership in El Al, Israel's national airline; Zim, Israel's major shipping line; Amidar, the state agency entrusted with providing and managing housing projects for socially disadvantaged populations; and Mekorot, Israel's national water company.[6] Although these were not formally state-owned industries in the strictest sense, they were still very much considered a part of the public sector and the dominant political order.[7]

The lack of state autonomy was further manifested in the ideological framework of the state. The Declaration of Independence opened with a proclamation that "the Land of Israel was the birthplace of the Jewish people" and proceeded to describe the process of "exile" and the "return" of the Jewish people to the land on which Israel was established. The Declaration then emphasized the right of "the Jewish people to be masters of their own fate, like all other nations, in their own state" and proclaimed "the establishment of a Jewish state in Eretz-Israel, to be known as the State of Israel."[8] By stressing the history of exile and return, the declaration made a commitment to fostering Jewish immigration and the principle of the "ingathering of the exiles," which was so prominent for the prestate leadership. It should be stressed that whereas the Declaration was signed by representatives of all the main organized Jewish streams, including the non-Zionist ultra-orthodox, it was not signed by any representative of the Arab minority, thus amplifying Jewish ownership of the state.

The foundational principles and the commitment of state builders to this ideological framework created distinct boundaries of belonging to the national community. State-issued identity cards, distributed to all citizens of the state, had a nationality clause that distinguished between members of the Jewish nation and other citizens. State symbols reflected Jewish identity exclusively. The state's flag, featuring the Star of David, was similar to the flag of the Zionist movement and was "inspired by the Jewish prayer shawl."[9] The Jewish menorah, a candelabra with seven branches, became the state emblem. And the state anthem was substantively and exclusively Jewish, focusing on the Jewish soul's longing to return to Zion in order to be a free people. The Jewish Sabbath was made the official day of rest, and newly introduced state holidays were essentially Jewish holidays.[10]

The lack of state autonomy influenced state practices and translated into policies that centred on continuing the pursuit of the objectives of the Jewish national movement. Ultimately, the state was an instrument in this pursuit; as Prime Minister Ben-Gurion stated before the Knesset when introducing his government's basic principles in 1949, "The establishment of the State of Israel was merely the first stage in the fulfilment of our historic vision. The ingathering of the exiles is a prerequisite to its full realization. Israel's principal task today is, therefore, to gather in the exiles."[11] Hence, an important area in which the policy preferences of the state elites were manifested was the laws pertaining to immigration and citizenship, which differentiated between Jews and non-Jews. The Law of Return, which was introduced in 1950, granted every Jew in the world the right to immigrate to Israel and obtain citizenship. This is not to say that immigration policies were not selective even among Jews: many Jews, particularly from Arab and Muslim countries, were disqualified on medical grounds or because they were seen as an economic liability.[12] Nevertheless, one should not lose sight of the forest by focusing on a small number of trees. Hundreds of thousands of Jews immigrated to Israel after its emergence in 1948, mostly from Arab countries. Israel's population almost doubled (from 650,000 to 1,300,000) by the end of 1950 and more than tripled by 1955, mostly as a result of immigration. From the "ingathering" perspective, whereas 6 percent of the world's Jews lived in Israel on its emergence, estimates give approximately 9.7 percent there by the end of 1950, nearly 13 percent by 1955, 17 percent in 1965, 21 percent in 1975, 27 percent by 1985, 34.8 percent in 1995, and 40.6 percent by the end of 2005.[13]

Approximately 156,000 Arabs who remained in Israel after the 1947–1949 war became Israeli citizens, although not without difficulties, and for many it took several years.[14] Obstacles were imposed when the government demanded that applicants for citizenship provide evidence that they were Palestine citizens in the period immediately preceding the establishment of the state. This was often a difficult obstacle to overcome because many Arabs did not hold identity cards or passports.[15]

The Citizenship Law, enacted in 1952, provided for naturalization of non-Jewish immigrants, who could become permanent residents if they renounced their prior nationality and demonstrated knowledge of the Hebrew language. It was at the discretion of the minister of immigration, and later the minister of interior, to grant such a permanent resident visa. Aside from 35,500 war escapees who were allowed to return after the war in the process of family reunification, the overwhelming inclination of the responsible ministers was not to grant citizenship to Arabs seeking to move to Israel, even those who left during the war, unless they married an Israeli citizen. This tendency is revealed by the low approval rate of applications for citizenship. Between 1952 and the end of 1955, Israeli citizenship was granted to only 309 applicants under the provisions of the Citizenship Law, although the ministry of interior handled 3,810 applications in 1955 alone.[16]

The impact of the immigration and citizenship laws was a reduction in the relative size of the Arab minority from 19 percent of the entire population in 1948 to 11 percent by 1951, a percentage that changed very little until the 1967 War.[17] It was only due to a slowdown in the inflows of Jewish immigrants (most eligible Jews from Arab countries had either already immigrated by the mid-1960s or chose to migrate elsewhere, while Soviet restrictions enabled no more than 160,000 Jews from the USSR to immigrate in the 1970s[18]) that the relative size of the Arab population picked up again to 15 percent in the mid 1970s, over 16 percent by the early 1980s, and closer to 20 percent in the 2000s.[19]

Land policies, too, reflected the inherent lack of state autonomy from the Jewish national organizations. For a long period, the JNF, whose role in the prestate period was discussed in the preceding chapter, continued to function as the land-purchasing agent of the state, reflecting the principle of land redemption, which, like the ideal of the ingathering of exiles, did not expire with the emergence of the state. Gradually, the functions of the JNF passed on to the state. The two sides signed a covenant in 1961, according to which the administration of land purchased in the past and to be purchased in the future by the JNF would be concentrated in the hands of the Jewish state through the newly established Israel Lands Administration (ILA), which was to be under the authority of a government ministry.[20] In practice, this arrangement provided for the nationalization of land. The agreement about the administration of land was instituted in the Basic Law: Israel Lands, which also anchored the principle by which land was not sold but distributed on lease, thus keeping it under state control.[21] Although this law (and all other laws pertaining to land distribution and housing) did not explicitly distinguish between Arab and Jewish citizens, the fundamental imperatives of the JNF were instilled in the new arrangement and passed on to the state as an unwritten rule. Thus, nationalization of land related to Jewish ownership of it and essentially equated with the "Judaization" of the land. The ILA and JNF had discretion over to whom they would lease land and for how long. Subsequently, whereas Jewish communities and individuals normally received land on the basis of forty-nine-year leases, the practice was to sign short-term leasing contracts, usually annual, with Arabs.[22] Although this was not stipulated as a formal regulation, it was a customary behavior pattern that emerged from the institutional framework and the norms embedded in it. Moreover, the JNF continued to collect donations from world Jewry and to purchase land, sometimes from the state itself in order to generate income for the state.

To be sure, control of the land was initially also influenced by security concerns. There was fear of future irredentist claims by Palestinian Arabs and apprehension that Arab villages along the new borders could serve as penetration points and become bases for subversive militias. After all, many of the PAI families had kin ties with Arab refugees in neighboring countries, and some were remnants of hamulas that were artificially divided during the war.[23] It was conceivable that some sympathy and loyalty would be displayed toward their co-nationals. Jewish society and the governing institutions, in turn, tended to associate the PAI minority with their enemies.[24]

The Jewish state sought to create a demographic presence that would increase its capacity to exercise sovereignty in frontier areas that were seen as potentially contentious, particularly along the border line. At the time, the Arab population was mainly concentrated in three geographical areas: the Galilee, where in 1948 approximately 58 percent of the Arab population resided; the Negev, inhabited by about 8 percent of the Arab population (mostly Bedouin); and the area known as the "Little Triangle" along Israel's northeastern armistice line of the West Bank of Transjordan, where about 18 percent of the Arabs lived.[25] One of the most useful ways to extend state control to these areas was to nationalize Arab-owned land through expropriation, and then to build new Jewish settlements on the expropriated land.[26] This practice was consistent with the desire to settle the enormous inflows of Jewish immigrants and the demand for more land for cultivation in Jewish agricultural settlements.[27]

In 1949 the Knesset passed the Emergency Land Requisition Law and in 1953 the Land Acquisition Law; both laws allowed the state to expropriate land for security needs. The definition of "security needs" was left vague, allowing the state all but unchecked authority to seize Arab lands. Oren Yiftachel has argued that the government identified areas with large concentrations of Arabs, including areas that were abandoned during the war, as "internal frontiers" that needed to be controlled by the Jewish majority.[28] These regions included the Galilee region (where only 12 percent of the population in 1949 was Jewish), the Little Triangle, the Negev desert, and the Jerusalem area. Land nationalization, or expropriation, took place primarily in these regions, and the nationalized land was used for the establishment of new Jewish settlements, revealing the close relationship between nationalization and Judaization. The predominantly Jewish Shlomi, Upper Nazareth, Carmiel, Maʿalot (all in the Galilee), Givaʿt Yearim, Shoresh (both in the Jerusalem area), and Omer (Negev) are all examples of new settlements that were built on nationalized land previously owned by Palestine Arabs.

The Absentee Property Law, passed in 1950, further allowed the state to seize land abandoned during the war by Arabs, even those Arabs who became legal citizens of Israel. Tens of thousands of Arabs were internally displaced in the aftermath of the war, and many received the incoherent legal status of "present absentees," which under the provision of the law made their land susceptible to nationalization by the state. The exact amount of land nationalized over the years is hard to determine. Several scholars have estimated that the Arabs in Israel lost about 70 percent of the land they owned.[29]

The same pattern of land policies continued several decades after state establishment. Not a single new village, town, or settlement was built for the PAI since the state declared its independence, whereas dozens of Jewish settlements were constructed. In the Galilee, for example, a "Judaization" plan, called "The New Development Plan for the Galilee," was introduced in 1975. According to the plan, privately owned land was to be expropriated and designated for building new settlements. In the six years that followed (1976–1982), more than 40 new settlements (also called *Mitzpim*) were built in the Galilee, all for the benefit of Jewish populations.[30] By the late 1970s, approximately 90 percent of the land in Israel was owned by either the state or the JNF and administered by the ILA.[31]

Although Yiftachel and Rumley found that the Judaization policy had some benefits for the Arabs, particularly employment opportunities in newly established industrial estates and the acceleration of the modernization process that began in the 1950s, there is little dispute that the overall social and economic impact was seriously damaging.[32] The compensation given for the expropriated land never matched its value.[33] The land that was confiscated was often the best land for agricultural cultivation. Because many of the PAI depended on agriculture for their livelihood in the 1950s, their means of livelihood was thus severely affected. Add to that the discriminatory land-leasing practices that generated disincentives for investment and development of the leased land as well as discriminatory water allocation policies, and the outcome was expanding underdevelopment.[34]

A related effect of the land policies was that many Arabs were compelled to work as hired labor in Jewish villages or in more modern Jewish-owned industries. This transition, however, was not without its difficulties because PAI mobility within Israel was restricted under the Military Government, as shall be elaborated upon in Chapter 4, and many did not have the skills required by the various industries. In the short and medium terms, Israeli land policies compelled the PAI minority to take steps toward integrating into the Jewish economy. By 1961, more than half of the Arab workers were employed outside their local village, in occupations such as drivers, waiters, unskilled construction workers, or other low-skill jobs.[35]

For the Negev Bedouins, in particular, land policies had destructive effects. Much of the land they inhabited, mostly in the northern part of the desert, was apportioned for Kibbutz settlements and new development towns in what the state perceived for a long time as frontier territory. As a result, the majority of the Bedouins were relocated and concentrated in a much smaller portion of the territory. Furthermore, their sources of livelihood dwindled as the economy was oriented toward absorbing the new Jewish migrants who settled in the Negev.[36] Scores of Bedouin villages, located outside the contained relocation area, remained unrecognized as legal by the state. By eschewing recognition, the state relieved itself of providing basic infrastructure, such as running water, electricity, health services, and schools. Lack of formal status for these villages also gave the state legal tools to continue to "redeem land" by demolishing buildings, evicting residents, and planning projects on these lands as if they were uninhabited. State authority to ignore the existence of these villages was entrenched in the 1965 Planning and Construction Law. The law classified lands on which these villages existed as agricultural lands on which construction was illegal. Although new Jewish settlements were not usually built on these lands, they were designated for agriculture (and thus often transferred to the administration of agricultural Jewish local authorities) and nature reserves.

The complex relationship between religion and state also reflected the embedding of Jewish dominance in the state. Israel adopted Judaism as its official religion. Although the substantive meaning of this relationship, the balance between civil individual rights and the role of religion in the public sphere have always been subject to contestation, the Jewish religion nonetheless gained an official status as attempts at intra-Jewish accommodation were made.[37] The state formed a government ministry for religious affairs and integrated religious courts into its judicial system to deal with matters of personal status. Religious holidays were incorporated into the national calendar and declared official public holidays. The Sabbath became an official day of rest in which public services were not supplied and labor was restricted.

Anchoring religion into state institutions made it far easier for the non-Zionist orthodox community, already troubled by the establishment of the Jewish state, to become members of the community. On the other hand, this arrangement also somewhat blurred the lines between Jewish religion and Jewish nationality; comparative research reveals that when national boundaries are informed by divisions along the lines of religion, boundaries of exclusion become even less permeable for minorities.[38] Thus, even though the leaders of the Jewish national movement and Israel's state builders were secular and not motivated by religious faith, the institutional arrangement they agreed on in order to accommodate intra-Jewish diversity accentuated majority-minority differentiation.

As the main motivation behind this arrangement was an attempt to reconcile different perspectives among the Jewish majority, state elites did not formulate a coherent and comprehensive policy regarding the non-Jewish minority. At the time, the vast majority of the PAI minority were Muslim. Muslims constituted about 70 percent of the non-Jewish population (Christians were about 21 percent and Druze slightly more than 9 percent).[39] "The status of Islam in the Jewish state was never a priority and was rarely a matter of discussion at high government levels."[40] Nonetheless, the integration of religion into the state had an impact on the relatively large Muslim population in particular. State religious Muslim courts were introduced, with jurisdiction over the Muslim community in matters similar to those addressed by Jewish courts. The Muslim Supreme Council, responsible for religious affairs, was dissolved; state bureaucrats were appointed in its place, engendering severe resentment among religious Arab elites.[41] Jurisdiction over Muslim communal institutions was divided between various government ministries, including the ministries of Minority Affairs, Religious Affairs, and Education, and the Office of the Advisor to the Prime Minister on Arab Affairs. Fragmentation, rivalry over areas of responsibility, and short-term measures, rather than a coherent vision, characterized the practices of the various arms of the Israeli bureaucracy and prevented the development of a comprehensive policy on communal institutions.[42]

Yet another facet that shaped the walls of exclusion was military-society relations. Not only were the security forces converted from the pre-state Jewish Haganah, but the prolonged conflict with Israel's Arab neighbors, which was perceived by most Israeli Jews as existential, made the army an institution of paramount societal importance. The need to maintain a strong armed force was a core consensual issue in Jewish discourse in Israel. In the first two decades of the state's existence, between 8 and 16 percent of the annual GNP was spent on defense (during the wars of 1956 and 1967, defense spending was higher).[43] Mandatory enlistment of most Jewish men and women, coupled with annual reserve duty for Jewish men for as long as thirty days a year, sometimes even longer, resulted in the army being not insulated from society but rather embedded in it, and contributed to the blurring of differences between soldier and citizen.

The army played two relevant roles in society. First, it was a means to construct a more cohesive Jewish nation from the diverse Jewish populations that arrived in Israel from numerous countries. It fulfilled this function through enlistment as well as through activity in civilian spheres. Uri Ben-Eliezer describes, for example, how the army was involved in the ma'abarot, the camps in which most of the new immigrants were initially housed; in providing education to new immigrants; and in childcare, medical care, and other welfare and social services.[44] This involvement was seen as a way for enhancing the connection with the recent arrivals. Second, the army served as a means for upward mobility in Israeli society and for improving individual and group standing. Yagil Levy demonstrated how, over the decades, individuals from previously marginalized groups within Jewish society have been able to integrate into the military and play increasingly more important roles in its ranks.[45]

Furthermore, the prominence of security questions has given the army a high public standing that allowed it to be involved in setting policies pertaining to the Arab-Israeli conflict, as well as in other civil spheres.[46] An officer class emerged in Israel, whose opinions on political and social issues mattered in public opinion. To attract voters, political parties often recruited retired generals and former members of the security apparatus to their ranks. Conspicuous examples include, among many others, Moshe Dayan, who served as chief of staff between 1953 and 1958, and Lieutenant General Yigal Alon, who retired from the army in 1950.[47]

Because of their delicate situation as both Israeli citizens and Palestine Arabs, and because they were widely associated with the state's external enemies, the Arab citizens of Israel (with the exception of the Druze) were exempted from mandatory army service. The impact was that the PAI were excluded from a crucial aspect in the continuation of the nation-building process after the state was formally established, and had no access to an important channel for upward mobility in social and political life.

There were many other areas in which state policies privileged the dominant group. According to some scholars, the welfare system purposefully discriminated against the Arab minority.[48] Others found discrimination in allocation of resources to PAI schools and local authorities.[49] Beyond adding more specific examples, the general point is that the intrinsic lack of state autonomy from the Jewish national movement translated into state rule-making and policies that disadvantaged the PAI minority. The state, over which the Jewish national movement exercised propriety, set rules that facilitated Jewish domination and gave the dominant majority clear preference in access to resources and opportunities in numerous ways. The state was practically impenetrable to the minority.

State Autonomy Since the 1990s

The lack of state autonomy has remained largely intact in almost all major dimensions well into the 1990s and the 2000s, when ethnonationalist mobilization was accelerating. The foundational principles remained relatively resilient to PAI demands. Jewish ownership of the state remained reflected in the ethnic identity of the personnel at the lower level and senior ranks of the bureaucracy: In 1992, Arabs constituted only 2.1 percent of all civil service employees in Israel.[50] According to the NGO Sikkuy: The Association for Advancement of Civic Equality in Israel, only thirteen of 966 people sitting on the boards of directors of government companies and only one of 604 senior executives in government executives were members of the PAI minority in the year 2000.[51]

The social identity of the military apparatus has also continued to be significant for state-ethnicity relations. PAI exclusion from mandatory conscription appears inevitable as long as Israel is still in conflict with other Arabs and Palestinians—and indeed PAI elites have persistently rejected suggestions of conscription.[52] And yet, the prominent role that the army has continued to play in civil and political life has remained significant. Ben-Eliezer has suggested that the protracted conflict has engendered a society that is a "nation-in-arms," characterized by mutually penetrating civic-military relations.[53] Questions of security and politics have continued to be intertwined in Israel and the security apparatus is still held in high regard in the eyes of the Jewish majority.[54] As a result of the military's high social standing, leading figures in the security apparatus have continued to be recruited into the highest ranks in politics upon retirement.[55] Only five of eighteen chiefs of staff who served since Israel's creation did not enter politics. Conspicuous examples of retired generals that served in senior government positions over the last two decades include the late prime minister Yitzhak Rabin, Prime Ministers Ariel Sharon and Ehud Barak; Shaul Mofaz; Moshe Ya'alon; Binyamin Ben-Eliezer; Matan Vilna'i; Danny Yatom; and many others. Some of those who choose not to engage in formal politics often appear in the media to provide what is deemed professional analysis on questions that cross into the civilian sphere. Some form reserve-officers associations, for example, the Council for Peace and Security, as pressure groups to express what are claimed to be authoritative views on questions of security that are central in Israeli politics. Of course, the military's authority in the military-civil relations should not be overstated. Civilian oversight of the armed forces is not in jeopardy the way the French Fourth Republic's civilian authority was.[56] At the same time, military personnel continue to be highly influential in society and politics.[57]

Just as in earlier decades, the lack of state insulation from the interests of the dominant majority affects policies of resource distribution. For example, service in the army continues to be tied to social benefits. While in many countries soldiers receive compensation for an enduring and often very demanding military service that sometimes involves putting one's life at risk, in Israel some benefits are also extended to the immediate family of the soldiers.[58] One of the most significant areas in which differentiation in the distribution of these benefits come into play is in allocation of National Insurance Institute (NII) allowances to families living underneath the poverty line. At the turn of the twenty-first century, NII allowances reduced the overall number of families living in poverty among the general population by about 45 percent. The number of PAI families living in poverty as a result from NII allowances, however, was reduced by only 23.3 percent.[59]

The ongoing lack of state autonomy has continued to get reflected in land policies as well. By the early 2000s, about 93 percent of the nonresidential land was already owned either by the state or the JNF and administered by the ILA, and still no new PAI settlement was built compared to dozens of new Jewish settlements.[60] Although expropriation of Arab-owned land has slowed down considerably since 1976, it was mainly because close to 90 percent of the nonresidential land had already been nationalized by the 1980s.[61] A more subtle way of increasing majority control over land has been the transfer of PAI-owned land to the jurisdiction of Jewish local governments through amalgamation of local authorities. According to Yiftachel, by the mid-1990s, only 2.5 percent of the country's local government area was under the jurisdiction of PAI local government.[62] Such amalgamation projects have provided legal mechanisms to utilize the land in the way that is advantageous to the majority of the population under the jurisdiction of the enlarged local government while preventing PAI expansion and construction of new neighborhoods.[63]

Likewise, scores of PAI villages retained their "unrecognized" status. There is no official data regarding the number of unrecognized villages, but the Association of Forty, a PAI NGO concerned with the issue, estimated that at the beginning of the twenty-first century about 70,000 Bedouins lived in unrecognized villages, mostly in the Negev Desert (approximately 10,000 were said to inhabit unrecognized villages in the North).[64] One of the most direct implications has been that the highest rates of unemployment and poverty in the country exist among the Negev Bedouin.[65]

Finally, Jewish ownership of the state has continued to be reflected in immigration policies as immigration laws have continued to embody the goals of the Jewish national movement exclusively, just as they did since the enactment of the Law of Return and the Citizenship Law in the early 1950s. The proportion of Jews living in Israel increased from around 27 percent of world Jewry in 1985 to over 40 percent by 2005, largely a result of mass immigration of over one million Jews from the former Soviet Union throughout the 1990s.[66] As a consequence, the relative size of the Arabs in Israel (20 percent in 2009) has increased far less than it would have despite high natural growth rates that saw the population increase from around 800,000 in the late 1980s to close to 1.5 million in 2009.[67]

Furthermore, a 2003 legislation that prevents Palestinians from the West Bank and Gaza who marry Israeli citizens from obtaining citizenship or a permanent resident status has placed further constraints on the PAI. According to figures released by the Ministry of Interior to the Israeli press, between 1993 and 2002 about 100,000 Palestinians immigrated to Israel through marriage.[68] Rouhana's observation that in times of conflict the Jewish identity of the state intensifies appears to get reflected through reformulation of immigration rules.[69] The head of Israel's security service, the Shin Bet, reportedly revealed that about 11 percent of the PAI who were involved in terror activity during the second *intifada* (literally, "shaking off"), which started in the fall of 2000, entered Israel through marriage to a PAI partner.[70]

While lack of state autonomy has persisted, it should be noted that the relationship between the organizations of the Jewish national movement and the state has loosened over the years as the state sought to limit the role of alternative organizations. The UJA, which in the prestate period and in the early days of statehood, transferred most of its donations to the JA and Israel, has incrementally reduced its allocations to Israel to below 40 percent.[71] Similarly, the JA, although still active in immigration, absorption, and settlement, has been downsized considerably and its scope of activities, particularly in the economy, has been reduced as a result of economic liberalization and privatization in Israel.[72]

Furthermore, access to civil service employment somewhat improved in the 2000s. The proportion of Arabs serving on boards of directors of state companies grew to 6.7 percent in 2003 and 8 percent in 2005.[73] The number of PAI employees in the civil service has also increased. If in 1992, only 2.1 percent of all civil service employees were PAI, by the end of 2002, Arabs accounted for 6.1 employees of all civil service employees (mainly in health and education services).[74] The number then declined to 5.5 percent in the mid-2000s.[75] The overall rise has been a product of two pieces of legislation that aimed to address structural discrimination.[76] Likewise, the first PAI board member of the ILA was appointed in 1999; the Supreme Court had its first Arab judge, Justice Salim Jubran; Oscar Abu-Razek was the first Arab to be appointed to the position of director general of a government ministry (Ministry of Interior); and Arab ministers have been appointed to junior posts on occasion: Labor's Salah Tarif, a Druze, served as a minister without portfolio between March 2001 and January 2002, and Labor's Raleb Majadele served as minister of science, culture, and sport from 2007 to 2009 (Majadele also served as a minister without portfolio for a short period).

The changes that have taken place in the state apparatus, however, have not been linear. Sustainable, irreversible movement in the direction of inclusion has yet to be consolidated. Arab presence in the bureaucracy is still far from reflective of this minority's relative size. More significantly, the situation in the civil administration does not appear to constitute a consequential structural change that gets reflected in resource allocation.[77]

The significance of this description of state institutions and policies is to stress that, despite variation on the margins, state autonomy and PAI exclusion have remained relatively consistent from state inception. Distribution of resources was and remains overwhelmingly in favor of the Jewish population. And yet, minority political activism has transitioned considerably. Thus, the Jewish character of the state cannot solely account for transitions in PAI political activism.

Grievances

If the Jewish character of the state cannot account for transitions in minority political mobilization and demands, grievances might. One potential explanation for Arab quiescence in the first two decades is that living under the jurisdiction of the Jewish state did not, in fact, generate unyielding grievances. An argument can be put forth, and has sometimes been made by observers, that compared to the conditions of life of their co-nationals living in refugee camps in the West Bank, Lebanon, Jordan, and other neighboring countries, the situation of the Palestinian Arabs in Israel was significantly better as a result of modernization and could have encouraged positive attitudes toward the state despite the ethnically exclusive national identity that it embodied.[78] After all, the effects of state policies and state-driven modernization were not exclusively negative. For example, improved access to clean drinking water, the introduction of modern agricultural techniques and new machinery, and the growth in income from agriculture from the mid-1950s (due to the increase in value of Arab products in Israeli markets) contributed to a rise in the standard of living for some.[79] Likewise, the introduction of a free universal education system had dramatically increased Arab access to education and literacy rates. Between 1948 and 1955, the number of state primary schools in the Arab sector rose from 59 to 112 (by 1960, there were 139 Arab primary schools), the number of teachers grew from 250 to 740, and the number of pupils grew from 10,000 to 24,863.[80]

Available sources, however, suggest that it is not contentment that accounts for lack of mobilization. A disclaimer that should be stressed immediately is that the tools available for a thorough evaluation of the sentiments of the minority in the first two decades of Israel's existence are limited. In the 1950s and 1960s, there were very few systematic studies about the PAI that engaged this minority, and almost no public opinion surveys of Arab attitudes.

One invaluable source is field research by Don Peretz, a Middle East scholar, in the mid- to late 1950s. Informed by personal contacts with members of the PAI, Peretz's study reveals deep misgivings.[81] Peretz noted that many Arab citizens of Israel complained they were second-class citizens. Discriminatory immigration and citizenship laws, socioeconomic gaps, land expropriation, employment policies, the government's stance on Palestinian refugees, and new local administrations all generated bitterness, resentment, and suspicion toward state authorities.

Peretz's findings are confirmed by a public opinion survey conducted by Yochanan Peres in 1967. The survey found that most of the Arab citizens of Israel felt that in the first two decades of Israel's existence, they made less progress than Palestinians in the West Bank in the spheres of economics and education. This finding debunks the proposition that the PAI were satisfied with the positive impacts of state-led modernization.[82] Furthermore, 48 percent of the PAI responded that they would feel more at home in an Arab state than in Israel, while only 37 percent responded that they feel better in Israel.[83]

A final source that can provide some evidence on sentiments among PAI elites, and which has been used by Ian Lustick in his influential work on the Arab minority in Israel, is Arab literature.[84] Much of the Palestinian Arab poetry and literature during this period dealt with victimization, the exile of refugees, regaining the lost homeland, and pride and self-empowerment.

The late Palestinian intellectual Abdul Latif Tibawi suggested that much of the Palestinian literature of the time emulated key motifs in the Zionist narratives that dealt with similar issues in the Jewish context.[85] For example, some writers and poets framed the questions of refugees and the retrieval of the lost homeland in a manner that resembled the way in which Zionism in the pre-state period envisioned a return.[86] Influenced by the success of the Zionists, Tibawi even adopted the terms *new Zionism* and *Arab Zionism* to describe Palestinian national aspirations, building on the idea of a dispersed and persecuted minority that will eventually return to and liberate its homeland.[87]

Others wrote of national pride in the face of government policies and discrimination. Probably the most noteworthy writers in this context were the author Emil Habibi, who was also a Communist Party Member of Knesset (MK), and the poets Mahmud Darwish and Samih al-Qasim. In one of his most acclaimed and widely referenced poems from the mid-1960s, "The Identity Card" (a reference to the nationality clause in the identity card that distinguishes between Jewish nationals and non-Jews), Darwish expresses national pride as well as his conviction of the Arabs' rightful ownership of the land appropriated by the Jewish state:[88]

> Write down, I am an Arab!
> Fifty thousand is my number,
> Eight children, the ninth will come
>   next summer.
> Angry? Write down, I am an Arab . . .
>
> You stole the vineyards of my
>   parents,
> The lands I used to plough,
> And left us nothing but these rocks—
> Will your government take them too,
>   as has been said?[89]

In "Our Threadbare Shirt," al-Qasim, in a defiant voice, stresses deep PAI connections to the land, as well as the imperative of not giving up on Arab rights to it despite the lack of material opportunities. The idea of return also features:

> Our staying in this land is suicide,
> Bookworms crowd my books,
> A feeling of death clouds my heart,
> I have searched for work until my
>   shoes are worn out.
> Employment Bureaus always say:
> "Wait, wait, wait!"
> I have been insulted, despised
>   and cursed.
>
> It is a disgrace to sell our ancestral
>   lands.
> Our roots in the womb of this land

Are strong and stretch out far.
As long as our threadbare shirt
Streams in the wind of misery,
The banner of return will remain
    on high.[90]

In 1960, Habibi, in an article in the Arab literary periodical *al-Jadid,* expressed sentiments of Israel as an imperialist power that builds a nation by depriving and victimizing the weak and vulnerable Arabs: "The total rejection of the rights of the Arabs, and the curious belief in the eternity of imperialism—are like two rats nibbling away at the foundations of peace and brotherhood that we are trying to hold on to with our full force . . . it is impossible to build one nation on the rubble of another."[91]

It should be stressed that poetry and literature are less reliable as a source for evaluating national beliefs and political sentiments, because they are indicative of political sentiments among a segment of the intelligentsia only, rather than the mass population. On the other hand, intelligentsias have been identified by several scholars of nationalism as being a main driving force behind the spread of nationalist sentiments among masses in the first place.[92] Intense ethnonationalist sentiments expressed by the intelligentsia that are not accompanied or followed up on by the establishment of political organizations and mobilization are still very much within the framework of the phenomenon that needs to be explained.

Ultimately, taken together, the evidence suggests that PAI passivity in the first two decades should not be attributed to contentment or an absence of distinct sentiments of minority nationalism. Bitterness and a strong desire to reconstitute the institutional framework existed from very early on despite the relative political passivity that characterized the 1950s and 1960s. Similarly, transition to independent political mobilization cannot be accounted for by changes in political and material inequality and grievances. The absence of large-scale independent political activism to mount a significant challenge to the lack of state autonomy and the transition to activism through the Communist Party are accounted for in the next chapter.

4

From Quiescence to the Communist Party

Arab politics transitioned dramatically within three decades. The ethnically defined nationalism of the prestate period was replaced by relative quiescence in the first two decades that followed Israel's independence. In the 1950s and 1960s, most Arab elites were concerned with guaranteeing immediate local interests and complied with ruling stratum practices. Ethnonationalist claims were made only by a handful of unorganized, if outspoken, intellectuals. Initial passivity then gave way to mobilization in the binational Israel Communist Party (ICP), which throughout most of the 1970s and 1980s was the single most popular political organization among Arab voters. Changing patterns of mobilization were accompanied by changing political demands When the Communists came to the forefront of independent Arab mobilization, they articulated national level political demands, which largely focused on distribution of resources. The transition, as the previous chapter demonstrated, is not correlated with grievances or the degree of Jewish hold on the state. It was in large part a result of broader changes in state-society relations in Israel and the beginning of a trend of dispersion of political power.

Patterns of Arab Mobilization

To observe that PAI politics was characterized by relative passivity in the first two decades is not to say that Arabs were absent from politics altogether. First, there were Arab MKs in party lists affiliated with the governing Mapa'i Party. These were clientelistic lists that toed the line of the governing party and were in no way independent (how these lists came about and were controlled will

be discussed below in the section on centralized power). When proposals to
ease PAI difficulties were put to a Knesset vote, for example, propositions to
role back the Military Government that administered Arab inhabited regions
until 1966, these Arab MKs typically voted with the government against removing the restrictions. Otherwise, the PAI were almost invisible in the Israeli political scene during the 1950s and most of the 1960s.

The Early Days of the Communists

The little Arab involvement in politics that was in opposition to the central
government in the first decades of Israel's existence was pursued through
the ICP. The party incorporated Arabs into its ranks and usually had one or
two Arab MKs. The ICP, however, was not an ethnically based PAI organization that claimed to advance an ethnonational agenda on behalf of the Arab
community, even though its MKs continuously protested against the discrimination suffered by the minority. Ideologically, the ICP claimed to be an
internationalist, or at least a communally neutral, non-Zionist party focused
on class politics. Sociologically, most of the party leadership at the time was
Jewish, a characteristic inherited from the prestate period.

In the first place, the Communist Party was established by Jewish immigrants from Russia who took part in the 1917 Communist Revolution and
exported its ideas.[1] It participated in the Jewish Yishuv politics but was marginal and usually received between 1 to 3 percent of the votes to the Yishuv's
Electoral Council. In 1924, the party was accepted by the Soviets to the Co-
mintern. Its ongoing Jewishness earned it rebuke from the Executive Committee of the Communist International (ECCI), which frequently criticized
the party for not doing enough to incorporate Arabs.[2] In 1944 the ICP began
publishing a weekly paper in Arabic, *al-Ittihad* (the Union) in an attempt to
reach out to the Arab population. Nevertheless, the sociological characteristics of members of the party remained primarily Jewish for a long time.

Taking their cues from the Soviets, the Communists formally opposed
all forms of nationalism and, before the UN partition resolution in 1947,
advocated the establishment of a secular communist state for both Jewish
and Arab workers in the whole of mandatory Palestine. The party's opposition to Zionism and adherence to the Soviets resulted in expulsion from the
Histadrut in 1924.[3] Likewise, Arab nationalism in Palestine was viewed by
the party as detrimental to the unified class struggle against imperialism.[4]

Opposition to it sometimes went beyond the Soviet position. For example, whereas the Soviets characterized events such as the 1929 Arab riots as a "revolutionary uprising," the Communists in Palestine viewed this event as a nationalist-driven pogrom.[5]

Although claiming to oppose nationalism, the Communist Party, following Soviet directives, accepted the UN plan of 1947 to partition Palestine into two states, Jewish and Arab.[6] Meir Vilner, the party's elected representative to the People's Electoral Council, signed Israel's Declaration of Independence on behalf of the party. Despite signing on to the Jewish state, the party, now called the Israel Communist Party, protested from the outset against the constitution of the new state in a manner that marginalized the Arab minority. Its Hebrew publication *Qol ha-Am* (voice of the people) was particularly vocal in condemning the Military Administration, imposed in Arab regions, as oppressive and even fascist.[7] However, the ICP did not object to the Law of Return when it was enacted. Publicly expressing understanding, shortly after the Holocaust, for a genuine need to ensure the protection of Jews, the ICP chose instead to focus on the difficulties faced by Arab residents of Israel in attaining citizenship.[8] Thus the ICP called for extending the Law of Return to include the Palestine Arab refugees and the displaced people of the 1947–1949 war.[9] Despite its acceptance of the Partition Plan and the Law of Return, the party called for a disengagement of the state from world Jewry and for the creation of a socialist regime, thus seeking to reconstitute the state and alter the norms guiding distribution of resources. On the whole, the ICP and its positions remained marginal in Israeli politics.

Although the ICP was mostly dominated by a Jewish leadership stratum during the 1950s and early 1960s (the general secretary and the majority of the Central Committee were Jewish), Arab integration into the party slowly took place during this period. The Arabs who joined the party were mostly secular, educated urbanites who were less committed to the traditional hamula practices and were attracted to the egalitarian doctrine of the Communists. These Arabs were mostly nonpracticing Christians from Haifa, Nazareth, and Jerusalem. By the end of the 1950s, support for the Communists was greater among Arabs than among Jews.[10]

Growing electoral support from the Arab minority was not reflected in the composition of the party's central institutions. Like other communist parties in the world, the ICP's main institutions were a Central Committee of approximately twenty members, of whom, in 1961, there were only five Arabs; a Political Bureau of seven members, of whom only two were Arabs;

and a secretary general, who was invariably Jewish.[11] The parliamentary list also did not reflect the proportion of PAI support for the party. There were no more than two Arab MKs when the party won six or more seats in Knesset elections, and one Arab MK when it won four seats.[12] Tawfik Toubi and the author Emil Habibi, both Christians from the mixed city of Haifa, were the party's Arab MKs until 1965.

Rakah's Turn

In 1965, an Arab majority faction, joined by the veteran Meir Vilner and some of his pro-Soviet Jewish followers, seceded from the ICP to form the New Communist Party (Rakah) in protest over their marginalization in the ICP. The majority of the Arab party members moved to Rakah while most of the Jewish leadership remained in the ICP.[13] The split followed vociferous complaints by Arab party members that the Jewish majority in the Central Committee was excluding them from decision-making, practically setting up a Jewish controlled party.[14] Many felt that their underrepresentation was reflected in the party's position on regional issues. Most conspicuously, in a period of increasing regional tensions leading up to the 1967 war, the Jewish leadership of the ICP, notwithstanding minor exceptions, was no longer willing to conform to the Soviet position that identified Israel with western imperialism and viewed it as the sole culprit in the conflict. Instead, most of the Jewish leadership tended to view Egypt's Nasser and his allies as the primary source of regional tensions.[15]

The formation of Rakah was a turning point in Arab politics in Israel. It launched a process that changed the character of PAI involvement in Israeli politics as Arabs were increasingly at the forefront of an independent political organization. The new forms of political mobilization came with new demands on behalf of the PAI minority. The party argued against distribution of resources on the basis of ethnicity and in favor of redistribution on the basis of class and social need. They called for ethnically blind, instead of ethnocentric, state policies. Following the lead of the Soviets, their demands were cast around claims that universal citizenship and social criteria, rather than ethnic affiliation, should determine the allocation of resources by the state. Party officials insisted that Israeliness was an important part of the minority's identity and enhancing civic identity was an important priority.[16] The types of demands and claims made on behalf of the minority at the time led the well-regarded Minorities at Risk Project to classify the Arab minority in Israel as an ethnoclass rather than as an ethnonation or a national minority.[17]

Following the break-up from the ICP, party assets were divided between the splitting parties such that Rakah held on to the Arab newspaper *al-Ittihad*, and the real-estate in Arab populated areas (mostly towns and cities) and in the mixed urban vicinities of Haifa and Ramlah. The Jewish-led ICP received ownership over the Hebrew paper and the old party's assets in the Tel Aviv vicinity.[18] Gaining possession of these resources, the Arab political activists became less dependent on Jewish leadership for mobilization and could set new priorities; Rakah now focused on increasing its presence and mobilization capacity among the Arab population. Whereas the ICP had barely fourteen branches in Arab localities in the 1950s, Rakah had seventy-nine branches in Arab population centers by 1981 and ninety-five by 1985.[19]

At the same time, Rakah insisted that, in contrast to the old ICP, it was going to truly adhere to the principle of maintaining an overarching cross-communal identity. The party defined itself as binational rather than ethnically exclusive. It made provisions to ensure Jewish representation in its institutions, including in the position of secretary general, which was held by Vilner. Although the party traditionally kept information regarding its membership secretive, one source estimated that about one third of party members were Jewish shortly after the split.[20]

The composition of Rakah's Knesset faction reflected the structural changes and the new direction of the party. Following the 1965 elections, the party had two Arab MKs (the veterans Toubi and Habibi) and one Jewish MK (Vilner). A Jewish candidate was placed fourth on the list. Prior to the 1977 elections, Rakah joined forces with Jewish socialist groups, such as the Black Panthers and the Israeli Socialist Left, to form Hadash—the Democratic Front for Peace and Equality (DFPE), as it attempted to buttress its image as a socially focused party with an integrative Jewish-Arab composition.[21] Nonetheless, through the 1970s and 1980s, there would not be a situation where the party had more Jewish than Arab MKs. Within the DFPE, Rakah maintained its independence and set the tone. Only one of the seats the DFPE won in the elections held between 1977 and 1988 was allocated to a non-Communist member: Charlie Biton of the Black Panthers movement. The Communist Party in Israel was no longer Jewish-dominated. It was a party in which Arabs were at the forefront and were able to influence the agenda.

The presence of a visible and vociferous Arab leadership in an independent political organization was appealing to PAI voters. Rakah recorded a relative victory over the ICP in the 1965 elections when it won three Knesset seats and twice as many votes as the Jewish-led Communist Party, which managed to win only a single seat.[22] A similar allocation of Knesset seats followed the 1969 elections, although with a greater extent of ethnic voting: Rakah significantly increased its electoral support among Arab voters whereas the ICP, in contrast, won only minimal support in Arab populated areas.[23] By 1973, the Jewish-led faction lost its ability to compete altogether.

From 1977, Rakah surpassed the Labor Party, the descendant of Mapa'i, and its clientelist lists as the most popular choice among the Arab electorate, leading to the eventual demise of the clientelistic factions.[24] Table 1 demonstrates the transition "from clientelism to communism" and the rise in popularity of the Communist Party among Arab voters during the 1970s and 1980s, as the party gained the support of between one third and one half of the PAI electorate.

While the balance of power between Jews and Arabs changed from the late 1960s, the sociological profile of the Arab leadership of Rakah did not change at a similar pace. The Arab leadership remained composed of mostly educated urban Christians. It was only following the elections of 1973 that

Table 1. PAI Vote (%) for Communists and Labor and Clientelist Lists, 1949–1988 Elections

Year of election	Labor and clientelist lists (combined)	Communists (ICP, 1949–1961; Rakah, 1965–1973; DFPE, 1977–1988)
1949	61.3	22.2
1951	66.5	16.3
1955	62.4	15.6
1959	52.0	10.0
1961	50.8	22.7
1965	50.1	22.6
1969	56.9	28.9
1973	41.7	38.7
1977	27.0	50.6
1981	29.0	37.9
1984	23	33.0
1988	20.4	33.0

Data from Stendel, Arabs of Israel, 290 and Knesset Website, http://www.knesset.gov.il.

Rakah had its first Muslim MK, Tawfik Zayyad, a poet from Nazareth and the town's mayor from 1975. Most of the leading echelon remained disproportionately composed of Christians, who constituted a minority of 14 percent of the Arab population. It took fifteen more years and four more parliamentary elections for the party to have a second Muslim MK, Hashem Mahmeed, the former mayor of the Muslim town of Umm al-Fahm.

The electoral appeal of the party to Arab voters was not hindered by the distinctive social characteristics of the leadership, perhaps indicating that the religious background of activists was not a particularly salient issue. A large part of the party's electoral success can be attributed to the organizational capacity and resources at the hands of the party's leadership. Resource Mobilization Theory (RMT) in the studies of contentious politics has revealed that one of the most important conditions for success is the availability and mobilization of resources (material and nonmaterial), including personnel, money, media access, organizational infrastructure, and leadership skills and experience.[25] Increasing the circulation of its paper—throughout much of the 1970s and 1980s, *al-Ittihad* was the main newspaper in Arabic—and opening branches and increasing its activities in areas such as the almost exclusively Muslim Little Triangle gradually increased the party's outreach to Muslims and simultaneously enabled Muslims to become more conspicuous in the party.

The demands made by the Communists in relation to Israeli domestic policies during the 1970s and early 1980s were mostly framed in socialist and overarching civic rather than ethnonational language as the party conformed to the principles laid down by the Soviets.[26] Many of the claims in support of redistribution of resources were cast as a need to address social inequalities and what the party saw as the exploitation of the working class as a whole. Issues such as the struggle against land expropriation were not presented as a simple Palestinian national claim to the lands. Instead, it was justified on grounds of a fight against an imperialist policy by the central government and discrimination against the socially disadvantaged.

The agenda advanced by the party went beyond particular policy issues and related to the institutional framework of the state as well. The official intent was to advance a change in the character of the Israeli regime toward a more socialist type along the ideology espoused by the Soviets. Rakah openly called for a reform of state institutions along nonethnic lines in a way that would ensure equal access to opportunities to all individuals regardless of their ethnic or national background. The party's program, approved in the

1965 Congress, included an explicit demand for "proper participation of the Arab citizens in the central and local state bureaucracy" in order to reverse marginalization.[27]

While calling for recognition of the Arabs as a national minority, the party eschewed from demanding autonomy or a separate PAI sphere and did not question the state's legitimacy. Thus, the Israeli flag was regularly displayed and Israel's national anthem was played in the party congresses.[28] Rakah's alliance with other Jewish socialist forces in the DFPE was also intended to enhance its integrationist credentials.[29] Among its allies in Hadash were the Black Panthers, a grassroots movement formed in 1971 by young Jewish immigrants who arrived from North Africa and the Middle East (Mizrahi Jews) soon after Israel gained independence. Protesting against what they saw as the marginalization of their community, the Black Panthers challenged traditional state priorities in allocation of resources and social and welfare policies.[30] In this regard, the Black Panthers and Rakah shared their criticism of the central government. Both saw their constituents as disadvantaged by the Zionist-based principles of resource distribution that were defined by the old state elites. Both framed their demands around class-based concerns in opposition to the prevalent nationalist discourse. In one highly publicized and illustrative instance, MK Charlie Biton protested against the parliamentary discussion on Prisoner of Zion Ida Nudel, who was imprisoned in a Soviet penitentiary. Biton claimed that the Knesset should be debating the conditions in prisons and the rights of prisoners in Israel instead.[31] In this vein, the DFPE claimed to speak on behalf of the socially disadvantaged and the working class as a whole in Israel, it supported antidiscrimination and welfare-related legislation, and presented a program that called for terminating all laws and practices that advantaged Jews and excluded Arabs from public benefits.[32]

Overt ethnonational rhetoric by Rakah was reserved mainly for debates over the territories Israel captured in the 1967 war, an issue that grabbed much of the Communists' attention. Embracing UN Security Council Resolution 242, which called for Israel's withdrawal from territories conquered in the 1967 war, Rakah made it its top priority to advocate for a Palestinian Arab state and positioned itself as a pressure group on behalf of this cause.[33] Although prominent individuals, like the author Emil Habibi, had always been open about their national sentiments, the party's expression of a clear and formal position on the Palestinian issue was facilitated by changes in the soviet approach in the mid-1970s. The modified Soviet position enabled the party to endorse the formation of a Palestinian state alongside Israel and recognize the PLO as the representative of the Palestinian national movement. When the UN passed a resolution equating Zionism with racism in 1975, Rakah blamed discriminatory government policies and the Israeli military presence in the West Bank and Gaza for provoking the resolution. It was the only political party in the Knesset that refused to condemn this resolution, and placed the onus on the state to prove that the contrary was true.[34]

Extra-Parliamentary Mobilization

Alongside its parliamentary activity, Rakah was also involved in facilitating extra-parliamentary mobilization in the 1970s. The establishment of nonparliamentary organizations went hand-in-hand with sustained efforts by the party leadership to create more effective links with PAI masses, whose political consciousness was growing, and to carve a wider, nonparliamentary channel for Arab mobilization. Among the newly created organizations were the National Committee for the Defense of Lands (NCDL) (established in 1975); the National Committee of Heads of Arab Local Councils (NCHALC), an umbrella organization that was formed in 1974 for facilitating cooperation and coordination between Arab mayors and heads of local councils, which although was not formed by Rakah was nonetheless dominated by it for prolonged periods; and a variety of student and youth associations.

Of particular significance was the NCDL, which Rakah presented as a nonpartisan body.[35] The NCDL played a decisive role in mobilizing masses in March 1976 in response to the publication of the government's New Development Plan for the Galilee that would see thousands of acres of land expropriated in northern Israel, the largest land expropriation scheme since the 1950s. A general strike and mass rallies were organized in several Arab towns and villages in the Galilee on March 30, 1976 in what became known as the Land Day events. The government responded by imposing a curfew on some of the Galilee villages for where rallies were planned, a measure that had not been taken since the termination of the Military Government about ten years earlier. Defying the curfew, it was the first time in the history of state-minority relations in Israel that leaders of the PAI minority organized such large scale mass mobilization, which risked violent confrontation with state authorities. Indeed, the state's security forces and protestors clashed, leaving six Arab protestors dead and dozens wounded. These events had such an impact on state-minority relations that Land Day has been commemorated every year since 1976, usually with rallies and strikes.

Although the establishment of the NCHALC in 1974 was not a Rakah initiative, the new organization was co-opted by the Communists early on and cooperated with the political party. Originally the brainchild of Shmuel Toledano, the prime minister's advisor on Arab affairs, who sought to create a new vertical channel of communication between the regime and the Arab minority, the NCHALC soon acquired an independent status and was identified by the state's security establishment as a threat.[36] It co-operated with Rakah and the NCDL in the Land Day mobilization and was instrumental for mobilizing additional local protest activity for national-level goals.

Trying to create a united, nonpartisan image and including mayors and heads of local councils who were not affiliated with Rakah, the Committee's main mission was to act as a pressure group for eliminating the gap between government allocations to Jewish and Arab localities. At the same time, Rakah sought to increase its influence in municipal councils, traditionally controlled by hamulas, through the Committee. Indeed in the late 1970s, it managed to increase its presence on municipal councils.[37] In the run-up to the 1977 elections, the collaboration between the two became even more conspicuous as Hanna Mwais, the chairman of the NCHALC, was placed in a realistic slot on the DFPE list and ended up in the Knesset as a representative of the party. Later on, the relationship between the Communists and the Committee was largely influenced by the leadership style of the Committee's chairman as some preferred to maintain greater autonomy.[38]

In addition, Rakah was involved in initiatives to form a variety of other extra-parliamentary organizations in order to increase its outreach to PAI masses and to mobilize them. The party played a role in youth and student associations that engaged in cultural and sporting activities as well as political activism. These groups, together with the local Party branches, were imperative for mobilizing protest activities and demonstrations on campuses and in the Arab street. Thus, student associations were formed on the campuses of the Hebrew and Haifa universities and, later on, a national association was formed to recruit activists on campuses and advance Rakah's vision (the party is also said to have sent Arab students to study in Eastern European communist universities[39]) Likewise, Banki, the youth movement of the party, recruited many activists, and in the 1970s got involved in campaigns to change the standard of education in Arab schools.[40] Other associations included the Association of Merchants and Craftsmen, the Committee of Arab

High School Students, and the National Organization of Arab Academics and Students.

Ethnonationalist Trends

While most of the claims and demands associated with the Communists and nonparliamentary organizations that operated in the 1970s and throughout most of the 1980s were made in the name of social equality, a small, but nonetheless significant, component of PAI organized political activism was pursued in the name of ethnonationalism. Most organizations that took this direction did not have the resources and the infrastructure of the more established Communists, and they found it difficult to be competitive during these two decades.

One of the most conspicuous groups was Abna' al-Balad (Sons of the Village), set up in the early 1970s in the urbanizing Umm al-Fahm. Its declared goal was to entrench Palestinian identity among the PAI through the formation of local associations and cultural clubs. The movement explicitly identified the Arabs as members of the Palestinian nation, and its activities were oriented toward enhancing the minority's distinct collective consciousness.[41] Abna' al-Balad declared agenda diverged from that of the Communists, as the movement accused Rakah of blindly toeing the line, and serving the interests, of the Soviets and of lacking real commitment to Palestinian national interests. Adamantly supporting the PLO, Abna' al-Balad called for the replacement of Israel with a secular democratic state in all of mandatory Palestine in which a Palestinian Arab majority would emerge, thus enabling Arab dominance of the sovereign institutions.[42] The movement characterized the Zionist movement as an extension of imperialism. The state was labeled an instrument in the hands of the Jewish bourgeoisie, exploiting Palestinian cheap labor.

The movement refused to take part in general elections, arguing that its participation would grant legitimacy to the state itself and imply an acceptance of the rules it sets.[43] It did, however, compete in local elections in Arab vicinities, but remained only marginally supported in the 1970s. Ultimately, Abna' al-Balad did not have the infrastructure, resources, and appeal of its political competitors. Although by the 1980s the group managed to establish deeper foundations in a growing number of PAI vicinities, and ultimately to increase its support in local elections, it was, nonetheless, still unable to be widely competitive with the more established political forces.

On the more conservative side of the political spectrum, the Islamic movement emerged as an additional mobilizing actor with isolationist tendencies. The extension of Israel's jurisdiction to the West Bank and Gaza following the 1967 war opened up opportunities for a young generation of PAI to engage in religious studies in religious institutions and colleges in these territories. Such opportunities were otherwise unavailable within Israel proper. These students, most notably, Sheikh 'Abdallah Nimr Darwish of Kafr Qasim and Sheikh Ra'ed Salah of Umm al-Fahm, returned from their studies with increased enthusiasm, aiming to provide an alternative collectivist framework to the dominant secular trends. In particular, the Islamists advocated the creation of an exclusively religious sphere consistent with Islamist codes of conduct in isolation from the Jewish population.[44] In the early 1980s several of the movement's leaders were imprisoned after forming a paramilitary group called the "Jihad Family." Like Abna' al-Balad, however, the Islamic movement was not competitive in the 1970s and early 1980s with the well-established Communists. It was only by the second half of the 1980s that the Islamic movement gradually managed to become a weighty force in PAI politics as the movement shunned violence and began to be electorally competitive, first in local elections and, by the second half of the 1990s, in elections to the Knesset (this development is elaborated on in Chapter 5).

To sum up, two decades of relative quiescence were replaced by independent PAI political activism led by Rakah, which was not an ethnically exclusive party. The voice of the party, therefore, was largely the voice of the PAI minority. Since the agenda of the Communists was largely constrained by official Soviet ideology and sponsorship, the dominant Arab political organization came under criticism from groups with greater Palestinian and Islamic political orientations, which were still peripheral in the 1980s. Beyond the organizational infrastructure that Rakah had, what enabled the transition were changes in the institutional structure. Although Jewish nationalism remained firmly embedded within the state, declining levels of regime presence in Arab regions and fragmentation in the centers of political power decreased the capacity of the central government to control the minority and created opportunities for independent PAI organization and mobilization.

Centralized Power and Quiescence

Understanding PAI transition from relative quiescence to mobilization requires us to first examine the causes of initial passivity. The previous chapters demonstrated that (1) the passivity of the first two decades cannot be accounted for by PAI contentment; many among the PAI, including intellectual elites, were highly aggrieved about their situation in the 1950s and 1960s; and (2) the transition cannot be explained by inequality and grievances as both variables were present with intensity during the period of quiescence. Rather, it is institutional change that is largely responsible for the transition in PAI political activism.

Control

In his seminal work on Arabs in Israel, Ian Lustick identified a system of *control* as the means by which the Israeli regime prevented Arab mobilization.[45] Control was characterized by Lustick as a systematic and coordinated policy by which the central authorities of the state regulated Arab behavior. The system had three prongs. First, it involved the deliberate isolation of the Arab population from the Jewish majority and the internal fragmentation of Arab society so as to curtail within-group minority cooperation. Second, the system created Arab dependence on the state for economic and political resources through uneven economic development. And third, it involved co-optation of Arab elites through the distribution of rewards to those who collaborated with the regime. The relationships between the three prongs were interactive and mutually reinforcing. For example, Arab dependence on the regime for resources made Arab elites more susceptible to co-optation. Elite co-optation facilitated the fragmentation of the Arab population, while fragmentation, in turn, enhanced dependence on the Jewish authorities.[46]

Lustick's analysis has made an indispensable contribution to the advancement of knowledge on the causes of minority quiescence. Although he stressed that his analysis never intended to imply "a massive and brilliant conspiracy on the part of Jewish officials responsible for Arab affairs,"[47] his discussion of the programmatic elements of the control system could give the impression that the political core had a master plan or a grand scheme for controlling the PAI. To be sure, such a master plan never existed. The Israeli government never formulated a coherent policy for dealing with the Arab minority. According to Nadim N. Rouhana, "it was not until almost thirty years after Israel's establishment that the Israeli cabinet examined, for the first time, the relationship between Israel and its Arab citizens and the situation of the Arab population."[48] More recent research reveals that Israeli policy at the time was far from monolithic. Practices were often determined at lower levels of the bureaucracy and the security apparatus, and depended on the bureaucrats in charge or the relationships formed between an Arab village and the local military officers in charge.[49]

These findings stand in contrast with earlier work produced by the likes of Elia Zureik and Sabri Jyris, whose writings indicated that Israel's policies were monolithic and resulted from a grand vision to deprive Arabs of land and create PAI economic dependency.[50] Lustick himself emphasized that his analysis was "not offered as a description of a comprehensive image held by Israeli bureaucrats."[51] Comparative politics scholarship has long revealed that the ability of leaders to control politics and anticipate outcomes is overstated and far from uniform.[52] Political outcomes are seldom the product of precise planning by state leaders. There are plenty of instances in which state leaders are unable to get their way or in which government actions have unintended consequences.[53]

Rather than take as a given the existence of an omnipotent leadership with a well-formulated master plan and unmitigated capacity to get its own way, the task is to identify the state-society characteristics that enabled the central government to establish dominance. What kind of state attributes and social features were conducive to the relative absence of independent PAI political activism during the first two decades following state establishment? Most significantly, there was a relatively high degree of state extensiveness and centralization of authority at the core. These were aided by a socially fragmented minority, providing the central government with significant capacity to curb independent PAI political activism.

State Extensiveness and Centralization of Authority

Probably the most significant institution to facilitate regime presence in PAI society was the Military Government. From the outset, the state was facing practical questions about reconciling democratic procedures with the security considerations engendered by the Arab-Israeli conflict.[54] The central government treated the Arab minority as a component in this regional dispute and as a potentially subversive element. This view was clearly illustrated in Ben-Gurion's expressed fear of what the PAI "might have done if they had been given the chance."[55] Relying on the Defence Emergency Regulations enacted in 1945 by the Palestine Mandatory government to fight Jewish and Arab insurgency, the Israeli government delegated most of its civil authority in areas populated by Arabs to the army. The new administration became known as the Military Government. Three military zones were established: in the Galilee, the Negev, and the Little Triangle. The slightly more than 10 percent of the Arab population who resided in mixed towns with a Jewish population were spared from the governance of the Military Administration.

The Military Government (which was formally under the authority of the Ministry of Defense) had far-reaching power to restrict the movement and activities of people residing under its jurisdiction. Of great consequence was the authority of the military governors' offices to regulate movement within, into, and out of the areas under their control. Citizens residing in these regions required travel permits to leave their villages, be it to seek employment in a bigger town, to visit family and friends residing in a different village, or otherwise. Often requests for permits were turned down, formally for security reasons, but as Ze'ev Schiff, a reputable journalist in the independent daily *Ha'aretz* observed, in practice, the discretion of officials was extensive. Favoritism and local quarrels with a government official could and frequently did influence the outcome of permit requests.[56]

Furthermore, in regions under the rule of the Military Government, the army had the authority to enter any privately owned property, seize anything that they suspected could undermine public security, demolish homes, banish individuals to other parts of the country, and carry out administrative detentions for up to one year. It also had the authority to cut off essential communication services, such as telephone lines or postal deliveries. Military courts had exclusive authority to try suspects in closed sessions for violating the regulations of the Military Government. Reviews of military courts rulings by civil courts were rare. And when they did take place, "the military often flouted the court's orders."[57]

The authority of the Military Administration to impose curfews and to declare areas closed military zones was also highly consequential for curtailing free movement. Of particular notoriety was the event in Kafr Qasim in 1956 when forty-eight villagers, including women and children, who were returning from work in their fields and were unaware that a curfew had been imposed, were shot and killed. The event led to contained protests by Arab intellectuals and politicians and a temporary reevaluation of the Military Administration, but eventually the central government decided to prolong it (albeit with some minor relaxations that were introduced in 1957).

Although the Kafr Qasim event was the exception, curfews as a whole were an effective means of hindering mobilization. Because technological means of communication were few—in 1970, still only 3.4 percent of Arab households owned a telephone—and because long-distance mobility by private means was not easily accessible—only 3.1 percent of Arab households had a private car in 1970—restrictions on travel and personal mobility severely impeded the minority's capacity to collectively organize beyond the local village and even within it.[58] The expansive presence of the security apparatus curbed the ability of the Arab minority to mobilize.

Probably the most well-known example of the effectiveness of this aspect of state extensiveness in preventing PAI mobilization was the case of the pan-Arab movement with the symbolic name, al-Ard (the Land). This organization was officially formed in 1959 by young, educated Arab intellectuals, most visibly lawyers and students, who saw themselves as followers of Egyptian president Gamal Abd al-Nasser. The movement did not recognize the legitimacy of the Israeli state and sought its abolition.[59] Notwithstanding the significance of other constraints, the security apparatus played a decisive role in bringing about the demobilization of al-Ard and its eventual demise. First, the group was denied a license to publish a newspaper or register as a financial company on security grounds. Attempts to bypass this restriction by publishing under different names were forcefully halted. Furthermore, activists were often denied travel permits to attend gatherings, and prominent leaders, such as Salah Baransi, Mansour Qardush, Habib Qahwanji, and Sabri Jiryis, were arrested on allegations of undermining state security. In 1964, the minister of defense used his authority, relying on the 1945 Emergency Regulations, to declare al-Ard a hostile organization and ban it altogether. Its assets were confiscated, and the group eventually disintegrated.[60]

In addition to the penetrative security apparatus, the central government's ability to control public discourse and use it to shape the boundaries of national identity in ways that were consistent with the Jewish national movement's objectives was also an indispensable component in the "extensive and cohesive" configuration. Public holidays, school textbooks, and educational radio programs were all used to consolidate a national narrative that would advance Zionist ideals and legitimate Jewish national hold on the state. The Israeli sociologist Uri Ben-Eliezer has argued that state elites were particularly successful at advancing popular perceptions that the Jewish citizens were actively participating in the construction of the state through their labor and military service.[61]

The capacity to infuse such images and perceptions is not a given. State control of radio (television was not introduced until 1968) and the public education system were crucial for enabling the leaders of the Jewish national movement, who were now the new state elites, to control the flow of information and transmit messages that anchored norms and values that legitimated their authority. The leadership did not leave much public space for opponents and critics to question state character and practices. Most of the newspapers published in Arabic were sponsored by Zionist political parties and the Histadrut, with the exception of the Communist al-Ittihad.[62] In the first decades, official censorship of the press was rampant, and there was only state radio, the Voice of Israel, which until 1965 was attached to the prime minister's office and was under the supervision of its director general, enabling easy control of content. Thus, for example, the Kafr Qasim event was not reported on in the media until approximately two months later.

Likewise, the Arab education system was tightly controlled by the state. The curriculum of Arab schools was dictated and ensured that the Zionist narrative, including the biblical roots of Jewish presence on the territory, was taught to Arab pupils, while at the same time omitting any reference to Palestinian Arab national identity or connection to the territory. In many cases, Hebrew textbooks were simply translated into Arabic.[63] Employment of teachers, too, was a tool for controlling the content of education. A considerable share of the teachers in Arab schools in the 1950s and 1960s was Jewish, and Arab teachers had to undergo security checks.[64] Those who were suspected of possessing nationalist or communist sympathies were rendered unqualified for teaching, and in some cases teachers were fired. According to one source, about half of all the Arab teachers received letters in 1953 warning them that their employment was not guaranteed.[65]

More broadly, the combination of centralization of authority in the hands of a small elite, on the one hand, and statist practices on the other, were essential for consolidating control at the center. Much has been written about statism under Prime Minister Ben-Gurion, largely reflected in Ben-Gurion's concept of mamlachtiyut, which sought to bring all the organized social actors (including all political parties), citizens, and social organizations under the authority of the state, and there is no need to review the literature and all the various aspects of the debate on this topic.[66] It is important to stress, however, that the extent to which all society-level actors were subordinate to the state has been overstated. The state was neither elevated from society nor a neutral actor, as at least one organized political force, namely Mapa'i, dominated state institutions. This feature was largely inherited from the prestate period and enabled the party to get its own way.

Indeed, not only did the state lack autonomy from the Jewish national movement, but, despite the attempts of the leadership—not least Ben-Gurion—to convey the opposite image, it was also not insulated from the dominant political party within this movement.[67] Appointments to the state bureaucracy, military and civil, were frequently linked to loyalty to the party and its vision.[68] The leadership of the ruling party exercised a large degree of control over the state, and affiliates often occupied senior positions in the state apparatus and public sector institutions, such as the Histadrut. It was only in 1959 that the Civil Service Law, which limits the engagement of senior civil servants in political parties, was passed.[69] Sociologist Baruch Kimmerling suggested that the Mapa'i elite justified its tight control of the state and its resources by pointing to its accomplishments in a variety of areas that Zionist values endorsed: the creation of the state, the absorption of immigration, the strengthening economy, the development of a common Hebrew culture and language, the establishment of a modern and powerful army of Jewish warriors, and so forth.[70]

Probably the most significant area in which this state-Mapa'i relationship was consequential was the economy. The Mapa'i-dominated state was very active in the economy and had significant capacity to allocate resources. Many analysts have characterized the economic structure that existed at the time as "state-led" or "statist."[71] There were many ways in which the state was involved in the economy. First, the government made it a priority to create a large state-owned industrialized sector. Many of the elites in this sector were Mapa'i associates.[72] Private entrepreneurship was highly regulated. Preferred industries, sometimes determined on the basis of personal acquaintance with senior bureaucrats or the minister of trade and industry, received subsidies and protection from foreign competition.[73] This is not to say that economic considerations did not play a significant role in policy-making. The state did adopt an export-oriented industrialization strategy, regulate foreign exchange, and set quotas and impose tariffs on imported goods to promote domestic economic growth. Israel, in this regard, was a successful developmental state.[74] Successful development, however, did not preclude Mapa'i favoritism.

Other ways in which the Mapa'i-dominated state was involved in the economy included the redistribution of land and determination of the relative price of capital and labor (the state's role in determining the price of labor largely derived from having the bureaucracy employ more than half of the labor force, as well as from setting wage standards[75]). Furthermore, the country was divided into development zones in which prices and government-levied taxes varied. Allocation of resources and investment subsidies also varied from region to region according to the priorities of the government.[76] Partisan and power politics considerations played a significant role in prioritization.[77] Thus, for example, the Kibbutzim that were associated with Mapa'i were generally in high-priority development zones and were ranked high for land allocation and government subsidies. Arab localities, on the other hand, were typically left out of the high-priority development zones.

Mapa'i's economic power was largely facilitated by its control of the Histadrut. The Histadrut remained most significant in shaping the economic and political landscape of the state. Following the establishment of the state, the Histadrut became the primary provider of accessible healthcare, and it increased the scope of its welfare activities to also include pension funds. Among other things, it also controlled Koor, the leading actor in Israel's industrial sector, which owned dozens of industrial, commercial, and financial firms and provided employment to tens of thousands of Israelis. As a result of its large economic base, many people depended on the Histadrut for their livelihood and for essential services. This dependence reinforced Mapa'i's political power, translated into political obedience to those who held power in the Histadrut, and increased the capacity of the ruling party to provide patronage to loyal constituencies. The significance of the Histadrut's role in consolidating Mapa'i's powerbase and control of politics was such that the secretary-general of the Histadrut stated during a 1955 Mapa'i Central Committee meeting that "if the British Labour Party had a healthcare organization and economic institutions like those of the Histadrut, it would remain in power forever."[78] The Mapa'i-led government, in turn, set rules that gave the Histadrut economic advantages and occasionally stepped in with subsidies and financial assistance. The government-Histadrut-Mapa'i nexus was such that Shafir and Peled concluded that "it was difficult to tell where the Histadrut 'ended' and the government 'began.'"[79]

Mapa'i itself had an internal oligarchic structure. As in the prestate period, the functionaries of the Histadrut also occupied the senior positions in Mapa'i. Hence, they were able to ensure their privileged position without in effect having to be elected on a regular basis. Indeed, party members did not elect their representative to the Knesset; rather, a commission composed of the party's leading echelon dictated to the general membership who would be on the list of the party's candidates. The leadership established networks of patronage with party activists (who themselves often extended patronage to clients at a lower level), the latter hoping for rewards, be it candidacy to the Knesset or a prestigious appointment in state-owned industry, in the Histadrut, or in one of its firms. Thus, a hierarchical structure to Israeli politics emerged, both within Mapa'i and between Mapa'i and others in society who sought access to state resources.

One important qualification to this portrayal of Israeli politics is required. The proportional representation electoral system, with a 1 percent threshold, produced an average of twelve factions in the Knesset throughout the 1950s and 1960s; as a result, all of the Mapa'i-led governments were coalition governments that typically included six or seven political factions representing diverse groups and interests. These included religious parties (Zionist and non-Zionist), Jewish ethnic parties (*Sepharadim*), parties with a socialist worldview, and parties with a more liberal position on economic issues. The Communists were ruled out.[80] The pluralistic nature of Jewish society led the governing party to strike important compromises with other factions in order to ensure its rule. This development was reflected in both the allocation of resources and delegation of authority to political allies in certain areas. Most conspicuously, compromises with religious political representatives provided the elites of this sector with some authority over areas such as religious education and family law. Some observers have also explained the decision not to adopt a constitution as an additional step taken to accommodate the religious public—who are said to be uncomfortable with a written constitution—and have characterized the emergent arrangement as consociational.[81] That said, those compromises served to consolidate central government strength and the support base of the dominant faction in the coalition government, as well as to enhance the willingness among smaller factions to accept the leadership role of Mapa'i.

The large degree of centralization of authority in the hands of the dominant political party, combined with the extensive presence of the regime in public life, yielded dependence and co-optation that were conducive to lack of independent PAI ethnonational mobilization. To be sure, the conditions faced by the Arab population that remained in Israel after the war were already not conducive to political activism. Most of the minority's religious, intellectual, economic, and political urban elite fled or were forced to leave during the war and were now on the other side of the border.[82] The hamulas that remained in Israel after the war were usually not of a national stature and were often preoccupied with internal rivalries.[83]

Furthermore, the communist ICP, always on the margins of politics, did not have the resources to seriously compete with Mapa'i. One consequential area in which this was evident was the ICP's attempt to organize trade unions outside the Histadrut. Up until 1953, most PAI workers were members of the ICP-dominated Arab Trades Union Congress. This organization, however, was much smaller and weaker than the Histadrut, and it was far less encompassing in its scope of activity. When the Histadrut started to accept Arab workers into its trade unions in 1953 and as full members with access to all Histadrut services in 1957, the communist trade unions collapsed. Barely three months after the Histadrut opened its doors to Arabs, approximately two thirds of Israel's Arabs workers (an estimated 11,600) applied for membership.[84]

Although this initiative was seen by many commentators as one of the most important steps toward integrating Arabs into Israeli society, it also served to weaken the already marginal Communists and create greater dependence on the Histadrut and Mapa'i for essential services.[85] In practice, the incorporation of PAI into the Histadrut resembles what Alfred Stepan has referred to as "exclusionary corporatist policies."[86] In this state of affairs, the elites who control the state, identifying a potential source of opposition, combine coercive means of control with exclusion of rival associations from politics. The governing elite "then seeks to integrate the excluded groups into associational organizations designed and controlled by the state."[87] Such practices have been pursued in many countries in order to demobilize potential dissenters.[88] In Israel, incorporation into the Histadrut facilitated demobilization by weakening opposition. Because the Histadrut was the only organization capable of delivering healthcare services and employment in remote areas without regard to economic considerations, the dependence of the PAI population on Mapa'i for its most basic needs was enhanced, thus cultivating political subordination.

The hierarchical structure of patronage that emerged following the extensive degree of centralization of power is crucial for understanding the absence of independent PAI political activity. The logic of the relationship of patronage relied on the extreme vulnerability of the Arabs, who were subjected to a penetrative state and the Military Government, on the one hand, and the significant capacity of the dominant state elites, on the other. Those who controlled resources were always able to generate an image of having the means to alleviate PAI suffering through patronage. The ruling party, utilizing the vast resources at its disposal, created Arab dependence and managed to co-opt Arab elites.

The preexisting traditional network of extended families lent itself to this purpose because the hierarchical organization of the hamula network already involved dependence of members of the clan on the heads and elders of the hamula. Mapa'i and state authorities had only to co-opt some hamula elders, a relatively small number of people, to be linked to the bulk of the Arab population. The Palestine Arab population was used to the practice of dealing with the regime through its hamula elders. Already during the period of Ottoman and British rule, hamula notables served as intermediaries between the central government and the indigenous population.[89] When Israel was established, these preexisting networks of relations between the central government, the traditional clan elites, and the local population were utilized.

The intense internal rivalry for influence made the hamulas further susceptible to cooperation with the government. A traditional hamula leader hoped that maintaining good relations with representatives of the government, particularly those responsible for distribution of funds in the Arab sector, would improve his hamula's situation and influence in the local village. Distribution of privileges and material resources by the ruling party and the bureaucracy it controlled, as a reward for political loyalty, were a common practice and included such things as travel permits, access to land, loans, modern agricultural machinery at cheap prices, employment in the Histadrut, civil service, or the education system, and even positions in local councils.[90]

One of the most coveted spoils in these patron-client relations was a seat in the Knesset. Prior to parliamentary elections, Mapa'i formed lists composed of Arab candidates. Invariably, these candidates were hamula leaders who had far-reaching influence in their communities, such as Sif al-din al-Zu'abi, mayor of Nazareth and influential head of several related hamulas; Salah Hasan Hanifas, a Druze leader from northern Israel; and Deib Obeid, a wealthy merchant and member of the local council of Taibeh in the Little Triangle. The selected Arab clients usually reflected the geographical distribution and religious make-up of the Arab population. The clientelistic lists were given attractive names, such as "the Democratic List of Israeli Arabs," "Progress and Labor," "Agriculture and Development," and "Cooperation and Brotherhood," but they did not have party infrastructure or official platforms. Their internal composition was determined solely by Mapa'i, which also funded them.[91]

Those who managed to win seats in the legislature were never appointed to the cabinet and, more often than not, found themselves on relatively marginal and uninfluential parliamentary committees, such as Environment or Labor and Welfare. Nonetheless, for Arabs competing for positions within their own communities, a seat in the legislature could translate into friendly ties with bureaucrats, which in turn could affect the implementation, or lack thereof, of policies pertaining to the Arab population in various regions. More broadly, affiliation with the dominant force in Israeli politics meant access to some public resources to be dispensed to one's hamula members and their allies.

Because of the intense internal competition for a seat in the Knesset, the Arab parliamentarians' loyalty to the ruling party was secured. Disloyalty could easily result in the removal of rewards and replacement with another candidate. Thus, the Arab MKs from clientelistic lists invariably sided with the central government. One of the most conspicuous indicators of the Arab MKs' obedience was their support for the continuation of the Military Administration in conformity with Mapa'i's position. In 1961, the prolongation of the Military Administration hinged on the votes of these Arab MKs.

Ultimately, through these patronage relations, the ruling party managed to attain the indirect support of most of the Arab electorate while co-opting the Arab leadership with the lure of immediate, if limited, gains, thus securing demobilization. And while there were many who referred to the co-opted elites by the derogatory title *adhnab* (tails), high voter turnout suggests that most complied. Indeed, to prove their value to Mapa'i, hamula leaders made great efforts to ensure high voter turnout; voter turnout was typically higher than in the Jewish sector, indicating the success of this strategy. Table 2 shows the very high Arab voter turnout and the number of clientelistic lists and the seats they won in elections during the first two decades of Israel's existence.

While the patron-client relations relied on preexisting factionalism within the Arab community, they also exacerbated them. The status of Mapa'i as the sole patron stimulated rivalry between hamulas for favors and privileges that only Mapa'i was in a position to give. One important arena where internal rivalry was intense is local councils. Traditionally, local decisions were made collectively by a group of elders representing the different clans. With the introduction of modern local governments, which had a limited number of elected decision-making positions while controlling access to important resources, there was less room for consensual forms of governance and competition intensified.[92] Control over local councils could translate into diversion

Table 2. PAI Voter Turnout and Mapa'i Clientelistic Factions, 1949–1969

Year of election	Arab voter turnout (%)	Factions affiliated with Mapa'i	Knesset seats for affiliated factions
1949	79.3	1	2
1951	85.5	3	5
1955	91.0	3	5
1959	88.9	3	5
1961	85.6	2	4
1965	87.8	2	4
1969	82.0	2	4

Data from Knesset website, http://www.knesset.gov.il/description/eng/eng_mimshal_res.htm.

of resources to the governing hamulas, exemption from (or significantly lower) local taxes for one's hamula, employment in schools and the local civil service, and other possibilities for manipulating resources. The rivalry was enhanced not only because there was a lot at stake, but also because of parallel networks of patronage that were established by the ruling echelon. It was not uncommon for one hamula to be in clientelistic relations with Mapa'i's Arab Department while its arch rival hamula was engaging in clientelism with the Histadrut.[93] This way, Mapa'i could ensure that hamulas who lost local elections would continue having incentives to acquiesce.

By the latter part of the 1950s, more than one quarter of the Arab towns and villages in Israel, containing approximately one third of the Arab population, were administered by local or municipal councils.[94] After the first two and a half decades or so of Israel's existence, more than fifty local governments were set up in Arab localities[95] Although the local councils were usually elected by the local population, they were under strict supervision of the Ministry of Interior, which, being the councils' main source of income, used its authority as a means of co-optation. Those who tried to resist risked being frowned upon by the Mapa'i elite. Thus, when the chairman of the Kafr Yasif local council challenged the Military Government and refused to hold Independence Day celebrations in 1958, the village was "threatened that the current village administration was in the way of development in the village including connecting it to the electricity and water grids."[96] Chairs of local authorities who collaborated with the Jewish authorities, on the other hand, were looked upon more favorably by the regime. The prospects of receiving rewards encouraged compliance.[97] In some instances, voters were made to believe that friendly electoral behavior toward Mapa'i would result in material benefits to the residents.[98] In some instances, Mapa'i support of hamulas in local elections was exchanged for hamula support for the governing party in Knesset elections.[99]

Ultimately, considerable regime extensiveness, or presence in public space, and centralization of political and economic power in the hands of a small elite, coupled with a fragmented minority organizational structure, proved conducive to PAI quiescence despite this minority's grievances. It would take changes in these state-society attributes to facilitate independent political mobilization.

The Decline of Centralized Power

The emergence of independent Arab political mobilization was largely facilitated by a degree of liberalization of Israel's institutions and broader transitions in state-society relations. The internal dynamics of Jewish politics and growing contention over political power yielded an incremental process of decentralization of power that decreased central government capacity to control society, on the one hand, and reduced the extent of state presence in Arab spheres, on the other. State retreat from Arab areas was accompanied by a decline in willingness and capacity to act repressively against the minority, a factor often associated with the appearance of contentious politics.[100] At the same time, the Arab population experienced social transformation that led to the erosion in the social and political significance of the hamula. These structural changes increased the opportunities available for the Arab minority to engage in independent political activism.

The Demise of the Military Government

The decline of repressive capacity was associated most significantly with the termination of the Military Administration toward the end of 1966. The demise of the Military Government resulted from influences that were partly exogenous to relations between Jews and Arabs. One factor was changes at the international level and the emergence of human rights regimes that introduced new norms of interaction between states and minorities.[101] The

1960s saw a massive wave of decolonization, particularly in Africa, coupled with growing international endorsement of human and civil rights. In 1961, the UN General Assembly voted in favor of imposing sanctions against the Apartheid regime in South Africa. In 1966, at about the time of the abolition of the Military Government, the International Covenant on Civil and Political Rights was ratified by the UN General Assembly. In 1969, the International Convention on the Elimination of All Forms of Racial Discrimination entered into force. Thus, the evolving international community directed states to terminate discrimination against minorities and protect their human rights.

While these covenants and conventions were not enforceable laws, some states that were concerned about their international image were influenced by them. Israel, which sought to be accepted as an integral member of the international community, ratified the international covenants. Thus, although they cannot be said to have played a decisive role in shaping Israeli policies, international norms were nonetheless influential in pressuring the central government to abandon the Military Government at a time when the government was seeking to buttress Israel's international position in face of Arab boycotts. The restrictions on the Arab population provided ammunition for those seeking to obstruct Israel's path to international acceptance. On a number of occasions, Arab adversaries used the Military Government to denounce Israel in various international forums as a racist state that persecutes the minority living under its rule.[102] The criticism, in turn, did not go unnoticed by the central government in Israel. Explaining the governing coalition's willingness to abolish the Military Government, an MK from the governing coalition reasoned that the Military Government "has been exploited by our enemies to incite others against us."[103]

That said, comparative research on the politics of ethnicity and nationalism in Central and Eastern Europe has long revealed that the impact of international constraints on state-minority relations is conditioned by domestic politics.[104] In Israel, internal majority group politics were highly consequential for the annulment of the Military Government. The partners of the Labor Party, Mapa'i's successor, in the coalition government pressured the ruling party to hand over jurisdiction to civil authorities. The National Religious Party (NRP) and the socialist Mapam saw it as detrimental for Israel's democracy and defense. Mapam MKs, for example, argued that rather than facilitate security, the restrictions alienated the Arab minority to the extent of possibly engendering security risks by driving some to actions against the state.[105]

Those who were not partners in Labor's coalition government were blunter in their assessment of the impact of the Military Government on Israeli politics. Menachem Begin, leader of the Revisionists' Herut, the main opposition party, argued that the Military Government served no security purpose and was exploited by Mapa'i to further its political objectives.[106] One of Begin's party colleagues echoed the position that "the maintenance of the Military Government sustained the rule of a certain party" by enabling it to distribute favors to its supporters, while fostering the illusion that it contributed to security so as to justify its existence before the Jewish public.[107] Labor's coalition partners agreed with this assessment. Thus, domestic political pressure to discontinue the Military Administration came from all major wings in Israeli politics, including indispensable coalition partners. And by the mid-1960s, it was obvious that the Military Government did not serve a security purpose and was harmful for Israel's international standing.

A change in the leadership of Mapa'i was imperative for the willingness of the ruling party to relinquish an indispensable tool for the clientelistic relations it established with the Arab population. The ascendance of Levi Eshkol, Ben-Gurion's successor as Mapa'i's leader, who at a later point became his internal rival within Mapa'i, to the prime minister post was vital for the cessation of the Military Government. In 1963, Eshkol became Israel's prime minister and until 1967, he simultaneously served as minister of defense. Among other things, Eshkol differed from his predecessor in two important respects. First, he was far less of a centralist of power and had a more liberal vision of the state. Second, he was more conciliatory in his attitude toward those ostracized by his predecessor. For example, in 1964, as a good will gesture toward the Revisionist Herut Party (the precursor of the Likud), Labor's bitter rivals, Eshkol allowed the corpse of Ze'ev Jabotinsky, the founder of the Revisionist movement, to be brought to Israel for burial. To advance national unity, he also incorporated the Revisionists into a quasi power-sharing government on the eve of the 1967 war, something which was unacceptable during Ben-Gurion's tenure.

Although Eshkol was unwilling to consider including the Communist Party in his government, he nonetheless took a less repressive approach toward the Arab minority. During his term, he incrementally relaxed the restrictions imposed by the Military Government in Arab populated areas, until the administration's total annulment. In a speech before the Knesset, Eshkol justified this change in policy by stating that the Military Government was simply no longer needed for security purposes.[108] Minding political pressure from indispensable coalition allies, Eshkol agreed to waive an essential tool for keeping the Arab minority tied to his party in clientelistic relations, a change in policy that Ben Gurion's loyalists vociferously opposed.

Ultimately, the impact of this change was paramount. The abolition of the Military Government significantly reduced regime extensiveness and meant that Arab movement was no longer restricted, political planning and gatherings could be more easily conducted, and leaders were subject to less scrutiny. Opportunities for political mobilization and organization opened up as Arabs could travel around the country freely and no longer had to fear the harsh measures that the military governors could impose on them. Of equal significance, as will be elaborated upon later, they became less dependent on the powerful ruling apparatus for much of their basic needs, in turn reducing the essentiality of participating in patron-client exchanges.

Decentralization of Authority

During Eshkol's tenure, other important consequential steps toward decentralization of political power decreased the capacity of the central government and the ruling party to control Israeli society in general and the Arab minority in particular. One such important example was in the electronic media field. The Voice of Israel, which at the time was the only radio broadcaster (aside from the army radio), moved from the Prime Minister's Office (PMO), where it was under the supervision of the director general and served as a government tool to disseminate information and analysis, to the newly established Israel Broadcasting Authority (IBA) in 1965, where it gained a little more autonomy.[109] The Israel Television was established three years later within the framework of the IBA. Prime Minister Eshkol viewed these as important steps toward liberalizing Israel.[110] Although the IBA faced plenty of political pressures and its practices initially retained many of the characteristics of media that is accountable to the country's ruling echelon, control gradually loosened.[111] In the 1970s and 1980s, more radio stations were added and space for debate about central government policies and practices increased. As the control of the governing apparatus over the content of public broadcasting gradually declined, although by no means dissolved, societal space was generated for alternative positions and narratives and a more critical discussion of political and social life in Israel and of government policies, including on issues pertaining to the Arab minority.

The process of liberalization and dispersion of power during the third decade of Israel's existence had several consequential prongs for the minority. In Israel, the process of decentralization was accompanied by an emergence of a vibrant civil society that challenged state supremacy vis-à-vis society, questioned the legitimizing norms that supported Labor's dominance, and subsequently contributed to the emergence of limited societal space, if unintentionally, for the Arab minority to independently politicize against its marginalization. A number of predominantly Jewish social and protest movements appeared in the 1970s—not least following the 1973 war—and early 1980s, questioning the central government's functioning and policies. For example, mass protest movements forced the establishment of the Agranat Commission following the 1973 Yom Kippur War to investigate the functioning of the Israeli military in the war. While this national commission of inquiry, headed by the chief justice of the Supreme Court, focused its findings and recommendations on military personnel, public protest forced Prime Minister Golda Meir to resign. Peace Now (established in 1977 to advocate territorial concessions in the pursuit of peace with Egypt and led the protests against Israel's invasion of Lebanon in 1982), Yesh Gvul (an organization backing soldiers refusal to fight in the Lebanon war and later on in the territories captured in the 1967 war), and the Black Panthers were all movements that challenged the nationalist ethos and the supremacy of the state over their civic and social rights, thus contesting the rules of state-society interaction that were set by the old state elites.

Of these movements, the impact of the mobilization of Mizrahi Jews in the Black Panthers (which would later join forces with Rakah in the DFPE) and beyond was particularly significant for the ability of Arab organizations to mobilize and challenge the central government for two main reasons. First, the Black Panthers focused on priorities in allocation of resources by the state, a burning issue for the Arab minority. Much like Rakah, the Black Panthers called for a redistribution of resources based on social needs rather than the national objectives that were defined by the ruling Labor elites. For the first time, a Jewish-based grassroots movement managed sustained protest mobilization that challenged the subordination of social goals to Jewish ethnonational ones, as defined by Labor.[112] They demanded higher priority in budget allocation for impoverished neighborhoods and peripheral development towns rather than the sectors associated with Labor and its agricultural settlements that were said to fulfill the Zionist ideal of "land redemption."[113] This was a direct challenge to the legitimizing norms that supported Zionism as practiced by the power-holders in the state as well as to the state-society power balance. Thus, the Black Panthers were helping to break the normative taboo about allocation of resources in a way that was consistent with Rakah's demands on behalf of the PAI.

Mizrahi protests were consequential for independent Arab mobilization beyond the impact of the Black Panthers. This Jewish constituency contributed to Labor's loss of dominance, a development that adversely affected the ability of Labor to co-opt hamula elders. Indeed, one of the primary causes for Labor's defeat in the 1977 elections was that the second generation of Jewish immigrants from North African and Middle Eastern countries, the parents of whom voted for Mapa'i, the precursor of Labor, turned against the ruling party. Labor was accused of preventing this population from fully integrating and from having equal access to opportunities, including severe underrepresentation in the Knesset, government, and senior posts in state bureaucracy. State elites during the first thirty years of statehood had salient sociological characteristics inherited from the prestate period: they were all of East European origin (Ashkenazi) and had immigrated prior to the establishment of the state.[114] The Mizrahi immigrants, on the other hand, were socially and geographically isolated from the veteran community. Frequently settled in development towns in the Negev or in new isolated neighborhoods, they relied on social services separate from those of the veteran community. Because of their en mass arrival (the population of Israel doubled itself in the first three years of the state's existence), the state was unable to ensure their comprehensive absorption in the labor market, and their housing was often functional at best. Hence, not only were their social services separate, but they relied on them much more than the veteran community.[115] They practically comprised a distinct, lower social stratum and many felt that the boundaries of exclusion were not permeable and that the holders of political power were not interested in providing access to those who arrived after state founding.

Thus, the younger generation of Mizrahi Jews rose up against the societal order they felt marginalized them. Turning against the ruling party, many second-generation Mizrahi Jews voted for Labor's primary challenger, the Likud, which in 1977 managed to depose Labor as the governing party.[116] It is beyond the scope of this study to examine why those Jews who challenged the social order chose to express their discontent with the ruling party by voting for Likud rather than the Black Panthers, who were at the forefront of many protests, were far from supportive of the Likud agenda, and chose to align with the Communists. Suffice it to note that already in the 1973 elections, Likud, carried by the wave of support of Mizrahi Jews, emerged as a major challenging force, winning 30.2 percent of the general votes, in comparison with Labor's 39.6 percent.

The turnover of 1977 was facilitated by another source of discontent within the Jewish majority: Jews of European descent, traditional Labor supporters from the prestate period, who became skeptical of Labor governance due to economic hardships. As long as economic performance was satisfying— annual inflation rates were in single digits until 1970—the statist economy of Labor was by and large accepted, despite its known ills, as a necessary means for building and promoting a viable independent economy.[117] In 1971, however, inflation rates soared into double digits: 12 percent in 1971, 39.7 percent in 1974 (in the aftermath of the 1973 war), and 31.3 percent in 1976.[118] The economic transgression caused widespread public concern regarding the costs of the Labor economy, its priorities, and the privileging of its friendly sectors, primarily the Histadrut. Add to that scandals revealed within the governing party and a critical assessment of the government's performance in the 1973 war, and the result was widespread yearning, even among many traditional Labor voters, for a new political force that would reform government and liberalize the economy.

A new political party, the Democratic Movement for Change (DASH) took Labor to task on these issues. In the 1977 elections, DASH managed to attract many Labor voters, gaining 11.6 percent of the total votes, which translated into fifteen Knesset seats. Labor had declined to thirty-two Knesset seats (24.6 percent of the total votes) while Likud won forty-three seats (33.4 percent).[119] Had traditional Labor voters not switched to DASH in the 1977 elections, it would have been plausible for Labor to remain competitive in these elections (although by no means retain its dominance, given the new trends among Mizrahi voters). DASH proved to be a temporary force, and its almost immediate dissolution resulted in most of its votes returning to Labor in subsequent elections. Throughout the elections that followed in the 1980s, Labor and Likud ran neck-and-neck.

Significantly for the Arab minority, Labor's loss of grip on the state and its resources hindered its ability to deliver spoils and co-opt hamula leaders. It no longer monopolized resources. There was now another Jewish political party who could potentially compete with it for providing patronage. The theoretical lesson to be drawn from this experience is that internal majority politics influences the constraints faced by the minority. Majority fragmentation reduced the ability of the governing apparatus to co-opt minority elites.

The Collapse of Patronage

Labor's loss of power and the rise of Likud as an alternative governing party were critical for the demise of the patronage networks that were so imperative for constraining Arab political activity. Interestingly, while the collapse of patronage networks in Africa is more often than not attributed to a loss of interest by patrons, in the Israeli case, clientelist linkages collapsed despite the interest of the Labor patrons in prolonging it.[120] In his study of patron-client relations in Africa, Christopher Clapham has observed that a necessary prerequisite for a clientelistic relationship is that patrons be able to deliver "or create the expectation that they can deliver the means to alleviate the vulnerability or achieve the goals of their prospective clients."[121] In Israel, not only was Arab vulnerability reduced when the Military Government was abolished, but Labor's access to resources suffered after it lost the elections and its image as a hegemonic force was undermined.

In addition to no longer being in a position to manipulate government resources according to its political interests, Labor's ability to mobilize and utilize the Histadrut for its political objectives was adversely affected. In the early 1980s, Histadrut firms still generated more than a quarter of the country's products and produced two thirds of Israel's agricultural products. The Histadrut's Koor company was still the country's largest industrial exporter, employing more than 30,000 people.[122] The Likud-led governments formed following the elections of 1977 and 1981, however, treated the Histadrut as a Labor powerbase and did not look favorably on its role in Israel's economy. Hence, they were far more reluctant to come to the Histadrut's aid when the organization experienced financial stress. The Likud administration conditioned any assistance on reforms and cutbacks of Histadrut activities; government regulation of Histadrut pension plan investments; privatization of nonprofitable Histadrut firms; a considerable downsizing of the Histadrut's bureaucracy; reduction in the number of employees; and other steps the government believed would make the Histadrut economically more efficient. The government also took over some of the company's less profitable ventures, such as Bank Hapoalim. Furthermore, in 1980 the Likud minister of finance stopped the subsidies to Hevrat ha-Ovdim, the overarching company that controlled all of the Histadrut's economic enterprises and in which the Histadrut invested the pension funds of its members.[123] With the scaling back of its activities and subsidies, Hevrat ha-Ovdim collapsed and many employees were laid off. As a consequence, the Histadrut lost much of its impact on the state and its ability to assist Labor in distributing material rewards for political support declined considerably. Thus, Labor's ability to determine distribution of resources and sustain its patron-client relations with hamula leaders was seriously undermined.[124]

By and large, Likud did not possess the same capacity as Labor to distribute resources and was unable to replace Labor's extensive networks of patronage with its own. One reason was the relative autonomy of the bureaucracy from the Likud. Students of patron-clientelism have discovered that in competitive democracies, alliances with the civil bureaucracy are imperative for people at the top of a patronage pyramid to establish and maintain networks of clientelistic relations.[125] Although it won the 1977 and 1981 elections, Likud did not have the same ties with the bureaucracy that Labor had managed to establish during almost fifty consecutive years of Yishuv and state rule. Many in the Israeli public administration had job security and affinity to the previous government. They were disinclined to assist Likud governments to increase its reach to followers by using state resources as rewards for political support. It would require plenty of time before Likud could conceivably penetrate the bureaucracy, replace the apparatus associated with Labor and have sufficient control over the public administration for it to cooperate with a Likud-led practice of informal distribution of resources to followers. Furthermore, the Election Law, enacted in 1969, stipulated that civil servants in the high ranks as well as police and military personnel were not permitted to engage in electoral politics, further distancing the state bureaucracy from the political parties (a 1959 law already limited the engagement of senior civil servants in political parties).[126] In short, in the late 1970s and early 1980s, Likud did not have the same tight control over the state apparatus and public resources that Labor had in earlier decades.

In addition, the Likud was not politically dominant in the same way that Labor was prior to the power shift. The 1980s saw Israeli politics transition to genuine competitiveness. Power was shared in unity governments between Likud and Labor from 1984 to 1990. Competition between patrons, accompanied by lack of monopoly over resources, is known to produce competing networks of clientelism that are far less stable and more difficult to sustain

Table 3. Electoral Support (%) for Labor, Likud, and Clientelistic Lists Among
Israeli Voters and Number of Knesset Seats Won by Clientelistic Factions,
1969–1988 Elections

Year of election	Labor	Likud	Clientelistic Arab factions (approximate support among Arab voters only)	Knesset seats won by clientelistic factions
1969	46.2	21.7	3.5 (40)	4
1973	39.6	30.2	2.4 (36)	3
1977	24.6	33.4	1.4 (21)	1
1981	36.6	37.1	>1 (12)	0
1984	34.9	31.9	0	0
1988	30.0	31.1	0	0

Computed based on data from the Knesset website.

than networks in which the patron is hegemonic.[127] Although the Likud did
try to form clientelistic lists to compete in elections, these lists relied on a
narrow support base and never succeeded in passing the threshold required
for representation in the Knesset. At most, the Likud managed to attract
around 7 percent of the Arabic speaking voters, mostly among the Druze
population.[128]

In short, internal contestation within the majority group led to the erosion
of centralized control at the core of the regime and, subsequently, to the collapse of the patron-client networks that contained Arab political activity. Fragmentation within the majority provided opportunities for breaking through
the barrier of clientelism and for minority political parties to independently
mobilize. Table 3 shows the relationship between the transition to Labor-
Likud competitiveness and the decline of the clientlistic lists.

Minority Societal Transformation

While the downfall of patron-client relations was largely facilitated by the
decline in the capacity of those at the top of the hierarchy to deliver rewards,
there were also transformations within Arab society that were imperative for
changes in mobilization patterns. Most notably, the political significance of
the hamula gradually eroded, undermining the position of the intermediary Arab patrons. Hamula practices and their impact on politics came under

scrutiny from within the minority group. A 1976 survey by Smooha found that only 23.3 percent of the PAI felt loyalty to the hamula should be maintained as it was traditionally, 31.8 percent thought it ought to be modified, and 44.9 percent believed it should be abolished altogether.[129] Strikingly, 76 percent of respondents felt that hamula loyalties inhibited PAI social development.[130] Hence there was minority awareness that traditional organizational structures needed to be transformed if the PAI were to make progress.

Ironically, it was state policies that unwittingly played a decisive role in bringing about a decline in the social and political significance of the hamula. First, the annullment of the Military Government significantly reduced the vulnerability of the Arab population and its reliance on local patrons for basic needs because many of the rewards delivered by patrons were associated with the Military Administration, including travel permits required for mobility outside the local vicinity. With easier mobility, employment opportunities outside the local village increased, and hence dependence on patrons for employment or other financial benefits declined.

Second, land policies, which were motivated by the desire to privilege the Jewish population, contributed to a process of social and economic modernization that decreased the dependence of many among the PAI population on patrons. The practice of land nationalization and redistribution by the state meant that many who previously relied on subsistence farming had to search for alternative means of livelihood elsewhere. This problem was acute because the land expropriated was often used for agricultural cultivation. If in 1954 about 54 percent of the Arabs in Israel were agricultural workers, only around 15 percent continued working in agriculture by the second half of the 1970s (See Table 4).[131] As a result, a growing number of Arabs hired themselves out as wage laborers to Jewish employers in Jewish localities. Since most of the Jewish economy was modern and industrial, searching for employment in the urban sector was generally more successful. An important share of the male workforce also became self-employed as contractors, subcontractors, and owners of small service businesses. A small minority became professionals and owners of big businesses. Developing a large-scale independent industrial sector to compete with Jewish industries faced significant obstacles because of government subsidies provided to industries in High Preference Zones (normally Jewish populated areas). Assistance provided by the JA and JNF also gave industries in Jewish populated areas an advantage that was difficult to overcome.[132] As a result, by 1975 most Arab male workers, who accounted for approximately 90 percent of the Arab workforce, were employed

Table 4. PAI Males Working in Agriculture out of Total Arab Male Workforce (%), 1954–1980

1954	1961	1975	1980
54	43	15.6	14.1

Data for 1954, 1961 from Wallach and Lissak, *Carta's Atlas of Israel*, 139. Data for 1975, 1980 from Israel Central Bureau of Statistics, *Statistical Abstracts of Israel*, 27 (1976), 299; 32 (1981), 332. The 1975 and 1980 data lump agriculture with forestry and fishing. Hence the share of agricultural workers is lower than indicated by the table.

Table 5. Occupational Distribution (%) of Arab Males, 1975 and 1980

Occupation	Distribution (89.4% of total Arab workforce), 1975	Distribution (81.7% of total Arab workforce), 1980
Agriculture, forestry and fishing	15.6	14.1
Construction (building and public works)	26.7	22.9
Industry (mining and manufacturing)	16.8	19.3
Commerce, restaurants and hotels	10.9	11.2
Public and community services	12.1	14.5
Transport, storage and communication	8.0	6.7
Financing and business services	2.0	2.3
Personal and other services	7.5	8.3

Israel Central Bureau of Statistics, *Statistical Abstracts of Israel*, 27 (1976), 299; 32 (1981), 332.

in Jewish urban areas in construction, transportation, cleaning services, waiting, and other relatively low-paying jobs.[133]

Nevertheless, the forced occupational transitions diminished basic economic dependence on the hamula, in turn reducing the political control of the local patrons, and thus facilitating the decline of dependent clientelistic electoral politics and central government capacity to control the minority. Tables 4 and 5 show the occupational transitions. Table 4 shows the decline in agricultural employment between 1954 and 1980. Table 5 shows the occupational distribution of Arab males in 1975 and 1980. The table demonstrates that by the mid-1970s more Arab males were employed in occupations related to the modern economy (most conspicuously in industry and construction) than in agriculture.

The integration of the PAI minority into the industrialized economy was complemented by a rapid urbanization process of the Arab localities. In 1961, Arabs in Israel lived in 2 Arab towns (Nazareth and Shafaʻamr), 6 mixed towns and cities, and 101 villages of 5,000 or fewer residents. The number of urban vicinities in which Arabs resided rose to 20 by 1972, 26 by 1977, and over 30 by 1979. In 1980, a majority of the PAI population inhabited 34 urban vicinities while about a third of the population resided in villages of 5,000 people or fewer.[134] Table 6 shows the urbanization process of the Arab minority in Israel.

State-driven modernization in the realm of education also had a considerable impact on the decline in political significance of the hamula. In 1949, the government enacted legislation making schooling mandatory and free of charge for all children between the ages of 5 and 13. A subsequent legislation extended the provision to age 16. While there were several independently run schools, the state was by far the main provider of education, including in Arab areas. The number of elementary schools operated by the state in PAI-populated areas grew from 59 in 1948 to 139 in 1960, 219 in 1970, and 312 in 1980. The number of high schools in Arab populated areas rose from 7 in 1960 to 35 in 1970, 49 in 1980, and 93 by the end of the 1980s. The rise in the number of high school classrooms built in Arab schools is most revealing. While there were 31 high school classrooms in 1960, there were 183 class-

Table 6. Urbanization of Arab Population in Israel (%), 1961–1979

Year	Arabs living in rural areas of total Arab population	Arabs urban dwellers of total Arab population
1961	74.3	25.7
1969	57.0	43.0
1974	41.7	58.3
1979	32.2	67.8

Data for 1961 from Wallach and Lissak, *Carta's Atlas of Israel: The First Years 1948–1961*, 137. Data for 1969, 1974, 1979 from Wallach and Lissak, *Carta's Atlas of Israel: The Third Decade 1971–1981*, 22.

rooms in high schools by 1970, 622 in 1980, and 1,223 by the late 1980s.[135] The number of Arab students attending high schools also increased sharply, from 1,956 in 1960 to 10,507 in 1970, to 37,276 in 1980.[136] In a period of two decades, when the Arab population as a whole grew by only 2.67 times (from 239,200 in 1960 to 638,900 in 1980) and the relative proportion of Arab school-age children among the entire Arab population remained relatively constant at 30 percent, the number of Arab high school classrooms increased by approximately 20 times and the number of Arab students attending high school grew by roughly 19 times.[137] By 1977, 92 percent of all school-age Arabs attended school.[138] The increase in the number of Arab university students also far exceeded Arab population growth, rising from 268 in 1966 to 2,000 in 1978 and 2,300 in 1981.[139]

In short, over a period of roughly three decades, the Arab minority underwent a transition from a rurally based and largely illiterate population that relies heavily on an agricultural economy to a far more urbanized and educated group that is mostly employed in the modern economy of urban vicinities in low-paying jobs as quasi-skilled labor. Modern means of communication facilitated transfer of information and enhanced intracommunal contact (the proportion of Arab households that owned a television set increased from 14.3 percent in 1970 to 70.9 in 1977, and telephone ownership significantly increased as well.)[140] The accumulation of these societal changes resulted in the decline of the dependence of most Arabs on the local village patrons for their necessities, and hence contributed to the decline of the patronage networks. The disintegration of the patron-client networks in turn created space for independent political activism. The Communists were the ones to take advantage of these new opportunities.

Regional Influences

No discussion of the PAI can be complete without some attention paid to the 1967 war and its implications. The war's aftermath saw a significant shift in the territorial boundaries under the jurisdiction of the Israeli state as Israeli rule extended to the West Bank and Gaza and led to renewed contact between the PAI and their co-nationals in these territories. Approximately one million Palestinians, many of whom were displaced during the 1947–1949 war and who for nineteen years or so lived under Egyptian and Jordanian rule, came under Israeli rule. With the annulment of the Military Government within

Israel, the PAI were now able to freely visit old relatives and friends, who themselves were now subjects of an Israeli Military administration.

To what extent and how exogenous factors, such as the regional war, influence state-minority relations is a debated question, as briefly discussed in the Introduction. In the case of the PAI, transitions in minority political activism came in proximity to the 1967 war. Willingness to openly self-identify as Palestinian and express ethnonational sentiments were widespread throughout the 1970s and 1980s. Public opinion surveys reveal this inclination.[141] Without reliable comparable survey data from earlier decades, however, it is impossible to establish trends.

An interesting 1976 survey found that 58.4 percent of the PAI viewed the term "Palestinian" as appropriate for their self-description, usually in conjunction with the broader Arab identity.[142] Over one fifth of the interviewees totally opposed Israel's right to exist and an additional 29 percent had reservations about the state's right to exist.[143] Over one quarter of respondents viewed being a part of a future Palestinian state alongside Israel as a desirable future for the PAI and over half saw recognition as a separate but equal people in Israel as desirable, indicating a desire for an ethnically neutral, but not blind, state in which allocation of resources is on a communal basis.[144] In this light, a significant majority of the PAI felt their community should have institutional autonomy in the spheres of education (including a separate Arab university), media, local government, and trade.[145]

It should be stressed that integrationist tendencies were also exposed in this survey. Roughly half of the PAI thought the title "Israeli," usually in conjunction with Arab or Palestinian, was appropriate for the collective identity of their group; most of the PAI viewed biculturalism as an important educational goal; and more than 90 percent supported retaining or even extending Hebrew language instruction in Arab schools.[146] Considering that approximately 63 percent of the PAI were wage-earners working for Jewish employers, these findings can be interpreted as practical means for increasing opportunities within the existing constraints.[147]

What is interesting for the purpose of this analysis is that the strong ethnonationalist preferences that existed in the 1970s were rarely reflected in PAI politics. The DFPE did ask that the PAI be recognized as a national minority but on the whole kept clear of isolationist demands. As this chapter has shown, Rakah went to great length to present itself as a Jewish-Arab party and stress an integrationist agenda. It was criticized by some among the PAI for neglecting the national question and submitting to the Soviets. Moreover,

according to the 1976 survey, only one year before the DFPE's great electoral success among the PAI, less than half of the minority population viewed
non-Zionist parties composed of Arabs and Jews, such as the DFPE, as the
preferable type of Arab political organization, while over one third viewed independent and exclusive Arab national political parties as the preferable form
of political organization for mobilizing on behalf of the minority.[148]

Minority political demands, however, are not necessarily a reflection of
popular sentiments. Ultimately, it is political organizations that engage in
activism and make demands on behalf of the minority. That Rakah, within
the DFPE framework, led PAI political activism without serious competition
from more ethnonationalist organizations suggests that if popular sentiments
of Palestinian nationalism were indeed influenced by the changing regional
environment, the impact of exogenous factors on minority political activism
is, at most, mediated by the domestic institutional framework.

Conclusion

In light of these processes, it was by no means inevitable that the ideology of
the Communist Party would be at the forefront, indeed dominate, minority
demands. Sammy Smooha's surveys in the 1970s revealed that the ideological
position advanced by the Communists—whereby the desirable solution for
the PAI is a secular Israeli state, where all citizens have equal rights as individuals regardless of ethnic background (an ethnically neutral and ethnically
blind state), alongside a Palestinian state—was not fully shared by the majority of the PAI electorate.[149]

And yet, until the mid-1980s, the Communists, and by extension their
demands, dominated Arab politics without serious competition from isolationist and ethnonationalist organizations. Undoubtedly, resources, path dependence, and historical legacies played a role in engendering this outcome.
Studies of contentious politics have revealed that the availability of resources
for mobilization is the key for sustaining mobilization.[150] Important resources
include, but are not limited to, party branches and organizational infrastructure, personnel, money, access to media, and leadership skills and experience.
The Communist Party, due to the legacies of preceding decades, was the only
organization with significant resources to mobilize when the opportunities
were opened. Its party branches spread throughout PAI population centers. By the early 1980s, the party's biweekly *al-Ittihad* had become the most

widely circulated Arab paper, and in 1983, the newspaper became a daily. The party's youth movements increased the party's presence. The National Organization of Arab Academics and Students and other affiliated student bodies were formed to assist the Communists with organizing and mobilizing the intelligentsia.

That the Communists were in a position to mobilize when opportunities arrived is largely a legacy of the preceding periods. The only non-Zionist party that integrated Arabs and had the necessary preexisting party infrastructure, resources, organizational foundations, and experience in politics to mobilize at the national level was the Communist Party. Independent national PAI organizations were unavailable in the immediate period following the abolition of the Military Government. Thus, at a time when state presence declined considerably due to the demise of the Military Administration and the collapse of the patronage networks, when internal majority divisions increased, resulting in the fragmentation in the centers of political power, and the minority experienced rapid societal transformation, the Communists were the only readily available option for the PAI. Therefore, the party had almost a monopoly on the articulation of minority demands.

Ethnically based organizations that made more isolationist or ethnonationalist claims tried to emerge, but they lacked organizational infrastructure and resources. Hence they were unable to mobilize effectively and offer an alternative agenda to the vision of the Communists, despite indications that a large segment of PAI society might have supported a more assertive ethnonationalist path had there been a viable ethnically exclusive political organization pulling in that direction. By the 1990s, however, such organizations would emerge, challenge Rakah's dominance, and advance different claims on behalf of the minority.

5

The Ethnonational Turn

In October 2000, thousands of Arab citizens of Israel took to the streets to demonstrate in solidarity with the second Palestinian uprising, or intifada, which had erupted several days earlier in the West Bank and Gaza. The protests soon turned into a violent clash between the police and the demonstrators, resulting in the death of twelve PAI protestors. Marking a significant deviation from PAI behavior during the first intifada, which amounted mostly to general strikes, the October events left a deep wound in Jewish-PAI relations in Israel.

On one level, episodes of communally related violence are sparked off by proximate precipitants.[1] The second intifada and television images of Israeli soldiers engaging in brutal confrontation with Palestinians in the West Bank and Gaza undoubtedly fueled sentiments of anger among many PAI. At the same time, a precipitating event is not a cause independent of broader underlying currents and transformations in a deeply divided society. To put it succinctly, the last two decades have witnessed a significant surge in the salience of PAI ethnonationalism. Whereas in previous decades the Communists spearheaded an integrationist strategy that sought to advance an overarching civic identity and according to which ethnic background ought to be irrelevant for resource distribution, throughout the 1990s and 2000s a growing number of PAI political organizations have been increasingly promoting Palestinian consciousness, advancing ethnonationalist objectives, and demanding recognition of collective group rights. PAI elites have reframed their demands using the language of indigenousness. "They are demanding an official recognition as an indigenous people entitled to collective rights that should be translated into self-government."[2] The Vision Documents, composed by new elites in multiple organizations that have emerged over the last two decades, demand autonomy in the spheres of education, religion, culture, social welfare, planning and development, and control over resources. They simultaneously demand proportional allocation of resources and veto power on state policies that affect the PAI. Furthermore, as indigenous people, they view themselves as integral members of the Palestinian people and a component of the broader conflict as a whole.

PAI collectivist politics have largely been manifested in the establishment of ethnically based organizations in several spheres, in demands to increase the ethnically exclusive sphere and their authority in it, and in willingness to take a more confrontational stance when asserting their demands. In the parliamentary arena, exclusive PAI political parties with ethnonational platforms have emerged, challenging the successor of the Communist Party, the DFPE. The DFPE has responded to the intensifying competition by increasing its appeal to the collective national sentiments of the PAI community and forming alliances with hardcore PAI ethnonationalist movements, thus downplaying the party's biethnic side. In the extra-parliamentary sphere, too, there is growing ethnicity-based PAI civil society activity that presents communalist challenges to the state. Religious and secular organizations have proliferated and are politically active in making communalist demands on the state. Alongside demands for increased autonomy and an exclusive social sphere for the minority, many new civil society organizations have been acting to increase the ethnic neutrality of the state while demanding proportional distribution of resources based on group size. Thus, rather than advocate civic, or bi-ethnic, collaboration, the new political actors are now practicing politics that revolve around communal affiliation and are demanding formal recognition of collective minority rights.

This chapter discusses the ethnonational phase of PAI involvement in Israeli politics. The chapter begins with a discussion of recent expressions of minority ethnonationalism, including the publication of the Vision Documents and the October events. The discussion then proceeds with a survey of the main political organizations that have emerged over the last two decades (both in the parliamentary arena and in the expanding civil society sphere) and have been involved in advancing PAI communalism. Chapter 6 will evaluate the conditions conducive to this transition of minority political activism. In a nutshell, the investigation reveals that majority resistance to minority integration and to attempts to make the state more neutral, coupled with a decline in state cohesion and extensiveness—factors that cause a decline in central government capacity to control society in general and contentious

minority activism in particular—provided favorable conditions for communalist politics. The emergence of a new PAI elite to take advantage of these
institutional changes and act as mobilizing agents has also been imperative to
these developments.

The Vision Documents

The most audacious nonviolent assertion of PAI ethnonational claims to date
has been the publication of four documents, collectively known as the Vision
Documents, in 2006 and 2007 by a number of different PAI organizations
that have come to the forefront of PAI politics in recent decades: The National Committee for the Heads of the Arab Local Authorities (NCHALA);
Mada al-Carmel: The Arab Center for Applied Social Research; Adalah [jus-
tice]: The Legal Center for Arab Minority Rights in Israel; and the Mossawa
[equality] Center: The Advocacy Center for Arab Citizens in Israel). These
four documents, *The Future Vision of the Palestinian Arabs in Israel, The Haifa
Declaration, The Democratic Constitution*, and *An Equal Constitution for All?
On the Constitution and the Collective Rights of Arabs Citizens in Israel*,[3] present the PAI as the indigenous population of the land, provide a PAI narrative
of state-minority and majority-minority relations, and present an ideological program for addressing the minority's status and future state-minority
relations (and by extension, majority-minority relations). Significantly, the
documents identify the Jewish identity of the state as the root cause of the PAI
plight and make demands for major institutional changes that will address
the distinct ethnonational identity of the PAI.

Arguably the most significant of these publications, and the one that has
attracted most attention, is NCHALA's *The Future Vision*. This position paper
constitutes the most outspoken organized and collaborative effort by PAI
elites from across the political spectrum to offer an alternative to the existing
institutional framework. Thirty-eight prominent PAI academics, intellectuals, and political activists contributed to the composition of the document,
which was endorsed by the High Follow Up Committee for the Arabs in Israel (HFUCAI), an organization composed of many elected representatives
of the PAI (including Knesset members and heads of local councils) and leaders of NGOs and other movements. Because of the extent of this collaborative effort, *The Future Vision* is widely seen as representative of the collective
position of the new PAI elite that has arisen over the last two decades (the

team of contributors also included Adalah activists who contributed to *The Democratic Constitution* and Mossawa's Yousef Jabareen, who composed *An Equal Constitution for All?*). *The Future Vision* has been described by experts as challenging "for the first time . . . most of the foundational premises of the Jewish state" and as constituting "a watershed in the history of Jewish-Arab relations in Israel."[4] Taken together, all four documents present serious challenges to majority-minority relations.

Despite important differences, the four documents share many ideas and positions. One of the most eye-catching features is the presentation of the PAI as the native people of the land, who are an integral part of the Palestinian people elsewhere and who were coercively separated from their co-nationals by the establishment of the State of Israel. *The Haifa Declaration* opens with the statement

> We, sons and daughters of the Palestinian Arab people who remained in our homeland despite the *Nakba*, who were forcibly made a minority in the State of Israel after its establishment in 1948 on the greater part of the Palestinian homeland; do hereby affirm in this Declaration the foundations of our identity and belonging. . . .
>
> Despite the setback to our national project and our relative isolation from the rest of our Palestinian people and our Arab nation since the *Nakba*; despite all the attempts made to keep us in ignorance of our Palestinian and Arab history; despite attempts to splinter us into sectarian groups and to truncate our identity into a misshapen "Israeli Arab" one, we have spared no effort to preserve our Palestinian identity and national dignity and to fortify it. In this regard, we reaffirm our attachment to our Palestinian homeland and people, to our Arab nation, with its language, history, and culture, as we reaffirm also our right to remain in our homeland and to safeguard it.[5]

The Future Vision and Mossawa's *An Equal Constitution for All?* use indigeneity explicitly. The preface to the latter publication states that "The Mossawa Center advocates for both minority status recognition in Israel and indigenous rights."[6] The constitution proposal proceeds to dedicate a subsection to a discussion of this status:

> [The Arab minority] is the indigenous, original Arab Palestinian population, living in its homeland even before the state was established,

when it was the majority group together with the rest of its people. The State of Israel was established on the ruins of the Palestinian people, for whom this event was a national tragedy—the Nakba. The indigeneity of the Arab population, therefore, is an integral part of the way in which it experiences its situation in Israel.[7]

Similarly, *The Future Vision* begins with the declaration, "We are the Palestinian Arabs in Israel, the indigenous peoples, the residents of the State of Israel, and an integral part of the Palestinian People and the Arab and Muslim and human nation."[8] Finally, Adalah's *Democratic Constitution* states that

> The Palestinian Arab citizens of the State of Israel have lived in their homeland for innumerable generations. Here they were born, here their historic roots have grown, and here their national and cultural life has developed and flourished. They are active contributors to human history and culture as part of the Arab and Islamic nations and as an inseparable part of the Palestinian people.[9]

Conceiving of the PAI as an indigenous national minority and as an integral part of the Palestinian and Arab people lays the basis for the type of demands and political claims made by the PAI.[10] First, the documents demand that the state formally recognize the PAI as the indigenous people of the country and as a national minority and to bestow on it a fitting legal status.[11] A formal title, in turn, provides a source of legitimacy to claims to language protection; distinct and autonomous political, legal, economic, social, and cultural institutions; self-government in the spheres of education, control over resources, planning and development, social welfare, and communication; and freedom to maintain ties with Palestinians and Arabs elsewhere. The increasing diligence with which the PAI have been asserting their group demands is strikingly correlated with the codification of related norms in international conventions and declarations, as the labels *national minority* and *indigenous people* have gained normative and practical significance. Norms for the entitlements of national minorities and indigenous peoples have been codified in the burgeoning body of declarations adopted by international organizations over the last two decades. The UN 1992 Declaration on the Rights of Persons Belonging to National or Ethnic, Religious and Linguistic Minorities; the UN 2007 Declaration on the Rights of Indigenous Peoples, which was adopted after many years of deliberations; and other declarations (for example, the Council of Europe 1995 Framework Convention for the Protection of National Minorities) endorse the rights of groups that fall under the relevant categories to enhanced collective rights, variable group autonomy and control over resources, protection from intervention by external state authorities in their affairs, and protection from forced assimilation and integration.[12]

If the PAI are viewed as an indigenous homeland minority and members of a larger national group, the idea of a trans-state Jewish nationalism with premodern ties to the land goes unacknowledged. There is a general acceptance, implicit and explicit, that a new category of a Jewish-Israeli nation has been created by the Israeli state and has a right to reside on the territory.[13] However, recognizing the existence of a recently formed Jewish-Israeli category, which is currently residing in Israel as a result of immigration, is significantly different from accepting that there are national ties between Jews in Israel and Jews elsewhere or that non-Israeli Jews are entitled to claim historical ties to the land. The Jewish state is depicted in some of these documents as an outcome of colonialism without any reference to a Jewish national claim to age-old connection to the land. *The Future Vision* states that

> Israel is the outcome of a settlement process initiated by the Zionist-Jewish elite in Europe and the west and realized by Colonial countries contributing to it and by promoting Jewish immigration to Palestine, in light of the results of the Second World War and the Holocaust. After the creation of the state in 1948, Israel continued to use policies derived from its vision as an extension of the west in the Middle East and continued conflicting with its neighbours.[14]

Israel, thus, is conceived of as an extension of the West in the Middle East rather than an expression of Jewish nationalism. Less blunt in its rejection of Jewish national claims to the land, but still adopting the traditional Palestinian nationalist narrative that Israel is an outcome of colonialism and imperialism, *The Haifa Declaration* states that

> Towards the end of the 19th century, the Zionist movement initiated its colonial-settler project in Palestine. Subsequently, in concert with world imperialism and with the collusion of the Arab reactionary powers, it succeeded in carrying out its project, which aimed at occupying our homeland and transforming it into a state for the Jews.[15]

Using the parameters of indigenousness and colonialists, the documents are advancing what Donald Horowitz refers to as *differential legitimacy*.[16] Horowitz has observed that "The claim to primacy by dint of indigenousness is both widespread and powerful; the term 'sons of soil' is used in a great many countries of Asia and Africa. . . . In general, the closer the identification of the group with the soil the more powerful the pretension [to legitimacy]."[17] Indeed, the indigene-outsider narrative has been employed in many cases to demonstrate belonging and to gain advantage in claims against politically dominant groups. Examples include the Kalenjin and Kikuyu strife in the Kenyan Rift Valley, the Beti and Bamileke in Southern Cameroon, Luzon Christians and Muslims in Mindanao (Philippines), Papuans and Javanese in Papua (Indonesia), and many others. In Israel, too, the narrative implies that if Jewish presence in the region is an exclusive result of colonialist settlement and has no foundation in historical national ties, then Jews are not native and the moral basis of their national claims are not on par with those of the native Palestinian people. According to *The Haifa Declaration* and *The Future Vision*, it is only due to historical mishaps that a national home for the Jews was established in Palestine, and it came at the expense of the indigenous population's national entitlement.[18]

It should be stressed that unlike *The Future Vision* and *The Haifa Declaration*, Mossawa's *An Equal Constitution for All?* and Adalah's *Democratic Constitution* do not discuss the origins of Israel's state formation and Jewish nationalism and claims. By steering clear of this issue, these two documents manage to avoid presenting the relationship between Palestinian nationalism and indigeneity claims, on the one hand, and Jewish national identity (broader than the Jewish Israeli category), on the other, in zero-sum terms. Nevertheless, these two documents stress the moral significance of prior presence on the land on group entitlement.

Horowitz notes that in many cases, differential legitimacy on the basis of exclusive claims to indigeneity has led to widespread perceptions that members of the nonindigenous group are alien and their presence on the land is, or should be, temporary (in some cases, there have been demands to deport the "aliens"), and that differential legitimacy was used to justify exclusivist practices on behalf of the "natives." In the case of the PAI, characterizing Israel as an extension of the West in the Middle East does not yield demands for the relocation of the Jewish populations. However, it does challenge the legitimacy of majority group national claims, and therefore the state's Jewish identity, while providing the moral basis for minority group demands. Hence, in addition to minority national institutions and self-government, the documents are also demanding to de-Judaize the state and formally reconstitute it as a binational state. The demand to fundamentally transform the foundational principles of the state is facilitated by the perception of the alien roots of Israel's state formation and by viewing Jewish Israelis as a new group while ignoring Jewish national claims to historically based ties.

Underlying the demand to de-Judaize the state there is an overwhelming negative moral assessment of state practices, and by extension, Jewish dominance (as one interviewee who participated in the work on *The Future Vision* explained, "the state reflects the will of Jewish society"[19]). Israel is described as having "enacted racist land, immigration, and citizenship laws, and other laws that have allowed for the confiscation of our land and the property of refugees and internally displaced persons."[20] Discussing extensively the socioeconomic, political, and cultural discrimination that the PAI face in Israel, the documents attribute the cause of this subordination to the Jewish definition of the state. *The Future Vision*, for example, states that

> official discrimination on a national basis is the core of all forms of discrimination against the Palestinian Arabs in Israel. It is the root cause from which Palestinians in Israel suffer, individually and collectively. Thus, the official definition of Israel as a Jewish state created a fortified ideological barrier in the face of the possibility of obtaining full equality for the Palestinian Arab citizens of Israel.[21]

The negative moral evaluation of the Jewish state is present not only in the discussion of state-minority relations, but also in the context of the Arab-Israeli conflict as a whole. *The Future Vision* and *The Haifa Declaration* depict Israel as solely responsible for the Israeli-Arab conflict. Israel's portrayal is of an imperial bully looking for a fight.[22] At the same time, the Arab and Palestinian role in the conflict—for example, the rejection of the UN 1947 partition plan, calls for the destruction of Israel, and Arab violence against Jews—goes unmentioned.

Juxtaposing the negative moral evaluation of the expression of Jewish nationalism through the state with the positive evaluation of Palestinianhood, indigeneity, and victimhood provides the foundations for calls to transform the national identity of the state. The (sometimes implicit) group comparison leads to demands for making the distinct group identities into the basis of formal social organization, politics, governance, and resource distribution in a new institutional configuration. The documents are calling for a binational state and advancing variants of power-sharing and consociational arrangements that will highlight group distinctiveness. Each of the documents provides a different name for the institutional arrangement that it proposes, but the main characteristics are similar. *The Future Vision* calls it a "consensual democracy" whereby the "State has to acknowledge that Israel is the homeland for both Palestinians and Jews."[23] *The Democratic Constitution* uses the phrase "democratic, bilingual and multicultural state." *The Haifa Declaration* calls it simply a "democratic and bi-national state," implying that Israel is not currently seen by the writers as a democracy (a position asserted bluntly in *The Future Vision*[24]). *An Equal Constitution for All?* does not provide a label. All documents call for official bilingualism and legal protection for minority languages. The documents also call for changing all state symbols, such as the flag and national anthem, as well as laws, such as the Law of Return, that stress the state's Jewish identity. Another shared demand is proportional representation of the PAI in the bureaucracy, government and public institutions, and decision-making bodies. In addition, the documents call for a right to veto decisions that affect the PAI population. Finally, they call for proportional allocation of material resources on a collective basis, with additional provisions for affirmative action as a means for applying corrective justice and compensating for past injustices.[25]

Adopting the Palestinian narrative of Israel's state formation and depicting the PAI as an integral component of the Palestinian people, the documents suggest that a comprehensive resolution to the Palestinian-Jewish Israeli conflict as a whole necessitates addressing the PAI problem as well. Interestingly, in discussions leading up to the publication of *The Future Vision* and *The Haifa Declaration*, some participants sought to explicitly propose a single state from the Mediterranean to the Jordan Valley as a solution to the Israeli-Palestinian conflict. This opinion, however, was held by a minority. Thus, it was decided to leave this proposal out of the documents but to nonetheless maintain an explicit link between the conflict's resolution and the PAI's position in Israel.[26]

The Haifa Declaration presents the occupation of the Gaza Strip and the West Bank in 1967 as a historical continuation of Israel's establishment in 1948 and an extension of its overall mistreatment of the Palestinian people.[27] In the opening paragraph, the writers of *The Haifa Declaration* posit, "We . . . put forward our conception of the preconditions for a historic reconciliation between the Palestinian people and the Israeli Jewish people, and of the future to which we aspire as regards the relationship between the two peoples."[28] The *Declaration* goes on to state,

This reconciliation requires the State of Israel to recognize the histori-cal injustice that it committed against the Palestinian people through its establishment, to accept responsibility for the *Nakba*, which befell all parts of the Palestinian people, and also for the war crimes and crimes of occupation that it has committed in the Occupied Territo-ries. Reconciliation also requires recognizing the Right of Return and acting to implement it in accordance with United Nations Resolution 194, ending the Occupation and removing the settlements from all Arab territory occupied since 1967, recognizing the right of the Pales-tinian people to self-determination and to an independent and sover-eign state, and recognizing the rights of Palestinian citizens in Israel, which derive from being a homeland minority.[29]

Similarly, Adalah's *Democratic Constitution* links Palestinian-Israeli conflict resolution to settling PAI-Jewish relations when it states that

In order to build an equal and democratic society, free of repression and violence, and as a basis for historic reconciliation between the State of Israel and the Palestinian People and the entire Arab nation, the State of Israel must recognize its responsibility for past injustices suffered by the Palestinian People, both before and after its establishment, [and] its responsibility for the injustices of the Nakba and the Occupation.[30]

In short, the Vision Documents daringly articulate Palestinian national-ism in Israel and portray a picture whereby Palestinian nationalism stands on a higher moral ground than Jewish national claims, a position that provides a platform for calls to de-Judaize the state and claims to self-government in im-portant realms. According to the documents, until these issues are addressed satisfactorily, a comprehensive resolution to the Palestinian-Israeli conflict as a whole cannot be complete.

The October Events

One of the monumental events manifesting PAI transition away from passiv-ity and growing identification with Palestinian nationalism was what became known as the October events, an episode of unrest that erupted in October 2000, shortly after the outbreak of the second intifada. This affair expressed willingness to engage in confrontational activism to challenge state social boundaries.

A comparison of PAI behavior during the first Palestinian intifada of the late 1980s in the West Bank and Gaza with that during the second intifada is particularly instructive for evaluating the transformation of PAI mobilization. According to Sammy Smooha, none of the characteristics of an uprising—which include casualties, curfews, confrontation with security forces, throwing of stones and Molotov cocktails, mass arrests and detentions, the disruption of daily life, and a decline in the standard of living—existed among the PAI during the first Palestinian intifada.[31] The main act of solidarity was a one-day strike in which about 60 percent of the PAI participated.[32] Although localized cases of stone throwing took place during this strike, PAI support for the intifada was by and large confined to parliamentary lobbying, expressions of public sympathy, and humanitarian aid.

Contrast this behavior with the unrest of October 2000. Two days after the eruption of violence in the West Bank and Gaza, thousands of PAI took to the streets. The protests were intense; they were widespread in the Galilee and the Little Triangle and went on for several days. They were labeled in some PAI quarters as a local "intifada."[33] One Israeli Jew was killed when his car was stoned near the Arab village of Jisser a-Zarka. The police responded to the unrest by using a variety of means, including the firing of rubber bullets and, in some cases, live ammunition at the protestors, killing thirteen of them and eventually managing to suppress the violence. The State Commission of Inquiry into the Clashes Between Security Forces and Israeli Civilians, known as the Or Commission, investigated the violence and observed that

> The riots in the Arab sector inside the State of Israel in early October were unprecedented. The events were extremely unusual from several perspectives. Thousands participated, at many locations, at the same time. The intensity of the violence and aggression expressed in the events were extremely powerful. Against security forces, and even against civilians, use was made of a variety of means of attack, including a small number of live fire incidents, Molotov cocktails, ball bearings in slingshots, various methods of stone throwing and the rolling of burning tires. Jews were attacked on the roads for being Jewish and their property was destroyed. In a number of incidences, they were just inches from death at the hands of an unrestrained mob.
> In a number of incidences, attempts were made to enter Jewish

towns in order to attack them. Major traffic arteries were blocked for long periods of time and traffic to various Jewish towns was seriously disrupted, sometimes even severed, for long periods of time. In a large number of instances, the aggression and violence was characterized by great determination and continued for long periods. The police acted to restore order and used a variety of means to disperse the crowd. As a result of the use of some of these means, which included firing of rubber bullets and a few instances of live fire, Arab citizens were killed and many more were injured. In the second wave of events, some places saw retaliatory Jewish riots against Arabs.

During the events, 12 Arab and one Jewish citizen were killed. One resident of the Gaza Strip was also killed. Such riots could have developed—heaven forbid—into a serious conflict between sectors of the population, such as the interracial conflicts with their attendant results that we have seen in distant locals. The fact is that, in a number of locations in Israel, these developments did lead to retaliatory Jewish riots.[34]

Significant changes in the behavior of political elites since the first intifada are also conspicuous. If during the first intifada PAI leaders generally called for expressions of solidarity without joining the uprising or committing acts of civil disobedience,[35] during the second intifada PAI leaders from a variety of streams delivered messages that, according to the findings of the Or Commission, delegitimized the state and inspired the PAI to take violent actions.[36] Leaders from a variety of political organizations with ethnonationalist orientations were accused of praising violent protests and encouraging the PAI to adopt this mode of action in their October protests.[37] Azmi Bishara of the Balad party, a rising political force from the mid-1990s, was found to have urged the PAI to learn the lessons of Hezbollah's success against Israel in southern Lebanon and to engage in a "popular *intifidah*."[38] Leaders from the strengthening Islamic movement urged the PAI to join what they termed the al-Aqsa Intifada, warning that the "*al-Aqsa* Mosque is in danger" and calling on the PAI to be willing to use force and sacrifice lives in defense of the mosque if the need arose.[39] Indeed, framing the events as a domestic intifada that coincided with the Palestinian intifada in the West Bank and Gaza served to highlight the ethnonational dimension of the mobilization.

PAI elites were further found by the investigating committee to have been responsible for spreading unverified rumors that spurred anxiety among the

PAI and provided fuel for violence. One rumor spoke about a "slaughter [of Palestinians] that is still taking place in the *al-Aqsa* Mosque."[40] The HFUCAI was blamed for spreading unverified rumors about police responsibility for the death of an Arab woman in earlier violent protests.[41] Another rumor dealt with alleged Israeli intentions to harm the al-Aqsa mosque. Experiments in psychology and evidence from comparative studies suggest that perceptions of hostile intentions and aggressive physical behavior on the part of an adversary increase the prospects of eliciting a violent response.[42] The significance of rumors in stirring anxiety and precipitating episodes of ethnic violence should not be underestimated. In his seminal work on ethnic riots, Horowitz notes that rumors play a critical role:

> They justify the violence that is about to occur. Their severity is often an indicator of the severity of impending violence. Rumors narrow the options that seem available to those who join crowds and commit them to a line of action. They mobilize ordinary people to do what they would not normally do. They shift the balance in a crowd toward those proposing the most extreme action. . . . Rumors, then, are not stray tales. They perform functions for the group and for individuals in it.[43]

Ascribing aggressive behavior to state authorities, the PAI were moved to an unprecedented form of action.

The systematic discrimination from which the PAI have been suffering and that was stressed throughout the Or Commission report undoubtedly played a significant role in spurring the October unrest, no less than imputing aggression to the Jewish state. Yet the timing of the riots was not random and suggests that broader underlying minority group transformations conditioned the impact of systematic discrimination and perceived Israeli aggression in the West Bank and Gaza on PAI behavior. Increasing minority mobilization in the name of Palestinian ethnonational identity led to the outburst at this particular juncture, namely the outbreak of the second intifada, and not during the first intifada or some other random point in time. The conditions that have produced this transformation will be discussed in the next chapter.

It should not be forgotten that the October riots were suppressed in a number of days by what the Or Commission found to be an unrestrained response by the security forces.[44] The relatively quick restoration of calm and the absence of any recurrences suggest that although central government capacity to control minority mobilization like it did in the first decades has diminished, state authorities still possess sufficient capacity to set firm parameters within which political activity must take place and that they can ward off minority violent contestation of the state's foundational rules that privilege the Jewish majority.

It is important to stress that even though there was no repetition of the unrest of October 2000, the events did have ongoing repercussions on PAI-Jewish relations in Israel. The PAI boycotted the 2001 national elections for the premiership to protest their repression by the state authorities.[45] One study revealed that in 2001, only about one quarter of the PAI were willing to fly an Israeli flag on Israel's Independence Day, as opposed to 43 percent in 1995.[46] Meanwhile, the Jewish public, taken aback by the magnitude of the PAI riots, has been shunning PAI places of business, which prior to the violence were frequently visited by Jews and relied on Jewish clientele. This unofficial boycott has contributed to an economic downturn and, according to one source, has "resulted in a 50 percent decline in the volume of Palestinian business in Israel."[47]

More significantly, a growing number of Jewish politicians, intellectuals, and academics have started to openly consider whether PAI-populated areas, given the vociferousness of their ethnonationalist expressions, should be transferred to the authority of a future Palestinian state. Such proposals did not come only from right-wing political parties such as Yisrael Beytenu.[48] The distinguished political scientist Shlomo Avineri, an Israel prize laureate and a former director general in the Foreign Ministry, proposed that following the formation of a Palestinian state in the West Bank, a referendum be held in PAI areas adjacent to the Green Line in which the PAI would be asked whether they wanted to be annexed to the Palestinian state.[49] This emerging discourse, coupled with hardening PAI alienation, reflected ethno-fortification and isolationism in the aftermath of the October events.

Ethnic Political Parties

Momentous events—such as the publication of the Vision Documents and the October events—highlight a longer process of transformation that can be observed in routine politics but whose meaning is sometimes overlooked because of the incremental character of the change. It sometimes takes exceptional events to direct attention to the significance of the nature of the change.

It is worth stressing, therefore, that PAI ethnonationalism is not an event that suddenly occurred in the year 2000. There has been an ongoing process in politics for more than two decades whereby ethnonational political organizations have steadily taken center stage.

In the parliamentary arena, the ethnonationalist turn has been reflected in gradual growth in the number and popularity of ethnic parties that have been touting Palestinian nationalism in Israel. These parties have posed challenges to the DFPE, which, as discussed in the previous chapter, was carrying the banner of Jewish-Arab cooperation and demanded a unifying civic Israeli identity. Whereas the DFPE tried to project an image of a nonethnic party, the new parties formed on an ethnically exclusive basis in an attempt to capitalize on group loyalties. As these parties increased in numbers and attempted to solidify their support base, they also engaged in intense competition for voters.[50] This internal competition, in turn, has led to an implicit outbidding war in which each party tries to persuade a limited pool of ethnic voters that it is the best representative of communal interests.[51] Thus, the parties' assertiveness has grown bolder over the years, and, like ethnic parties in many other deeply divided societies, they have not only reflected but also contributed to the growth of PAI ethnonationalism by appealing to the electorate in ethnic terms.[52]

The first serious electoral challenge to the DFPE came from the Progressive List for Peace (PLP), which first competed in the 1984 elections. The PLP was established after a group of activists and intellectuals splintered from the DFPE, charging that the Communist Party was too feeble in addressing PAI national identity. Like the DFPE, the PLP was formed as a joint Arab-Jewish list, but with an Arab as its head, namely the Muslim lawyer Mohammad Mi'ari. The party claimed to advance Palestinian national awareness among the Arabs in Israel, emphasizing the minority's ethnonational affiliation with Palestinians elsewhere.[53] The movement's main focus of activism, however, was advocacy on behalf of a Palestinian state in the West Bank and Gaza. Otherwise, the party was vague on how its proposed agenda of state neutrality should be pursued in Israel. Following two national election campaigns in 1984 and 1988, in which it won two seats and one seat, respectively, the party decided to "Arabize" and marginalized Jewish representation.[54] Facing competition from additional new PAI parties, the PLP was unable to retain its support among the PAI and was not reelected in subsequent elections.

The Arab Democratic Party (ADP) was the first independent political party to organize on an exclusive Arab basis. It was formed by Abdulwahab

Darawshe in the run-up to the 1988 elections, shortly after the first Palestinian uprising erupted in the West Bank and Gaza. Darawshe left the Labor Party, charging that it was complicit in repressing the Palestinians in the West Bank and Gaza.[55] Maintaining that Jewish parties were exploiting Arab voters without advancing the minority's interests or enabling integration, Darawshe reasoned that a separate Arab party had become a necessity to mobilize the PAI and promote the group's particularistic interests in conjunction with lobbying for a Palestinian state alongside Israel.[56] Despite its ethnically exclusive character, the party did not rule out cooperation with Zionist parties and expressed willingness to participate in Labor-led coalition governments following the national elections of 1992 and 1999, a stance that led some observers to view the ADP as an integrationist party.[57] The integrationist dimension was further reflected in the party's demand to have Arabs appointed to senior posts in the bureaucratic apparatus as a means for enhancing Arab participation in decision-making.

Integrationist aspects were combined with efforts to expand a separate Arab sphere. The ADP contributed to the establishment of organizations particular to the PAI and demanded that the PAI be recognized as a national minority with a distinct national identity.[58] Although these demands fell short of institutional autonomy, the party did raise the idea that the PAI community should be allowed some authority to manage its own affairs. By appealing to PAI voters in ethnonational terms, making ethnic demands on the government, and advocating for an ethnically exclusive sphere, the ADP both recognized and added to the significance of the ethnic national identity of the PAI for politics. Many of the PAI social and political forces that have emerged since the establishment of the ADP have built on the notion that communal empowerment is contingent upon separate organizational infrastructure.

After winning one parliamentary seat in the 1988 national elections and two in the 1992 elections, the ADP joined forces with the southern stream of the Islamic movement in the run-up to the 1996 elections.[59] The joint list managed to win 25 percent of the PAI vote, which translated into four Knesset seats. The 1999 elections saw the United Arab List (UAL) of the ADP and the Islamists depose the DFPE as the most popular political party among the PAI electorate, winning 31 percent of the PAI vote, which translated into five Knesset seats. Following a brief decline to two seats in the 2003 elections, as a result of internal disputes and splinters,[60] the UAL managed to rebound in the 2006 elections as the party coalesced with Ta'al, a party that broke into the parliamentary scene close to the turn of the century and is raising the

banner of Palestinian nationalism in Israel. The joint list won four seats, thus
regaining its status as the most popular choice among the PAI electorate. The
UAL-Ta'al alliance achieved similar success in the 2009 elections.

The alliance with the ADP in the 1996 elections marked the first time that
the Islamists, who up until the late 1980s did not have a significant political
following, competed in national elections. The willingness to participate constituted a sharp shift from the movement's traditional isolationist worldview,
according to which the group ought to minimize its interaction with external
state authorities. In the past, the Islamists' efforts were placed almost solely on
constructing a parallel sector that provides services for the community in the
realms of education, health, religion, culture, and sport. Earlier in the 1980s,
several of the movement's leaders were imprisoned after forming a paramilitary group called the "Jihad Family." However, following their release from
prison, the leadership declared that it eschews violence and turned to what is
known as the *da'wa* (invitation or call to the religious framework).

A fresh dual approach was adopted in the 1990s, according to which, despite the overarching isolationist strategy, interaction with the state or the
Jewish majority should not be totally spurned if such relations are believed
to benefit the minority and to improve the movement's standings among the
PAI. Although he admitted that his desire is to have a caliphate replace the
existing regime, Sheikh Ibrahim Sarsur, the political leader of the movement
in Israel, reasoned that such an objective is unattainable in an environment
where Jews constitute the majority.[61] Instead, the southern stream of the Islamic movement adopted a pragmatic attitude that combines acceptance of
PAI minority status in Israel with an attempt to create a religiously exclusive
local sphere consistent with Islamist codes of conduct and in which the state
does not intervene. Sheikh 'Abdallah Nimr Darwish, the spiritual leader of the
movement, expressed this vision when he proposed an arrangement—which
Nadim Rouhana terms "personal autonomy"[62] but which can more accurately
be defined as "institutionalized cultural autonomy"—whereby the minority
has constitutionally guaranteed authority to administer its own cultural affairs, education system, and media while respecting the state's laws.[63]

The decision to interact with the state in national elections caused a rift
in the Islamic movement. An opposition led by Sheikh Ra'ed Salah, mayor of
Umm al-Fahm, stuck with the position that participation in national elections would legitimize the institutions from which the movement wished to
disassociate and that, therefore, the practice of shunning national elections
should be prolonged. The disagreement led Salah and his followers to form

the separate northern stream. Meanwhile, joining forces with the ADP, the southern Islamists held two of the UAL seats following all the elections that were held since 1996 except for 2003.

Balad, the National Democratic Assembly, was the first parliamentary force to vociferously frame PAI demands in terms of indigenous national minority rights. Founded in the mid-1990s by Azmi Bishara, who holds a Ph.D. in philosophy and was a faculty member in the Palestinian Beir Zeit University, the party brought together remnants of the old Abna' al-Balad movement, which was discussed in the previous chapter, and various other left-wing PAI groups.

Identifying Zionism as a colonialist movement, Balad views the PAI struggle not only as a fight for civil equality but also as an endeavor of a native people for national liberation.[64] Balad sees the PAI as an integral part of the Palestinian Arab nation that happens to live under Israeli rule and to be separated from its Palestinian co-nationals as a result of colonization and externally imposed territorial boundaries. Because the struggle of the PAI is interpreted as integral to the Palestinian liberation struggle as a whole, a Palestinian state in the West Bank and Gaza does not go all the way to resolving the Palestinian-Israeli conflict. Rather, solving the conflict in the region depends on addressing the status of the Palestinian minority in Israel. As a result, Bishara and his followers did not support the Oslo peace process, which deals only with the West Bank and Gaza but leaves the character of the Israeli state unchanged. Oslo was interpreted by Bishara and his followers as a sign that the Communists' integrationist route was misguided.[65]

Balad decries the idea of "Israelization" of the PAI, which it views as inconsistent with maintaining a distinct Palestinian Arab identity[66] (one of its leaders stated that he will consider any Arab who volunteers for national service, an act seen as integrationist, a "leper"[67]). Instead, the party demands institutional autonomy for the PAI coupled with the de-Zionization of the state, making it "a state of all its citizens" rather than a Jewish state.[68] The party leadership has been calling for a reconstitution of the institutional arrangement along consociational lines whereby the state would be binational and decentralized; each national community would have extensive autonomy over its own affairs including, among other things, education, health, culture, religion, universities, housing, and media; and distribution of state resources would be done on the basis of relative communal size.[69]

In the run-up to the 1996 elections, Balad decided to form a joint list of candidates with the DFPE. Both parties had left-of-center ideologies on economic issues. This alliance, however, did not last long. From the outset, collaboration was motivated more by political calculations rather than ideological alignment, considering that Balad was new on the political scene and the DFPE was trying to improve its standing among PAI ethnonationalists in face of the growing competition from PAI ethnic parties. The joint list won five seats, two of which were allocated to Balad. Running independently of the DFPE, Balad managed to win two seats in the 1999 election and three seats in the 2003, 2006, and 2009 elections, thus anchoring its position as one of the major PAI political forces.

The political activism of the party's leadership has been characterized by its assertiveness and frequent controversies. For example, Bishara made several trips to Syria and Lebanon, met with Hezbollah leaders, and expressed Arab solidarity and sympathy toward old Nasserite ideas of Pan-Arabism. During the Israel-Hezbollah war in the summer of 2006, Bishara expressed sympathy toward Israel's adversaries. During "End Israeli Apartheid Week," which was held across Canadian university campuses in 2007, Jamal Zahalka, Bishara's successor, reportedly accused Israel of practicing apartheid.[70] Zahalka has also appealed for international protection for the PAI, identifying the Jewish character of the state as the source of danger.[71] And in 2010, MK Hanin Zoabi took part in the flotilla that sought to break the Israeli naval blockade of the Gaza Strip and was engaged in a violent confrontation with the Israeli navy. Bishara's flight from Israel, when an investigation was opened against him on suspicions of assisting Hezbollah's intelligence operatives during the 2006 war against Israel, further illustrates the polarization between the ethnonationalist PAI party and the state.[72]

Beyond electoral fortunes and daring assertiveness, however, Balad's main impact has been to force a change in the terms of discourse among PAI organizations as a whole. This is by no means a unique phenomenon of minority politics in Israel. The multiplicity of ethnicity-based parties both mirrors and affects the ethnonationalization of politics.[73] As an increasing number of ethnic parties emerge and compete for the support of the same pool of voters, each party tries to present itself as best suited to represent the interests of the ethnic group. This dynamic sometimes leads to what is termed *ethnic outbidding*, whereby the rival parties increasingly appeal to ethnic sentiments and assume more exclusivist positions on ethnic relations issues in order to demonstrate loyalty to the group and increase their attractiveness to members of the ethnic group.[74] Balad in particular had such an impact. The party's ideological program and outright appeal to the electorate in ethnonational rhetoric have changed the terms of political debate. Most noticeably, the Vision Documents adopted some of the core tenets of Balad's ideology. Framing Jewish-PAI relations around indigenes and colonialists, and the demand for a neutral state in which distribution of resources and access to power and decision-making revolve around ethnonational identities, can be traced back to Balad's ideology more than to any other political party.

The DFPE has been responding to the intensifying competition from ethnically exclusivist rivals by trying to buttress its nationalist credentials.[75] It should be remembered that the need to introduce ideological revisions would have been necessary anyway because of the collapse of communism in Eastern Europe.[76] And yet, the competitive political environment—combined with the rise in what Rouhana and his collaborators termed *identity voting* patterns, whereby "the issue of Arab and Palestinian affiliation plays an important role"[77] in the choices of the electorate—undoubtedly influenced the DFPE's political choices and led it to try to enhance its image as a party championing minority particularistic interests. The DFPE transformation has not been linear and has not always been reflected in the official manifesto of the party, although the platform calls for recognizing the Palestinian Arab population in Israel as a national minority with entitlement to national equality on top of civic equality.[78]

The greater emphasis on ethnonationalism can be more readily detected in the party's practices. First, alliances with more nationalist forces have been formed. The joint list the DFPE established with Bishara's Balad in 1996 was followed by collaboration with Ahmad Tibi in the 2003 elections. Frequently appearing in the Israeli media as a representative of the Palestinian perspective, Tibi, a former advisor on Israeli affairs to Yassir Arafat, is widely regarded as a symbol of Palestinian nationalism and possesses "the credentials of open service to the PLO."[79] His political party, Ta'al, is characterized by its personification: the leader is the party. The collaboration with Tibi, who has also called for proportional allocation of Israel's foreign aid between the Jewish and PAI populations,[80] came at the expense of the party's Jewish constituency; the sole Jewish candidate was relegated from the third spot on the party's election slate, which had previously been reserved for a Jewish representative. This partnership stood in stark contrast to one of the most obvious integrationist facets of the DFPE in previous decades, the Jewish-Arab composition of its slate of candidates. However, after winning more than 37 percent of the Arab votes in the 1996 elections, 14 percent more than its tally four years earlier, the DFPE experienced a relative decline in support in the

1999 elections when its association with Bishara expired. As intra-Arab competition for PAI votes was intensifying (and the party had been struggling to capture consequential Jewish votes for a very long time[81]), the desire not to be outbid by rival PAI ethnonational parties began to influence behavior. Thus, in 2003, the DFPE leadership was again willing to trade off some of its binational image in order to increase the party's appeal to the PAI electorate. The outcome of the 2003 elections left the party without a Jewish MK for the first time in its history, as the joint list won three seats.

This state of affairs caused discontent among some party members. In the lead-up to the 2006 elections, the party reinstated a Jewish candidate, Dov Khenin, to the third position and offered Tibi the fourth place on its list of candidates. Refusing to be demoted, Tibi suspended his ties with the DFPE and joined forces with the UAL instead.[82]

The characteristics of the DFPE's leadership have also changed over the last two decades, as a new generation of young Muslim leaders with greater communal sensibilities has emerged and replaced the old Christian guard while marginalizing the Jewish component. The disappointing outcome of the 1992 elections, when the party won merely 23 percent of the PAI vote, likely accelerated the process of making over the leadership.[83] Up until 1992, the DFPE had at least two Jewish parliamentarians in every Knesset. Since 1992, the party has had no more than one Jewish MK (and no Jewish MK between 2003 and 2006). Moreover, perennial communist MKs, like the Christian Tawfik Toubi and the Jewish Meir Vilner, who served in every Knesset since 1949, were replaced in 1990. Those among the party's leading apparatus who adopted a more nationalist rhetoric, such as current General Secretary Mohammed Barakeh, moved to the forefront of the party while more civic-oriented politicians, like Hashem Mahameed, found themselves either sidelined or completely pushed out.

Barakeh in particular embraced the ethnonational and rejectionist rhetoric. In 2005, for example, he participated with Bishara in a conference expressing support for the Syrian regime, referred to the United States and Israel as "the big spider" and "the little spider," and accused them of creating a crisis between Syria and Lebanon.[84] The centrality of ethnonational identity was stressed by Barakeh when he put forth the position that the DFPE's role is to find the balance between the PAI's interests as citizens in Israel and their Palestinian national affiliation.[85] This position demotes, if not discards, the idea of an overriding Jewish-Arab civic identity in Israel.

In short, the last two decades have seen the dominance of DFPE replaced

Table 7. Distribution of PAI Votes (%), 1984–2009 Elections

	1984	1988	1992	1996	1999	2003	2006	2009
DFPE	32.0	33.4	23.2	37.4**	21.8	28.3**	24.3	27.3
PLP	17.5	14.3	9.2					
ADP and UAL		11.3	15.2	25.4	31.5	20.0	27.4**	32.0**
Balad					17.0	20.9	20.2	22.3
Labor	26.0	16.4	20.3	16.6	7.5	8.8	12.8	4.6
Others	24.5	24.6	32.1	20.6	22.2	22.0	15.3	13.8
Total vote for ethnic PAI parties*	0	11.3	24.4	25.4	48.5	46.9	47.6	54.3

Data from Knesset website, http://www.knesset.gov.il/description/eng/eng_mimshal_res. htm. See also Lustick, "The Changing Political Role," 116; al-Haj, "The Political Behavior of the Arabs in Israel in the 1992 Elections," 151; Frisch, "The Arab Vote," 103–5; Ghanem and Ozacky-Lazar, "Israel as an Ethnic State," 123; Diskin, The Elections to the 13th Knesset, 35, The Elections to the 12th Knesset, 7–8, 60–71; Rouhana, Saleh, and Sultany, "Voting Without Voice," 234–35; Rekhes, "The Arab Minority in Israel and the 17th Knesset Elections," 167. There are marginal disputes over the precise percentage because of difficulties ascertaining PAI vote in mixed cities.
* The total does not include votes for the DFPE, even in elections when the party ran on a joint list with Balad and Ta'al and when there was no Jewish MK. The DFPE has been left out of the total tally to demonstrate that even when it is left aside, the rise in ethnic voting is still significant. The classification of the DFPE as a nonethnic party is, of course, controversial, as many analysts would consider it an ethnic party, particularly since 1996. Based on the main indicator provided by D. L. Horowitz, how the party's support is distributed among ethnic groups (rather than intentions of party founders), the DFPE should be considered an ethnic party, and the rise in ethnic voting becomes even sharper; see Horowitz, *Ethnic Groups in Conflict*, 291–93. PLP is included in the total for 1992 but not 1984 and 1988 because of the "Arabization" of the party. The total for 2003 includes 6 percent won by Hashem Mahameed's Progressive National Alliance Party, which splintered from the UAL and did not pass the threshold required for Knesset seats.
** In 1996, the DFPE coalesced with Balad; in 2003 it joined forces with Ta'al. The UAL collaborated with Ta'al in 2006 and 2009.

by intense internal competition and the rise of ethnically based parties that advance exclusivist ideologies, make ethnic demands, and appeal to the ethnonational sentiments of the electorate. The changes in the political party scene have been accompanied by changes in voting patterns. Tables 7 and 8 show the trend whereby ethnically based parties have increased their support among the PAI electorate. Table 7 in particular reveals that the DFPE has fared better when it formed joint lists with ethnonationalist parties (1996 and 2003). On the other hand, support for the Labor Party, the most popular non-PAI party among PAI voters, has declined considerably since the 1980s.

Table 8. Distribution of Knesset Seats Among Arab and Binational Parties, 1981–2009

	DFPE***	PLP	ADP (UAL since 1996)	Balad	Ta'al	Total won by ethnic PAI parties
1981	4					0
1984	4	2***				0
1988	4	1	1			1
1992	3		2			2
1996	3*		4	2*		6
1999	3		5	2		7
2003	2**		2	3	1**	6
2006	3		3**	3	1**	7
2009	4		3**	3	1**	7

* DFPE and Balad ran on a joint list that won 5 seats.
** In 2003 DFPE and Ta'al ran on a joint list that won 3 seats. In 2006 UAL and Ta'al ran on a joint list, winning 4 seats
*** In 1984 the PLP had one Jewish MK. For this table, PLP is considered an ethnic party only after it was "Arabized" in 1988. As in Table 7, the DFPE is not counted as an ethnic party, even though it has met most of the criteria since the 1990s.

Finally, the tables demonstrate that although PAI ethnically exclusive parties emerged in the late 1980s, a sharp rise in support for PAI parties did not take place until after the 1996 elections. Chapter 6 provides a comprehensive explanation for this surge. Suffice it here to briefly note that the surge of ethnic parties is strongly related to changes in the electoral rules that were introduced at the time and that enhanced segmentation. Already prior to the electoral reform, Israel had a multiparty system, which has been found in the political parties literature to provide fewer incentives for parties to appeal to median voters.[86] Israel's highly proportional electoral system, which had an electoral threshold of 1.5 percent at the time, encouraged political parties to form around particularistic interests. The electoral reform that first applied in 1996 created a two-ballot system. Voters could cast one ballot for a party list (as they did before) and a second ballot for a prime minister. As a result, voters increasingly engaged in split-ticket voting: voting for a prime minister from one of the two largest parties and for a party list that catered to their narrow group interests. By 1999, almost two thirds of the electorate split their votes.[87] The new electoral rules thus produced a general growth of sector-specific parties, including religious parties, new immigrant parties, and PAI parties.

Ethnic Civil Society

The ethnonationalist turn has been manifested in alternative forms of politics as well, primarily the proliferation of ethnically based nonparliamentary organizations. Over the last two decades hundreds of PAI NGOs have appeared. In 2004, more than 1,600 such organizations were registered in Israel, about 80 percent of which had been established since 1988.[88] Most of these NGOs engage in providing services to the Arab population at the local and national levels in issues such as culture, religion, education, and welfare.

Beyond providing local services, some ethnically based organizations have advanced broader political objectives. Claiming to address the structural causes of Arab marginalization in the Jewish-dominated state, activists in these associations almost unanimously convey the view that the uniethnic character of the state is the main cause of PAI marginalization.[89] The first signs of such extra-parliamentary activism began in the 1970s. This activity, however, was limited and often elite directed, as was the case of the National Committee for the Defense of Arab Lands, discussed in Chapter 4.[90] It has only been since the 1990s that ethnicity-based organizations that demand changes to the institutional order, which they believe is at fault for the structural inequalities that disadvantage their group, started to proliferate.

The term *ethnic civil society* is used in reference to civil society associations that make ethnic demands on the state and mobilize to advance the particularistic interests of their ethnic group.[91] Activists in ethnic civil society associations belong overwhelmingly to the identifiable ethnic group in whose empowerment they are interested. Comparative research reveals that there is a link between the extent of ethnic tensions and the structure of associational life in a multiethnic society. Ethnic conflict is more intense when associational life is organized along intraethnic lines, whereas civic engagement between different ethnic communities serves to mitigate ethnic conflict.[92] The formation of parallel, ethnically based civil society organizations is thus a characteristic tendency in a deeply divided society. At the same time, the ethnic demands on the state and attempts to increase the group's ethnonational consciousness also serve to reinforce cleavages. Ethnic civil society and a deeply divided society act on each other.

One of the main attributes of ethnic civil society activism is the priority that ethnic claims are given over rival civic liberties when the two collide. This situation is best exemplified in the position taken by Adalah: The Legal Center for Arab Minority Rights in Israel, one of the most visible PAI NGOs, on a proposition to amend personal status laws in Israel. Hassan Jabareen, Adalah's general director, objected to the reform even though it would have provided PAI women with access to civil courts by lifting the exclusive jurisdiction of religious courts on some personal status matters. (The amendments were supported by most civil rights groups, including the Association for Civil Rights in Israel, and women's groups in Israel.) Jabareen explained that he did not wish to provide legitimacy to state intervention in the traditional practices of the PAI minority, including those practices that hold back women's equality.[93]

At first glance, the label *civil society* appears at odds with organizations that pursue particularistic interests and are interested in expanding parochialism in the ethnic community. Many scholars conceive of civil society as in direct opposition to ethnic segmentation. Civil society activism is meant to advance the public good for the benefit of all individual members of society irrespective of ethnic affiliation.[94] By now, this idealistic view of civil society has long been discredited. Scholars have noted that the conception of what constitutes the public interest is highly contested: "struggles over the public interest are not between civil society on the one hand and bad guys on the other but within civil society itself."[95] There are many single-issue organizations that promote a particularistic agenda. Associations dealing with women's issues or diverse sexual orientations, for example, advance the interests of only particular segments of the population. Typically, most activists in such associations belong to the identifiable group that the organizations claim to represent. Many times they operate in tension with other organized groups who oppose their agendas and who have a contrasting idea of what constitutes the public good. Ethnic civil society's distinctiveness does not derive from its focus on particularistic ends but from its ethnicity base.

PAI ethnic civil society organizations make a variety of demands and advance several objectives. Some organizations aim to limit state extensiveness in the minority's public sphere by working to expand the minority's ethnically exclusive space. By establishing an alternative organizational infrastructure, mobilization that follows this path tries to offer spheres of political and social authority that parallel those of the state. The concrete pursuit of this objective is conducted through the establishment of a network of private voluntary organizations, such as charities, medical clinics, and education facilities. These welfare services are often supported by parallel commercial and revenue-generating enterprises. The Islamic movement best exemplifies this category. Others have been calling for the establishment of minority national institutions with exclusive authority over issues pertaining to minority culture, education, and religious and social life. This is best exemplified by the four Vision Documents. Some organizations prefer to place emphasis on state identity, privileging, and the promotion of binationalism of sorts. The objective of this type of mobilization is to influence state character and practices of distribution by making ethnic claims for equal distribution of resources on the basis of ethnic group size and fair group representation in the administrative apparatus. Some of the secular PAI organizations that will be discussed next are engaged in this form of activism. Of course, one form of activism does not preclude others. In practice, many organizations pursue multiple objectives simultaneously.

The Arab Center for Alternative Planning (ACAP), established in 2000, provides a good example of an organization that operates along two main avenues. Specializing in urban planning and land development (a large portion of ACAP's employees are professional urban planners and engineers), ACAP claims to routinely monitor state plans for development projects and devises alternative plans that, according to the association, represent the interests, needs, and "national identity of the Palestinian Arab communities."[96] In 2004, ACAP was recognized by the Ministry of Interior as an independent organization that is entitled to review planning procedures and file objections to government development plans on the minority's behalf. At the same time, the organization has been calling for an increase in PAI representation in the state apparatus, particularly in the areas of urban planning, housing, and land allocations. ACAP promoted a campaign that calls for PAI representation at all levels of planning organizations and building councils, in hopes of influencing distribution policies from within the state. Before getting elected to the Knesset on behalf of the DFPE, the organization's general director, Hanna Swaid, sat on the state's National Planning Board.

Mossawa: The Advocacy Center for Arab Citizens in Israel, another visible NGO, has been more vociferous than ACAP in its demands for a separate PAI public sphere in addition to greater state neutrality and equal PAI representation in state institutions. Before publishing *An Equal Constitution for All?* representatives of Mossawa (equality), established in 1997, participated in debates in the Knesset Constitution, Law, and Justice Committee on proposals for drafting a constitution and adopting a more inclusive national anthem. The association presented a position paper to the legislative committee that called for the inclusion of PAI representatives in the drafting stages of a constitution. Like the descendant document that was published with the other three Vision Documents, the position paper called for institutionalizing bilingualism; granting autonomous administration for the PAI in the realms of religion, education, and culture; proportional representation of the PAI in the civil administration and other state and public agencies; proportional distribution of material resources; and the inclusion of PAI identity in state symbols.[97] Mossawa has also been active in litigation on collective rights issues. The organization's legal experts have petitioned the Israeli Supreme Court against Israel's citizenship laws and have published position papers on this issue.[98]

One of the most visible ethnically based PAI NGOs is Adalah, established in 1996. Most of this organization's activism in pursued through litigation. In the view of Adalah activists, the purpose of their legal mobilization is to advance Arab communal rights. Previously in the Association for Civil Rights in Israel (ACRI), this organization's founder, law school graduate Hassan Jabareen, claims to have been disillusioned with ACRI's focus on individual civic rights rather than minority communal rights. Much like Darawshe when he left the Labor Party to establish the ADP, Jabareen reasoned that the process of minority empowerment requires a distinct PAI human rights organization that is exclusively concerned with the collective rights of the minority.[99]

Adalah's challenges of the government focus on unequal allocation of cultural and material resources on issues such as land, language, housing, education, and access to social services. Taking advantage of the empowerment of the judiciary in relation to the legislature and the executive, and the High Court of Justice's liberal attitude toward disadvantaged groups, Adalah works to influence state practices by submitting petitions to the Court on issues relevant to the PAI as a whole.[100] Several examples illustrate the collectivist character of Adalah's activism. On land issues and distribution of resources, there was a successful petition against the government's decision to exclude Arab localities from the National Priorities List, as well as several petitions dealing with unrecognized villages.[101] As elaborated upon in greater depth in Chapter 3 on state autonomy, there are dozens of villages whose existence is unrecognized by the state. Adalah petitioned successfully several times on behalf of residents of unrecognized villages for the right to an official address that will include the name of the unrecognized village and for access to state-maintained social services in the villages. The courts ordered that when the state formulates policies it should take into consideration that the land of unrecognized villages was inhabited. Particularly important was the *Sawaʿed v. Ministry of Interior* case, whereby the right to an address implied a de facto, if not de jure, recognition of the Arab village. Owing to the history of the state's land policies, Adalah considered these rulings important victories in its attempt to make state policies more ethnically neutral.

Through its litigation activity, Adalah explicitly and implicitly asks the court to recognize the collective rights of the PAI as a national minority, thus trying to codify the status of the PAI as a national minority. For example, two successful petitions to Israel's High Court of Justice in 2002 resulted in a ruling compelling municipalities of mixed cities and the Ministry of Transportation to use Arabic on municipal signs in mixed localities and on all national road signs.[102] According to one of the presiding judges, the court's ruling implied recognition of "the collective right of the Arab public to preserve its independent and separate cultural identity through its language."[103] It is the very character of petitions of this sort that forces the state to treat the Arab population as a collective national community while enhancing the self-image of the PAI population as a distinct national community. After publishing *The Democratic Constitution*, which demanded national and indigenous rights for the minority, Adalah was reportedly considering proposing a single constitution for a "supranational regime in all of historic Palestine."[104] Thus, it emphasized the connection to the Palestinian nation as a whole.

In addition, Adalah has taken upon itself to provide free legal representation to PAI public representatives. For example, the NGO appealed to the Supreme Court on behalf of disallowed PAI electoral lists and of MKs who were disqualified by the Elections Committee prior to the 2003 parliamentary elections.[105] This kind of activity is seen as significant for the PAI community as a whole.

The Arab Association for Human Rights (HRA) is more skeptical than ACAP, Mossawa and Adalah about the utility of interaction with Israeli institutions. HRA prefers to focus its challenge of what Peleg has referred to as the ethnic constitutional order on appeals to international agencies.[106] The organization's general director, Mohammad Zeidan, argues that disentangling the state from majority dominance is inconsistent with appealing to the state's judicial bodies because the legal framework in Israel has been formulated to serve the interests of the dominant Jewish majority in the first place.[107] Therefore, the battle for minority empowerment requires bypassing the state's legal system. Hence, instead of litigating within Israel, HRA claims to lobby external actors to apply international pressure on Israel to treat the PAI as a national minority.[108]

Likewise, Ittijah: the Union of Arab Community Based Organizations (established in 1995) promotes ethnic differentiation. The declared objective of this NGO is to provide an overarching framework for collaboration among PAI NGOs and facilitate a separate, ethnically exclusive civil society sphere for the minority. Ittijah attempts to stress its disassociation from Israel and Jewish society and highlight its distinct Palestinian identity have been reflected in several ways. For example, the sign on the building Ittijah occupies in Haifa is in Arabic and English only. Likewise, at the NGO forum that took place during the World Conference Against Racism, Racial Discrimination, Xenophobia and Related Intolerance in Durban in 2001, the Haifa-based organization identified its home country as "the Occupied Palestinian Territories." Furthermore, the organization's general director, Ameer Makhoul, has expressed opposition to accepting donations from transnational Jewish philanthropic organizations, which provide a large base of financial support to many PAI NGOs, because he suspects the donors are pushing toward cooperation with Jewish NGOs and are trying to co-opt and subordinate Arab activists to integrationist priorities.[109] The organization's articulated opposition to normalizing relations between Israel and the Arab world in the Cairo Conference of Arab NGOs in 2002 led the European Union to end its financial support for an Ittijah project dealing with the promotion of Arab civil society. And in May 2010, Makhoul was arrested on suspicion of espionage and contact with a Hezbollah agent. A plea bargain was struck between his lawyers and the prosecution.

Aside from these and other secular NGOs, there are Islamic organizations that operate in the civil society sphere. Since their early days, the Islamists have aimed to provide an alternative collectivist framework to the dominant secular trends, particularly those of communism and westernization.[110] The difficulty of treating the Islamists as a monolithic group has been alluded to in the earlier discussion of the split between the southern and northern streams. Despite their differences, however, both streams share the vision of having an expansive and exclusive Islamic domain to which state authorities will not have access. They do not possess a sense of belonging to the state and do not convey a sense of, or a desire for, an overarching civic identity.[111] Arguing that the plight of the Arabs is generated by the penetration of Western materialistic values, the Islamists, like Islamic movements elsewhere, are trying to recruit followers by transmitting the message that *al-Islam huwa al-hall* (Islam is the solution) and are aspiring to build a separate society with an Islamic identity that lives according to Islamic law.[112] They also advocate building linkages with Islamic movements elsewhere in order to create a kind of loose confederation of Islamic polities that transcends territorial boundaries.

The Islamist position does not support making an effort to construct a civic identity and shared institutions with a large Jewish population (particularly as Jewish presence in the territory is partly seen as an outcome of imperialist intrigues), because doing so would not advance the objective of creating a society that follows Islamic practices and traditions. As a consequence, the Islamists minimize their interaction with state authorities. Their preferred alternative to is to establish what Gerard Clarke calls a "virtual parallel state," or a quasi-Islamic state within the Jewish state, whereby affiliated organizations replace state institutions in providing services (primarily education, religious, and cultural services) as well as in their policing and judicial functions.[113] The Islamic movement operates a variety of community services including educational institutions, medical centers, a drug rehabilitation center, and other charity-based services. It has also been active in collecting donations that are used for creating a welfare system and supporting its enterprises, as well as for improving local infrastructure, for instance by paving local roads.[114] I'qra'a, one of the largest NGOs affiliated with the movement, "specializes in providing support to high school pupils and in preparing them for university studies [and it] has alone established kindergartens in more than 30 Arab towns and cities."[115] Moreover, they have been able to operate ethnically based organizations even in places where biethnic organizations are present. For example, the Islamists founded a separate Islamic soccer league in which twelve clubs compete separately from non-Muslims.[116]

Participation in elections to local authorities has helped the Islamists to emerge as a political force. In the first local elections in which they participated (1989), the Islamic movement managed to win the chairmanship in six localities, including in the sizable towns of Umm al-Fahm and Kafr Qasim. Local-level government, as Ghanem notes, provided the movement with financial sources to draw upon, including taxes and central government funding.[117] In addition, over the years, the movement has been able to operate revenue-generating enterprises that facilitated its activities.

Regarding the PAI position in the Arab-Israeli conflict, the Islamists view Zionism as the root of the conflict and as a movement that serves the interests of foreign empires that have perpetuated the conflict to advance their objectives. Their historical narrative resembles the one depicted in the *Future Vision* document, whereby the Zionist movement forcefully deprived the Arabs of Palestine through violence and coercion. The movement's leadership has expressed the position that a comprehensive solution must encompass the PAI community, the right of refugees to return to the land, and a Palestinian right to self-determination and self-government.[118]

Despite this position, the southern stream of the movement does not reject coexistence and some degree of cooperation. This stream accepts, at least temporarily, that Muslims are a minority in a Jewish state.[119] Indeed, the main differences between the southern and northern streams pertain mainly to the extent of interaction with the state and to operational issues, including the degree to which the struggle for change should be carried out within the framework of the Israeli law. Several hundred of the youth affiliated with the southern stream attend Israel's colleges and universities, including the College of Judea and Samaria in Ariel, a contentious Jewish settlement in the West Bank. The rift in the Islamic movement, which erupted in the mid-1990s between the spiritual leader Sheikh Darwish and an internal opposition led by Sheikh Salah was engendered by a disagreement on the extent of isolation and on whether to participate in the 1996 parliamentary elections, a position supported by Darwish and his followers. Darwish reasoned that the launch of the Israeli-Palestinian peace process and the attempts at reconciliation of Israel and the Palestinian national movement brought about mutual recognition of national rights and that, therefore, there was no purpose in sustaining the rejectionist approach toward Israel's institutions. Seen in this light, the peace process should be utilized by the Muslims within Israel to make social gains, even if the process entailed increased voluntary interaction with the state and the Jewish majority (including participation in elections).

The rival branches operate separate organizations. They are further distinct in that the southern branch publicly recognizes Israel's existence and seeks internal autonomy, whereas the northern branch is unwilling to recognize the state. The weekly publication of the northern branch, *Sawt al-Haqq Wal-Hurriya* (The Voice of Truth and Freedom), used to identify its place of publication as Umm al-Fahm, Palestine, and its offices as located in Nazareth, Palestine, indicating its rejection of the Israeli state.[120] The paper often used confrontational language against the state, demonstrated sympathy toward the Hamas movement, and sometimes expressed understanding toward the motivation of suicide bombers. Furthermore, the northern branch also maintained financial ties with Islamists in the West Bank and Gaza and claimed that the money is used exclusively for social welfare. In 2003, Salah and four other leading members of the movement were arrested on suspicion of transferring money to Hamas, and in 2005 the five were convicted of receiving money from outlawed organizations and sentenced to prison terms.[121]

Regarding Salah's involvement in spurring violence against the state, the Or Commission concluded that

> As the head of the northern branch of the Islamic Movement, the mayor of Umm al-Fahm and a public personage, he was responsible in the period preceding the October 2000 events, including in 1998–2000, for the transmission of repeated messages encouraging the use of violence and the threat of violence as a means to achieve the objectives of the Arab sector in the State of Israel. These messages also related to the objective defined as the liberation of the al-Aqsa Mosque. In addition, he held mass assemblies and used inflammatory propaganda to create a charged public atmosphere concerning this sensitive issue. As far as the above is concerned, he made a substantive contribution to inflaming the atmosphere and to the widespread eruption of violence that extended within the Arab sector at the beginning of October 2000.
>
> As the head of the northern branch of the Islamic Movement, the mayor of Umm al-Fahm and a public personage, he was responsible . . . for the transmission of messages that negated the legitimacy of the existence of the state and for presenting the state as an enemy.[122]

Thus, the Islamists, as a whole, are trying to constitute exclusive institutions distinct from those of the state. The southern and northern branches are distinct in that the southern branch maintains channels of communication with the external regime, whereas the northern branch rejects the authority of the state's non-Islamic institutions.

It is worthwhile to conclude this subsection by reiterating that what binds the activism of various ethnic civil society groups, secular and religious, is no less significant than what separates them. Ethnically based organizations work to institutionalize a collective PAI ethnonational identity by making ethnic demands on the state as well as through the creation of a separate public domain. They emphasize that an independent, intraethnic PAI civil society sphere is essential for building a strong, independent Palestinian society that can pursue a broad response to existing structures of Arab subordination in the Jewish-dominated state. As a result, in addition to activism that focuses on their relationship with the state, many organizations also operate vis-à-vis their own communities in order to increase PAI collective awareness and to provide members of the minority community with capacity to pursue collective objectives. For example, ACAP provides professional counseling to local municipalities on land-related issues, as well as planning and development issues. It has also been educating and providing professional assistance to PAI local councils with filing objections to government development plans.[123] Likewise, having identified weaknesses in PAI access to media, the general director of Mossawa claims to have contributed to the establishment and support of *I'lam*, an NGO dedicated to ensuring that the PAI perspective gets a fair share of media coverage.[124] The HRA claims to run educational programs in Arab schools that expose PAI students to their rights under international law. The Islamists have programs aimed at educating PAI for self-sufficiency. As Sheikh Salah was quoted as saying, "We mustn't make do with whining. . . . We have to build a society that supplies its own needs."[125]

Conclusion

The ethnonationalist turn and the audacious demands on the state elicited variable responses from the Jewish majority and state institutions. Much of the reaction has been defensive and oriented toward restraining PAI activism and ensuring that the Jewish stronghold on the state is not loosened. Thus, the Shin Bet, Israel's domestic security service, has overtly increased its presence among PAI activists, issuing cautions that it is committed to thwarting mobilization intended to harm Israel's Jewish character.[126] A new political party, Yisrael Beytenu (Israel Our Home), emerged, championing a plan for territorial and population exchange, according to which approximately 200,000 Arabs living in Wadi Ara and the Little Triangle will be transferred to the Palestinian Authority.[127] Along with other political actors on the Israeli Right, the party (which won eleven seats in the 2006 elections and fifteen in the 2009 elections) advances bills that will condition full citizenship and political rights on taking oaths to Israel's Declaration of Independence and Jewish symbols and on compulsory military service. In addition, citizenship laws that prevent Palestinian spouses of PAI from attaining citizenship have been put into force.

Others, however, have taken a more accommodating approach. Most notably, the High Court of Justice has been open to applying liberal principles to mitigate Jewish national dominance, such that many PAI activists praise it as the main state institution accessible to them. Court rulings have affected distribution of land and resources. ACRI, too, has publicly expressed criticism of the Shin Bet activities, which it sees as attempting to curtail PAI political activism, and has demanded their cessation. In short, reaction has varied as the state has become increasingly differentiated and Jewish society more fragmented on key questions of values.

Although the ability of the central government to control PAI mobilization has diminished considerably since the 1960s, central state authorities still possess a meaningful capacity to set boundaries that avert violent ethnonational activism, and the dominant Jewish majority is still capable of warding off challenges to the state's foundational principles. The circumstances that have yielded the ethnonational turn and these particular minority-state-majority relations are the focus of the ensuing chapter.

6

The Changing Israeli State-Society Relations

Distinctive mutability in some state institutions—and not in others—has been conducive to the rise of Palestinian ethnonationalist politics in Israel. Israeli society, economy, and politics further liberalized in recent decades and concurrently political authority continued to disperse away from the central government. State extensiveness has declined and the state is no longer present in public life as it was only a few decades earlier. The level of fragmentation at the core has increased considerably as more segments in society compete for political power. In this respect, transition in PAI political activism, the rise of ethnically based organizations, and parochial demands on the state mirror changes in Israeli politics at large as much as they are influenced by them. At the same time, one key state attribute has not changed; the state continues to be exclusively Jewish dominated while PAI marginalization persists. The parochialism advanced by PAI political organization has thus taken on a particular nationalist form.

Adaptive Preference

Chapter 3 described how lack of state autonomy form the Jewish majority has remained relatively consistent over the years and has continued to translate into policies of distribution that favor the majority national group. Sentiments of resentment about their subordinate status have always been widespread among the PAI. Minority demands in the 1970s and 1980s to renegotiate state-ethnicity relations have, however, encountered resistance.

Yoav Peled has explained how Israel's institutional structure reconciled

Jewish domination and democracy up until the early 1990s. His analysis differentiates between two concepts of citizenship in democratic settings: liberal and republican types of citizenship.[1] The liberal concept of citizenship recognizes only individuals as the bearers of universal equal rights. It does not recognize communities and relegates religion and other types of subcommunal affiliations to the private sphere. Thus, all individuals are equal before the law and have equal political rights as individuals. The republican concept of citizenship, on the other hand, recognizes a "public good" beyond the sphere of the individual. According to this perspective, "citizens are who they are by virtue of participating in the life of their political community."[2] The citizenship of members of a political community includes participation in determining, and access to, the common good as well as obligations, such as military service to protect the polity, that are accompanied by privileges.

In Israel, according to Peled, multiple layers of citizenship rights coexisted. The PAI had access to a liberal type of citizenship through the extension of political rights to all PAI individuals, but they were denied access to the public good, access which only members of the Jewish majority in Israel were entitled to. Thus, a republican type of citizenship was (and still is) extended to Jews only, allowing Israel to sustain a hierarchical institutional structure that is simultaneously democratic and Jewish-hegemonic. Some scholars have labeled this arrangement *ethnic democracy*.[3] Some prefer the label *ethnocracy*.[4] Peleg uses *ethnic constitutional order*.[5]

Attempts to elevate the PAI to republican citizenship status have been resisted with counter entrenchment of Jewish hegemony using formal and informal means. Thus, for example, the Jewish majority in the Knesset reacted to the electoral success of the PLP in the 1984 elections by amending the Basic Law: The Knesset in 1985. The law stipulated that a political party advocating the "negation of the State of Israel as the state of the Jewish people" will not be allowed to participate in elections.[6] Proposals put forth by the PLP and DFPE to add "and its Arab citizens" to this article were rejected.[7] In 1992, this principle was reinforced in the Political Parties Law that forbids the registration of a political party whose platform negates the right of Israel to exist as a Jewish state. (Both laws also disqualify political parties that incite to racism or oppose democracy.)[8] Public opinion surveys also revealed strong support among the Jewish majority for sustaining exclusive majority ownership of the state.[9] In 2009, the Knesset approved in a preliminary reading a bill that would criminalize calls to change the definition of the state as "democratic and Jewish" and would allow imprisoning violators for up to one year.

Thus, the demands made by PAI political elites to transform state identity have been usually rebuffed as the majority in the Knesset used the legislative tools in its hands to impede the ability of the minority to renegotiate state-ethnicity relations.

A more interesting example of attempts to elevate the PAI to republican status citizenship was made during the tenure of the government headed by Yitzhak Rabin in 1992. Rabin's government embarked on a peace process that was to negotiate the division of sovereignty over the territory in dispute between Israel and the Palestinians in the West Bank and Gaza. The government did not enjoy the support of the Jewish majority in the Knesset throughout most of the process that began in September 1993 with the Declaration of Principles on Interim Self-Government Arrangements, known as the Oslo Accords. Only fifty-six MKs from Jewish political parties supported the process on an ongoing basis.[10] To ensure majority support in the 120-seat Knesset, Rabin's government had to rely on the backing of the five MKs from the DFPE and ADP, four of whom were PAI. Thus, the peace process was dependent on the support of PAI MKs, albeit from outside the coalition government. The government, therefore, allowed the PAI to participate in, and determine, the formulation and implementation of crucial policy decisions on perhaps the most sensitive public good in Israeli discourse: borders and territory. It was arguably the boldest attempt to date to extend republican citizenship rights to the PAI.

This type of change to the conventions of communal engagement was greeted with immense animosity from a large segment of the Jewish majority. The Oslo peace process was already contentious and brought tens of thousands of protestors to the streets in numerous rallies to demand a halt to the negotiations. Many opposed the accord on ideological grounds, believing that the Jewish people had an ultimate religious and historical right to all the territory between the Mediterranean on the west to the Jordan River on the east.[11] Some organized protestors viewed the issue as fundamentally a matter of Jewish identity because, according to their belief, this land was promised to the Jewish people by God and Jewish return to it is linked to messianic redemption.[12] For many, therefore, the debate over peace and territory had identity questions at its core.[13]

That the government did not enjoy the support of the Jewish majority in the Knesset accentuated the controversy over where the boundaries of inclusion and exclusion between the Jewish majority and the PAI minority should rest. Benny Elon, one of the main leaders of the protest movement and later an

MK on behalf of the right-wing Moledet Party, explicitly stated that although he objected to any territorial concession, he was willing, albeit reluctantly, to accept such a verdict if it was made by a Jewish majority. According to Elon, a government that is dependent on Arab support is not morally permitted to make compromises regarding the territorial and social identity of the Jewish state.[14] Elon was goaded by the diplomatic developments to propose a constitutional change that would formally guarantee that only a Jew can become president or prime minister and that issues concerning the future of the state, its borders, and identity would be decided by a Jewish majority. Mainstream parliamentary parties and politicians endorsed the exclusion of the PAI from access to such a sensitive public good as well. Many demanded that Rabin's government call new elections because it did not have a Jewish majority. According to Smooha's surveys, even among the Jewish voters of Labor and the Israeli left, only a minority of less than 40 percent supported unconditional inclusion of Arab political parties in the coalition.[15] The criticism leveled at the Labor government and its reliance on PAI parties reflected the unease with which most of the Jewish population felt at the growing access of the PAI to the public good. And in the subsequent elections (1996), the slogan "Bibi is good for the Jews" was deployed on behalf of the Likud candidate for the premiership, Binyamin Netanyahu, and is considered to have been indispensable for his win in those elections.[16]

Thus, attempts at altering the barriers of political integration have generally been resisted. Research in political psychology and rationality has revealed that preferences are shaped by expectations: adapting preferences to perceived realities is a rational reaction by individuals, organizations, and groups when they conclude that a desired objective is not attainable.[17] When they no longer expect to have access to something they initially desired, people often change their preferences, rejecting the previously desired objective precisely because it is unattainable. The idea that a sense of being rejected can engender reciprocal sentiments of counter-rejection is well illustrated by Jon Elster using the fable of the fox who dismissed grapes that were out of his reach as sour. Elster terms this cognitive process "adaptive preference formation."[18]

In ethnic politics, firm boundaries of exclusion can lead to counter-rejectionism and active isolation by the excluded. As the PAI were denied political integration on the basis of ethnonational identity despite the efforts of the DFPE, minority activists increasingly embraced ethnocentrism and began to base their own collective demands on the basis of their communal identity. There is persuasive evidence that members of the PAI community do not trust state institutions and the central government and increasingly feel rejected by them. One public opinion survey conducted by Adalah in the early 2000s, for example, found that 92.5 percent of the PAI did not trust the central government, 80 percent did not trust the Knesset, close to 80 percent did not trust the police, and overwhelming majorities did not trust other arms of the state. The only institution that had the trust of the majority of PAI respondents was the Supreme Court.[19] Annual surveys conducted by Mada al-Carmel: The Arab Centre for Applied Social Research corroborate the findings that the PAI feel rejected by the state and the Jewish majority and are pessimistic about their future status in the state.[20]

PAI political organizations have responded to the persistence of exclusion by altering their collective demands. Demands for separate institutions, including a PAI parliament and distinct and autonomous educational and social institutions, have been on the rise along with the creation of ethnically exclusive parties, as elaborated on in the previous chapter. A growing number have stopped voting in elections altogether, particularly since the beginning of the twenty-first century (although voter turnout among Jews has also declined considerably).[21] At the same time, public opinion surveys have found that over the years, a steadily declining number of PAI find the reference "Israeli" suitable for their self-definition and a plurality of PAI define themselves as Palestinians or Palestinian Arabs living in Israel.[22] In the context of ethnic politics, therefore, the process of adaptive preference formation can turn the banal cliché "if you can't beat them, join them" to "if you can't join them, differentiate."

Accordingly, many shifted their affiliation and political support to distinctively Arab parties. One conspicuous example of adaptive preference formation at the local community level is the case of the Negev Bedouin. This community shifted its support almost singularly from the Labor party to the UAL, which brings together the Islamic movement-southern branch and the Arab Democratic Party. In the 2009 elections, 80 percent of voters in Bedouin communities voted for the UAL.[23]

The ability of the UAL to penetrate into the Bedouin community highlights the significance of organizations in the process of adaptive preference formation. The variable role that political leaders play in shaping the political identity and preferences of ethnic groups has been noted in numerous studies on the politics of ethnicity all over the globe.[24] In the PAI case, newly emerging elites and political organizations have been acting as agents for promoting distinct Palestinian awareness. As'ad Ghanem observes that the PLP was the primary force in the 1980s to instill Palestinian consciousness among the PAI as its message of "the Palestinian roots of Arabs in Israel" was absorbed by the Arab masses.[25] Azmi Bishara's Balad, which has been espousing a hybrid pan-Palestinian and pan-Arab ideology, has also worked to advance the trans-state ties of the PAI minority. The party identifies the PAI as members of the larger Palestinian people that only happened to be residing under Israeli rule due to historical circumstances. Its members travel to Arab countries that are in conflict with Israel, including Syria and Lebanon, and justify their travels as significant for enhancing PAI ties with their Arab co-nationals.[26] The Islamists, too, with the creation of a separate public domain with separate social and cultural organizations, have worked to enhance local religious consciousness. And likewise, secular civil society organizations have been acting as agents for advancing a national PAI collective awareness by challenging the state on issues of collective significance and emphasizing minority national and indigenous rights. Many view it as their mission to promote a PAI national collective identity among members of the minority group population.[27]

The new mobilizing organizations are composed of a new generation of PAI elites. Over recent decades, the elite of the PAI has undergone a significant transformation. A new, self-assured generation has emerged. Unlike its hamula-based predecessor, the contemporary stratum of PAI elite is composed of an educated class that exhibits ethnonational pride and independently pursues social and political activism that champions Palestinian nationalism.[28] This stratum has been referred to as the "stand tall generation."[29] Socially, members of the new PAI elite are largely a product of the urbanization, education, and occupational transition that were discussed in Chapter 4, although this social transformation did not immediately engender a new stratum of PAI elite. Rather, this was a longer process.

Unlike the traditional elite that they replaced, members of the contemporary PAI elite were born into the state in the 1950s, 1960s, and 1970s. They witnessed the compliance of their parents in their youth and their community's subordination. Sheikh Ibrahim Sarsur, for example, the political leader of the Islamic movement's southern branch, was born in Kafr Qasim shortly after the killing of forty-eight villagers, some of whom were from his extended family. He states that the event was always in the background of his upbringing with commemoration ceremonies and family photos of the deceased placed in his house.[30] Ameer Makhoul, who abandoned the DFPE and participated in the establishment of the more nationalist Balad, and who has served as the general director of Ittijah, claims to have come from a family that had much of its land expropriated.[31] Similar stories are common. The more general point is that the new elite grew up resenting the subordination of the preceding generation and participated in the Land Day protests at a young age. According to their own accounts, active involvement in the Land Day events was a crucial formative experience and, accordingly, some view themselves as the "Land Day generation."[32]

At the same time, they have continued to experience the rigidity of the social boundaries. This new generation of professional Arabs, who took advantage of education opportunities, was also frequently denied access to employment in the professions in which they were trained, in both the public and private sectors. Often, the security services prevented many from attaining teaching positions. NGO activism has become a route to which many could have and have turned. Indeed, the vast majority of NGOs are headed by university graduates. The proliferation of NGOs that was discussed in Chapter 5 was undoubtedly influenced by the lack of access to professional opportunities. ACAP, for example, employs urban planners and engineers; Adalah, Mossawa, and HRA employ lawyers. Many NGOs employ academics. For many of the activists, NGO work is a career for which they receive salaries. Thus, NGO activity has become a vocation that addresses two needs: It is a tool for promoting a social and political agenda, and it has also become an avenue for a professional career with all the associated material and psychological rewards.

Interestingly, education has had similar impact on the profile of the parliamentary political leadership of the PAI. According to Amal Jamal, between 1949 and 1984, only seven out of the seventy Arab MKs had an undergraduate degree. "In comparison, from 1984 to 2003, 53 of the 62 Arab MKs have had at least a B.A. degree."[33] Of the twelve Arab MKs that were elected to the 17th Knesset in 2006, four had a doctoral degree, two held a master's degree, five had a bachelor's degree, and only one Arab MK did not have postsecondary education.

In many cases, mobilizing agents and national sentiments operate in reciprocity, feeding off each other, when struggling against an exclusionary institutional setting.[34] The proximity to developments in the relations between Israel and the Palestinians in the West Bank and Gaza undoubtedly influenced the PAI.[35] Although it is difficult to ascertain the direct impact of individual events, it is plausible that the accumulation of regional events since the first intifada has been relevant for the growth in organized ethnonational mobilization. Events like the first intifada and the ensuing Oslo Accords were cast as manifestations of Palestinian expressions of national aspirations. Although the first intifada did not bring about mass protests similar to the October 2000 events, PAI newspapers generally tended to adopt the Palestinian perspective and editorials expressed solidarity with the uprising.[36] According to Rouhana and Ozacky-Lazar and Ghanem, PAI sympathy for the Palestinians in the West Bank and Gaza and support for the goals of the Palestinian national movement was widespread during this period and during the Madrid Peace Conference of 1991.[37]

The Oslo Accords had dual implications for the PAI. On the one hand, the agreement brought about widespread international recognition of Palestinian nationhood and established the legitimacy of the PLO as the representative of the Palestinians. The majority of the PAI, including the Communist Party, supported the agreement.[38] On the other hand, the agreement also entailed Palestinian recognition of Israel. It left the PAI outside the framework of the agreement and the national Palestinian institutions that were to be established. The institutions of the Palestinian Authority were to be established in the West Bank and Gaza; the PAI were to remain a domestic Israeli matter. Thus, some among the PAI leadership saw it as entrenching and legitimizing the Jewish identity of the state and as detrimental to the minority in Israel.[39]

The establishment of the National Democratic Assembly, Balad, was largely related to dissatisfaction with the Oslo Interim Agreement and the enthusiastic endorsement of the agreement by the Communists. Believing that the agreement was detrimental to PAI interests, some activists left the DFPE and together with activists from the defunct Abna' al-Balad movement, they established the Balad Party. Founding figures and supporters, such as Azmi Bishara, Jamal Zahalka, and Ameer Makhoul, voiced their concern that the two-state solution would sentence the PAI to a perpetual marginal status. According to Makhoul, the Oslo Interim Agreement indicated to the activists that the goal of integration, championed by the Communists, was not going to be achieved. The struggle for integration was lost and "a new approach had to be to build our separate institutions rather than seek integration."[40]

The al-Aqsa intifada would have likely also sensitized the Palestinianness of the PAI. Surveys by Ghanem and Ozacky-Lazar reveal rising sympathy to the Palestinians and their struggle shortly after the outbreak of the uprising.[41] Other surveys exposed a growing degree of mistrust between Jews and the PAI and between the PAI and state institutions.[42] Although the second intifada was not the underlying reason for the "October events," as explained in the previous chapter, the uprising in the West Bank and Gaza acted as a precipitant. In response to the call of the HFUCAI to protest against the death of Palestinians at the hands of Israeli security forces, thousands of PAI demonstrated in numerous locations, including mixed cities. In some locations, the protests turned violent. In what was labeled by some as a Palestinian intifada in Israel, protestors set up roadblocks, burned tires, and confronted the police with stones and Molotov cocktails.[43] PAI leaders were accused by the investigative Or Commission of disseminating inflammatory ethnonational messages that inspired the minority to challenge state authorities violently.[44]

Thus, elite behavior works in reciprocal relations with ethnonationalism. Mobilizing agents respond to ethnonational sentiments yet they also appeal to them and mobilize them. The rise of new PAI mobilizing actors to organize and lead a struggle against the existing institutional order while endorsing communal-based politics has been both reflective of adaptive preference formation and advanced it.

Institutional Fragmentation and Declining State Extensiveness

PAI disillusionment with integrationist strategies and adaptive preference formation tell only part of the story. They are not enough to explain mobilization. The transition from altering preferences to assertive articulation of these preferences through the means discussed in the previous chapter is contingent on changes in the overall state-society relations, and particularly the decline in extensiveness and cohesion at the core of the polity.

Political Fragmentation

One of the main factors driving changes in overarching state-society relations in Israel was the rising internal factionalism and competition for political power within the Jewish majority. Majority fragmentation led to decentralization of authority, a decline in state presence in many important spheres, and subsequently, a continuing decline in central government capacity to control society, including the PAI minority. Majority fragmentation intensified in the 1990s with the growing political salience of the religious-secular, Ashkenazi-Mizrahi, liberal-conservative, and left-right cleavages. In Israel, it should be remembered, these various divides largely overlap.[45]

Chapter 1 posited that when subgroups within the hegemonic group contest for institutional dominance among themselves, new institutional opportunities may unintentionally be created for bolder and more vociferous minority mobilization strategies. The growth in the political salience of the intra-Jewish divides was manifested in contestations over multiple issues. Intra-Jewish extensive contestation in turn resulted in the redesigning of the state's institutional framework in a variety of spheres, including electoral rules, constitutional engineering and judicial empowerment, economic liberalization, and laws regarding civic associations. These institutional changes contributed to further diffusion of public authority and state retreat from the public space.

One conspicuous area where this dynamic came into play is the shift of the Israeli party system from polarized competition between Labor and Likud, which characterized politics in the 1980s, to a fragmented system in which the power of the large parties declined (and this change, of course, came on top of the transition from the single-party dominance that characterized politics until the 1970s and was discussed in Chapter 4). The continuous stalemate throughout the 1980s between the dovish and mostly secular and Ashkenazi-supported Labor, on one side, and the more hawkish, conservative and Mizrahi-backed Likud, on the other side, increased the political bargaining power of small political parties, particularly the religious political parties, Shas and Agudath Yisrael, in coalition negotiations with Labor and Likud. Although these religious parties were more inclined to support the Likud due to the secular and liberal orientation of Labor supporters, they were nonetheless skillful at maintaining their bargaining power and could trigger a coalition crisis at will.

Israel's highly proportional representation electoral system with a low electoral threshold (raised to 1.5 percent in 1988) provided easy access to small factions.[46] As Michael Harris and Gideon Doron have observed "when a fragmented society has an electoral system that encourages many parties to form, it must expect that a majority government will be difficult to construct."[47] Because Labor and Likud were roughly of equivalent size, national unity governments, propped up with several smaller single-interest parties, became common in the 1980s. It was possible for the two parties to form national unity governments without additional parties, but by adding additional parties to the coalition, they could threaten to govern without the other. Thus, the 1980s saw a series of oversized yet shaky coalition governments that made sustaining effective government difficult. The 1981 coalition (not a national unity government) incorporated five parties and the 1984 and 1988 coalitions contained six parties each.

Following the 1992 elections, electoral reforms were introduced. Their purpose was to enable the creation of sustainable governments and to strengthen the executive. Up until the 1996 elections, Israeli voters cast a single ballot for a political party list. Under the reform of the Basic Law: The Government, voters were to cast two ballots. One ballot was for a party list and the second one for an individual candidate for prime minister. Although elected separately, the prime minister still required the confidence of the Knesset. A no-confidence vote supported by sixty-one members of the Knesset would lead to new elections for the Knesset and the prime minister. By giving voters the right to vote directly for the prime minister, it was thought that the authority of the executive would be enhanced and the prime minister would become less susceptible to pressure from smaller parties.

Altering electoral rules can change the behavior of voters, however, particularly in deeply divided societies.[48] The changes that were introduced had unintended consequences: they increased the popular vote for parties that represented a niche clientele. Thus, special interest parties were further strengthened, not weakened, under the new system, and the Knesset became even more fragmented. Because voters were able to express their position on the question of peace, security, and territories through their choice of prime minister, they were now more inclined to vote for a political party list that represented their particularistic interests rather than for the prime minister's party. In 1996, approximately 45 percent of the electorate engaged in this form of split-ticket voting; by 1999 almost two-thirds did so.[49] As a consequence of the reform, Labor and Likud's share of the votes decreased dramatically while political parties that represent particularistic interests grew in number and size.

In total, as can be seen in Table 9, the number of political parties that gained access to the Knesset grew from eleven in 1992 to fifteen in 1996 and nineteen in 1999 (counting separate parties running on a joint list as distinct parties).[50] Particularistic interest parties, representing, among others, various religious constituencies, new immigrants from Russia, Mizrahi Jews, Jewish settlers in the West Bank and Gaza, and labor unions, made considerable gains. A new Russian immigrant party, Yisrael Ba'aliyah, won seven seats in the 1996 elections and six in 1999 when an additional immigrant party, Avigdor Lieberman's Yisrael Beytenu, managed to gain access to the Knesset by winning three seats; Shas, representing Mizrahi religious Jews, grew from six seats in 1992 to ten in 1996 and seventeen in 1999; Shinui, a party claiming to

Table 9. Fragmentation of Party System and Rise of PAI Parties, 1992–2009

Year of election	Seats held by two largest parties together	Parties represented in Knesset	Seats held by PAI parties	Share of total vote won by PAI parties (including DFPE)
1992	76	11	5	4.0
1996	66	15	9	7.4
1999	45	19	10	7.9
2003	57	16	8	7.4
2006*	48	16	10	8
2009*	55	15	11	9.2

Based on election data available on Knesset website, http://www.Knesset.gov.il/description/eng/eng_mimshal_res.htm.

The DFPE is considered a PAI party in this table as the party underwent a significant transition since the 1990s. It fits D. L. Horowitz's fundamental indicators of an ethnic party (*Ethnic Groups in Conflict*, 291–92), as it derives its support overwhelmingly from the PAI and makes ethnic demands on the government.

*Since 2006, the newly established Kadima party, led by former prime minister Ariel Sharon, who seceded from the Likud in 2005, became one of the two largest parties. It won the 2006 election and became the governing party; it also emerged with the most Knessset seats following the 2009 elections, but Likud was in a better position to build a coalition government.

represent secularist Jews, won six seats in 1999 and fifteen in 2003. A return to the old voting system before the 2003 elections managed to somewhat halt the fragmentation trend but not to completely reverse it. The 2003 and 2006 elections resulted in sixteen political parties represented in the Knesset (including separate parties running on a joint list). As a result of the 2009 elections, the number of parties in the Knesset dropped to fifteen.

What was relevant to Jewish voters also applied to the PAI electorate with equal if not more force. The PAI were now able to vote for a prime minister representing the center-left while also casting a ballot for a PAI political party to represent their particularistic interest. In 1996 and 1999, roughly 95 percent of PAI voters voted for the Labor candidates for prime minister, Shimon Peres and Ehud Barak.[51] By 1999, over two thirds of PAI voters engaged in split-ticket voting and voted for a PAI political party. The total number of seats won by political parties claiming to represent the PAI (including the DFPE) increased from five in the 1988 and 1992 elections to nine in the 1996 elections, and ten in the 1999 elections.

After the old voting system was restored, the "leaking" of voters to PAI parties slowed down, but old voting patterns were not restored. Political parties representing the PAI won eight seats in the 2003 election (largely due to an internal split within the UAL that resulted in votes worth roughly two Knesset seats being lost to PAI parties that did not pass the threshold), ten seats in 2006, and eleven seats in 2009. The number of parties claiming to represent the PAI grew from two in 1992 to three in 1996 and to five in 1999, 2003, 2006, and 2009 (counting separate parties coalescing on a joint list as separate parties).[52] Table 9 demonstrates the relationship between the fragmentation of Israel's political party system (and the decline of two largest parties), following the electoral reform that was introduced after the 1992 elections, and the rise in number and electoral gains of political parties representing the PAI.

The case of the PAI is not unique. A fragmented party system is a variable that has often been associated with the rise of ethnic parties in other places around the world.[53] This is because the electoral rules that induce such systems provide incentives for voters to vote for ethnic parties and hence for parties to appeal to particularistic interests. When there is more than one party that claims to represent the minority, the dynamic that can sometimes occur is that of "outbidding," whereby each of the ethnically based parties tries to outbid its competitors in demonstrating loyalty to the group and commitment to advancing group interests.[54]

Thus, on the one hand, the new electoral rules in Israel created space for a greater number of niche clientele PAI parties. On the other hand, PAI political parties found themselves competing among themselves for the PAI vote. Considering that the pool of potential support for PAI parties is limited, the competition for the PAI vote became intense. Add to that that enough time had passed for the PAI to overcome the legacies of the military administration, for a new elite to emerge, and for parties other than the Communists to build organizational infrastructure that will enable them to compete with the DFPE. Some have even speculated that in the 1980s, the state enabled the Islamists to operate relatively unrestrained so as to enhance internal PAI competition and undermine the dominance of the communists.[55] This kind of policy would have undoubtedly contributed to the pluralization of PAI politics. The competition that has emerged between parties vying for the support of the PAI electorate provides incentives for the competing PAI forces to appeal to ethnonational sentiments in order to enhance their credentials as the most appropriate representatives of the minority's interests. It is for this reason that the DFPE, for example, formed alliances with Balad and Ahmad Tibi's Ta'al, the ADP joined forces with the Islamists, and representatives of all the parties have sharpened their rhetoric and are making bolder ethnic demands on the state as elaborated in the previous chapter.

The theoretical lessons generated by this experience relate both to the role of institutions as more than just conduits of preferences—they can harden preferences in a fragmented and highly competitive environment—and to the impact of internal majority fragmentation on minority politics and ethnonationalism. The intra-Jewish split and the subsequent changes in the electoral rules have enhanced an interactive, reciprocal process whereby the PAI were more likely to express ethnonational sentiments by voting for PAI parties. Concomitantly, competing PAI political parties, vying for voters, have greater incentives to increasingly appeal to ethnonational sentiments and make blunter ethnic claims in the name of Palestinian nationalism in Israel.

Interestingly, already in 1989 Ian Lustick predicted that the Arab minority was going to increase its political power because of the conflict-ridden attribute of Israeli politics.[56] According to Lustick, the intra-Jewish divide made PAI electoral support indispensable for Labor and its associates on the left, in turn making them more likely to court PAI voters and parties. When adding the relative population growth of the PAI and the possibilities of tactical maneuvering by Arab voters and politicians, Lustick anticipated that the bargaining power of the PAI would increase and enable this minority to become a decisive factor in Israeli politics. He wrote that "so long as Israel's Jewish majority remains deeply and evenly split on the main questions facing the state, Israeli Arabs will be in an increasingly strategic position to influence, if not ultimately control, the composition of Israeli governments."[57] Thus, Labor would be compelled to join forces with the PAI and accommodate some of the minority's demands, setting Israel on the road to binationalism.[58]

Even though for a while, the Rabin government did establish cooperative relations with PAI political parties, Lustick's prediction about the impact of intra-Jewish fragmentation did not materialize. The fragmented character of Israeli politics had the opposite effect to what Lustick anticipated and made accommodating PAI parties and their main demands highly improbable because of the increasing dependence of central governments on a growing number of coalition partners that were unwilling to compromise on Jewish dominance and could quit the coalition and bring down the government.

Since the 1990s, coalition governments relied on a particularly large number of parties. Each party in the coalition required a payoff for supporting the government and could at any point withdraw from the coalition and make the government fall. Binyamin Netanyahu's coalition government (1996–1999), for example, consisted of nine parties, including Likud-Gesher-Tzomet, the National religious Party (NRP), Yisrael Ba'aliyah, the Third Way, Shas, and United Torah Judaism (UTJ), which brings together Degel Ha'Torah and Agudath Yisrael. Several of the junior coalition partners eventually helped to bring down Netanyahu's government and joined Ehud Barak's Labor government following the 1999 elections. Similarly, Barak's government (1999–2001), which initially consisted of Yisrael Ahat (A joint list of Labor, Meimad, and Gesher), Shas, Yisrael Ba'aliyah, Meretz, the Centre Party, the UTJ, and the NRP, lost the UTJ following a dispute over the travel of an oil-transferring track on a Sabbath day. The government lost several other coalition members shortly after the failed Camp David peace summit in the summer of 2000. Even though it started off as a ten-party coalition (counting parties that coalesced on a joint list as distinct parties), Barak's government was left with a parliamentary minority, and eventually Barak resigned and lost the 2001 elections to prime minister to Ariel Sharon. The coalition formed by Sharon following the 2003 election consisted of "only" six political parties. As a consequence of the decision to unilaterally withdraw from Gaza, however, right wing parties left the government and the Likud split as Ariel Sharon and his followers, realizing that they had lost the support of most of the Likud, seceded to form the Kadima Party.[59] The Kadima-led coalition government (2006–2009), which consisted of six parties, also collapsed after it was bolted by Labor. Thus, the growing strength of smaller parties meant that dealing with contentious policy issues (including Jewish ownership of the state) entailed significant political risks. The central government became significantly weaker and less stable as governments could easily be brought down by the small political parties due to disputes over controversial policy issues.

The question of Jewish ownership of the state has remained very much a central issue in Israel and the Jewish majority is *not* evenly divided on this question. Public opinion polls have revealed consistent support for maintaining the Jewish identity of the state and Israeli leaders have made recognition of Israel as a Jewish state an important issue in peace negotiations with the Palestinians.[60] As a result, including PAI parties in the coalition and accommodating their ethnic demands, as Lustick predicted, has become even less likely than before. As the Rabin-headed government (which had only 2 formal members since September 1993, Labor and Meretz, and was supported by the DFPE and ADP from the outside) discovered following the Oslo Interim Agreement, having PAI parties as strategic partners that support the coalition comes with a heavy price, as demonstrated earlier in this chapter. With the increased fragmentation and further decline of the large parties, increasing the political role of the PAI has become even riskier as it would likely entail losing support of crucial Jewish coalition partners. Even prime ministers from the center-left, who needed to bolster their credentials as loyal to the interests of the Jewish majority when pursuing the peace process, have chosen to marginalize PAI political parties.[61] For example, in 1999 when Prime Minister Barak formed the government that would engage in the Camp David Summit, he distanced himself from the PAI parties and preferred to form a coalition with the religious and right-of-center Shas and National Religious Party. More recently, the rise of Yisrael Beytenu to the status of the third most popular party in Israel, when it won fifteen seats in the 2009 elections, was characterized by the party's pointed claims directed against the PAI. In short, political fragmentation has made the political risks associated with accommodating PAI ethnically based political parties higher than the benefits such a partnership is likely to bring.

Dispersion of Power and Declining State Presence

Political fragmentation has engendered dispersion of political power and authority and has prevented any single state institution, a large party, or the central government from concentrating political power and reestablishing ultimate control over society.[62] The process of diffusion of political power and authority has been accompanied by a reduction in state extensiveness, or presence, in the public sphere as well as growing incongruence between various agencies regarding public values, visions of society, and the treatment of the minority. A decline in state extensiveness and decentralization of authority has imposed limitations on the capacity of the central government to penetrate and structure society and has provided extensive public space for organized social groups, including PAI ethnically based groups, to operate outside the realm of the state and articulate ethnic demands more assertively.

It should be stressed immediately that at no point has the state lost its capacity to set firm boundaries in which all groups must operate—with the possible exception of settlers in the West Bank.[63] The state is still relatively well institutionalized and still possesses significant coercive capacity to prevent sustained domestic violent mobilization and secessionism. Nevertheless, majority fragmentation and the declining degrees of state cohesion and extensiveness have provided sufficient space for the consolidation of ethnic civil society and other forms of extra-parliamentary mobilization that were discussed extensively in Chapter 5 and that challenge the foundational principles of the state.

There were two axes of dispersion of authority that were particularly consequential for the emergence of PAI ethnic civil society mobilization: horizontal, between various state agencies, and vertical, between state and society. The most conspicuous aspect of the horizontal decentralization, aside from the changes in the legislature-executive relations that were discussed above, was the empowerment of the judiciary vis-à-vis the executive and the Knesset through increased judicial activism of Israel's High Court of Justice. The transitions in executive-legislature-judiciary balance of power highlighted differences in values and attitudes toward Israel's diverse social groups and the socially and politically subordinate, including women, same-sex persons, non-Jewish residents that arrived in the 1990s, and the PAI minority.[64]

Two of the most important junctures on the road to strengthening the judiciary were the introduction of Basic Law: The Judiciary in 1984, which in part also codified the High Court of Justice's authority to review government practices, and Basic Law: Human Dignity and Liberty and Basic Law: Freedom of Occupation, which were enacted in 1992 and deal with the protection of civic and property rights.[65] These basic laws have been interpreted by the High Court of Justice as a "constitutional revolution" that provide the courts with greater scrutinizing power for review of government policies that might infringe on the civic rights of citizens.[66]

As with changes in electoral politics, judicial empowerment was partly generated by intra-Jewish segmentation. According to Ran Hirschl, the empowerment of the courts was largely related to the loss of hegemony of Labor and the elites it represents.[67] In his comparative study of Canada, Israel, South Africa. and New Zealand, Hirschl finds that when a dominant segment of society realizes that it is likely to lose its hegemony, it tries to protect its privileged position by transferring authority away from elected government institutions to the courts through the constitutionalization of civic rights, particularly property rights. This is primarily true for segments that are not a numerical majority because without judicial review, parliamentary majorities can more easily transfer resources. That the secular Ashkenazi elites lost their hold on power has been discussed extensively in the literature, and there is no need to elaborate here more than what has already been written.[68] According to Hirschl, when the secular elites associated with Labor realized that the challenges posed by the religious and the more traditional communities were not transient, they opened the judicial avenue as protective means, empowering the courts to review government policies and protect their privileged social and economic positions.

Others have argued that the polarization of the secular-religious divide and the decline in the ability of the divided Knesset to resolve contentious issues since the early 1980s have enabled the courts to intervene and resolve disputes on issues of principle.[69] As the High Court of Justice was becoming more accessible to marginalized groups, the shift in the court-Knesset balance of power led to a refocusing of Israeli political mobilization in general. The 1990s saw a significant upsurge in litigation activism by organized groups, including civil rights organizations, women, immigrants, secularists, reform and conservative religious associations, and many others.[70] By 1999, 6 percent of all NGOs registered in Israel were dealing with law, advocacy, and politics.[71] Litigation has thus become a means for political participation as well as protestation against state authorities.[72]

The court's increasing involvement in sociopolitical disputes has made it an additional center of authority, or an alternative rule maker, as it brought to the forefront alternative liberal values that checked the authority of centralized, majoritarian institutions and claimed to uphold the rights of disadvantaged groups. Among the most conspicuous non-PAI examples of organization that mobilize through litigation were the Association for Civil Rights in Israel, the Israel Movement for Progressive Judaism, Israel Women's Network, and Hemdat (a movement concerned with religious pluralism).

One highly publicized example of the particular impact this transformation has had for policies toward the PAI is the case of the Qa'adan family. An application by the Qa'adan family to lease a plot of land in the community settlement of Katzir, built on land allocated to the Jewish Agency by the ILA, was rejected on the grounds that the family did not fit the community. In response to a petition by ACRI, the High Court of Justice ruled that the state cannot discriminate on the basis of nationality or religion when allocating state land to citizens.[73] In issuing its precedent-setting ruling, the High Court of Justice gave higher priority to the value of civic equality for individuals than to the traditional ethnonationalist priorities of the other centers of authority of the state.[74] The implication of the ruling was not immediately internalized as the ILA was not in a hurry to implement the court's decision.[75] In the longer term, however, subsequent petitions or threats of petitions forced changes in state practices. According to one report, in 2004 after initially resisting on ethnonational grounds, the ILA agreed to release seven plots of land to Arab families in a new neighborhood in Carmiel following a petition to the courts by ACRI and the ACAP.[76] Additional petitions by ACRI, Adalah, and ACAP have prompted the attorney general to rule that neither the ILA nor the JNF were entitled to discriminate against the Arab minority in land allocation.[77]

Beyond specific policies, the empowerment of the judiciary and its commitment to different norms has opened up opportunities for mobilization by litigation by PAI organizations as well. Organizations like Adalah, ACAP, and Mossawa have become what Charles Epp calls "support structures for legal mobilization."[78] The pursuit of rights through courts, according to Epp, has become possible through these support structures, "consisting of rights-advocacy organizations, rights advocacy lawyers, and sources of financing."[79] Ethnically based organizations create infrastructure for mobilization in the name of the collective and provide access to the courts for individuals and groups who would otherwise not have the resources to act on their own. For example, some workers in Adalah are responsible for locating potential cases with collective bearing to bring before the courts. Indeed, most of the abundant petitions submitted by Adalah, which were discussed extensively in the previous chapter, have been of a collectivist character. Likewise, Mossawa took it upon itself in 2005 to petition the courts against the lack of programming in Arabic on Channel Two in Israel, an issue of concern to many in the PAI community, but one that individuals would find difficult to pursue individually.[80] And ACAP has been at the forefront with petitions dealing with access to land. By 2001, about 7 percent of PAI NGOs were operating in law, advocacy, and politics, indicating the significance of the judicial avenue.[81]

The strengthening of the judiciary and incongruence between the values traditionally promoted by the central regime, on the one hand, and the judicial arm of the state, on the other, had come in conjunction with transformation in broader state-society power relations. Dispersion of authority simultaneously reflected and further modified power relations in society. It translated into a decline in the capacity of the ruling echelon in the central government to control society while further reinforcing the empowerment of civil society associations. Numerous non-PAI advocacy organizations emerged in Israel in the 1980s and 1990s to demand greater accountability from the regime. Some utilized judicial empowerment to pursue their interests; others preferred protest mobilization. Notable examples include the Movement for the Quality of Government and the Constitution for Israel Movement. Some challenged traditional practices of distribution of material and cultural resources, for example, Hakeshet Hamizrahit (the Mizrahi Rainbow), which wanted more material and cultural resources diverted to Jews of Middle Eastern origin. Some have even suggested that the Constitution for Israel organization, which mobilized tens of thousands of demonstrators in the late 1980s and early 1990s, was the main agent that led politicians to alter the electoral system and the introduction of the important Basic Law: Freedom of Occupation and Basic Law: Human Dignity and Liberty.[82]

All in all, Israel's civil society activity, the origins of which were discussed in Chapter 4, experienced tremendous growth in recent decades.[83] The challenges presented by the burgeoning civil society reflected and engendered changing power relations between state and society, whereby society increasingly demanded greater government accountability and created space for social participation in decision-making. Increasingly, society has been more able to scrutinize the state and influence it, rather than vice versa as was historically the case in Israel.

These challenges had an impact on the space available for PAI civil society mobilization. ACAP, for example, like many other organizations, could more legitimately criticize and file objections against government development plans when Hakeshet Hamizrahit was doing something similar. Adalah could more easily claim to legitimately question government policies through petitions as ACRI was mobilizing in the same way. And many other organizations could claim to be participating in existing public debates. As I stated elsewhere,

> The debates within the Jewish community over changing the hierarchical citizenship structure that privileged some groups and marginalized others, on the one hand, and the changing power relations between state and society in Israel, on the other, provided space for PAI participation in this discourse. Particularly noteworthy in this context is Mossawa's participation in the meetings held by the Knesset Constitution, Law, and Justice Committee on a future constitution. Mossawa's proposal aimed to challenge the PAI's position in the hierarchical structures in Israel. Adalah's "The Democratic Constitution" (2007) and the National Committee for the Heads of the Arab Local Authorities in Israel's "The Future Vision of the Palestine Arabs in Israel" (2006) also came about on the backdrop of intensifying debates since 2003 amongst the Jewish majority about drafting a constitution for Israel (the question of drafting a constitution gained in significance since 2003 when the Knesset Constitution, Law, and Justice Commit-

tee started to hold regular debates on the issue). Several Jewish non-governmental actors, including the IDI [Israel Democracy Institute], the Shalem Center, and others, either proposed drafts for constitution or participated in regular discussions in the Knesset on the issue.[84]

Thus, ethnically based civil society activism and the ethnic claims that accompanied it were largely facilitated by the public space that mainstream Israeli civil society carved open. It should be clear that not all Jewish NGOs shared an agenda. Many of the prominent organized social forces were non-liberal. Some were more conservative. Some advanced a Jewish nationalist agenda. Arguably, the most prominent of these was Gush Emunim, formed in the 1970s with the goal of settling the territories Israel captured in the 1967 war and promoting Jewish sovereignty over the territory. The important point to keep in mind, however, is not the agenda itself. It is the expanding pluralistic discourse, on the one hand, and the corrosive capacity that the extraparliamentary activity, liberal and conservative, had on the central government's capacity to pursue policies independently of social pressure and without being subjected to public scrutiny, on the other. One scholar observed that "the mushrooming of multiple Israeli social change and advocacy organizations . . . emulated in style and methods of action twentieth century American social movements. These non-profit, politically partisan and non-partisan organizations embraced American concepts of civil society."[85] And another distinguished scholar noted that organized societal groups that have been increasing their demands on the state, have "had a long-term corrosive effect on the state's ability to channel the diverse currents in society."[86]

The accumulative impact of these changes in state-society relations in Israel, the declining congruence in preferences and values among significant arms of the state (most significantly between the judiciary, on the one hand, and the legislature and executive, on the other), and the decreasing presence of the Israeli state in society was to accelerate the process begun in the 1970s of reduced regime capacity to control minority activism. As Israeli society and politics opened up, new channels became available for PAI mobilization. The new institutional setting provided the PAI with new opportunities through which to challenge the lack of state autonomy and practices of ethnic favoritism.

Under these conditions, ethnically based civil society activity could bourgeon, and it is not surprising that much of the patterns of growth in PAI ethnic civil society activism that was elaborated upon in the previous chapter followed the more general pattern of growth in civil society activism in Israel. Thus, at the beginning of the 1980s, PAI civil society activity hardly existed. By 2001, over 1,600 NGOs were registered, almost two thirds of which were founded in the 1990s (80 percent since 1988).[87] In 1990, PAI NGOs accounted for 3.1 percent of the newly registered NGOs; by 1999, the rate grew to 7.7 percent, "amounting to 4.4 percent of the cumulative total of Israeli third sector to date. The significant increases in 1999 can thus be regarded as a culmination of formal organizational activity among this minority group."[88] In the 2000s, the annual rate of newly registering NGOs began to exceed 7 percent. Table 10 lists the year of establishment of some of the most active and well-funded PAI NGOs involved with politics, litigation and advocacy.

The burgeoning PAI nonparliamentary activism has been facilitated by an upsurge in funding from international sources. That international organizations, trans-state money transfers, and transborder social activism have facilitated the intensification of ethnic group, and particularly minority, mobilization is conventionally accepted.[89] International activism contributes to the diffusion of ethnic claims on the basis of a human rights discourse.

International organizations such as the Ford Foundation, Oxfam, and the European Commission have long been involved in promoting civil society projects and democracy around the world, and they have also contributed to PAI NGOs. More intriguing is the upsurge in funding from transstate Jewish philanthropic foundations as well as Israeli support networks. The most active on this front are the New Israel Fund (NIF), the Moriah Fund, and the Abraham Fund Initiatives, who together have been donating more than U.S.$3 million annually to PAI ethnically based associations since the mid-2000s and the amounts are rising.[90] In 2008, Adalah alone was authorized a

Table 10. Year of Establishment of Prominent Ethnically Based PAI Nonparliamentary Organizations

Organization	Year of establishment
ACAP	2000
Adalah	1996
Ahali	1999
Association of Forty	1978
HRA (Arab Center for Human Rights)	1988
I'lam	2000
Ittijah	1995
Mossawa	1997

grant of over half a million U.S. dollars; ACAP $105,000, Ahali over $40,000, I'lam $31,000, and Mada al-Carmel $200,000.[91] Many of the donors are driven by the belief that strengthening minority rights in Israel, promoting pluralism, and counterbalancing state ethnic favoritism is normatively desirable and contributes to a better society in Israel as a whole.[92]

Within Israel, Shatil, founded and backed by the NIF, has been providing significant technical and financial assistance to ethnically based PAI organizations. The NIF (established in 1979) and Shatil were created in response to the rise to power of the Likud and the Israeli Right. The founders of these two organizations were liberal Jews, who sought to counterbalance what they perceived as the growing ethno-communitarian trends signified by the rise of the Israeli right and conservative-religious segments of society. According to its website, "SHATIL, The New Israel Fund's Empowerment and Training Center for Social Change Organizations in Israel, was established in 1982 to strengthen civil society efforts and promote democracy, tolerance, and social justice in Israel."[93] Initially, Shatil and the NIF were active primarily in the Jewish sector, advancing what they saw as a social justice agenda and assisting NGOs that dealt with marginalized populations in the Jewish sector, including women, nonorthodox religious organizations, immigrants, and other community-based groups. Shortly thereafter, they extended their support to the Arab minority and to PAI ethnically based associations. It should be stressed that all of the main donors endorse Israel's foundational principles.[94] Their support of PAI ethnic civil society should not be interpreted as endorsing PAI ethnonationalism or the demands expressed in the Vision Documents. And yet, the transition in Israeli politics and society over the last two and a half decades and the emergent sociopolitical fragmentation were accompanied by a more pluralistic discourse and greater public space for civil society to check the influence of the central state. These sociopolitical processes ended up being conducive to PAI ethnically based civil society activism as Shatil and the NIF have become major players in Israel's civil society sector, which now tolerates ethnic claims against the state and the Jewish majority.

Consequential declining state presence in the public arena occurred in several other places. In the realm of electronic media, for example, independent commercial and cable television and local radio stations were introduced in the late 1980s and early 1990s. The proliferation of media outlets had accelerated the process that began in the late 1960s and early 1970s and which was discussed in Chapter 4, whereby the center of governmental authority increasingly lost most of its control over the content of public discourse.[95] The transformation in the media landscape provided additional opportunities for PAI mobilization as PAI organizations that focus on advancing a PAI agenda in the media were formed. I'lam: Media Center for Arab Palestinians in Israel is arguably the most conspicuous of these organizations. This NGO characterizes its activities as oriented toward "empowering the Arab media landscape." [96] It does so partly through scrutinizing media coverage of the PAI, providing critical feedback to media outlets for their coverage of the PAI, and expressing concerns when they feel the PAI position is treated unfairly. I'lam also claims to work to advance the access and representation of Arab journalists to Israeli media. In 2008, it also launched a program aimed at improving the quality and level of professionalism of Arab journalism. How much influence this organization has is a debateable question.

One of the most important facets of declining state presence that proved consequential for PAI nonparliamentary ethnically based activism was in the social and economic realms. Since the 1980s, there has been a steady retreat of the state from the economy and a transition toward a liberal market economy, consumerism, free entrepreneurship, enhanced privatization of government companies, and deregulation of trade and investment. The number of government companies (defined as having at least 50 percent government ownership) declined from 189 in 1987 to 119 in 1995, and further still at the turn of the twenty-first century.[97] Likewise, the Histadrut practically sold most of its property holdings and privatized most of its firms.[98] Koor, for example, which was owned by the Histadrut and was the leading actor in Israel's industrial sector in the first several decades, was sold to private ownership as were Israel's major banks. The private domain considerably increased throughout the 1990s and 2000s as "the private sector produced an increasing share of national wealth."[99] According to Nitzan and Bichler, much of the economic power in Israel has shifted from the state to leading families and groups, including Arison, Dankner, Ofer, and Recanati, among many others.[100] Many of Israel's leading domestic firms came under partial foreign ownership.[101]

Furthermore, the introduction of the National Health Insurance Law in 1995 stipulated that individuals no longer needed to be members of the Histadrut to have access to its health care services. The new regulations ended this organization's all but absolute monopoly over health service, arguably the most important social service, as three rival health insurance providers, Maccabi, Leumit, and Me'uhedet, increased their share of clients. The Histadrut's historical role as a social, economic, and political power in Israel practically expired following these changes. Membership in the Histadrut, 1.8 million in 1994, declined by more than 60 percent by the end of 1997.[102]

When government agencies divest themselves of responsibility for providing services and when state presence decreases in the economic sphere, there is often growth in private sector and service activity.[103] The privatization of various aspects of Israel's economy and social services provided societal space for non-state actors to provide services instead of the state, the role of which in redistribution of resources had gradually decreased. According to Gidron, Bar, and Katz, as the state privatized many of its public services in the 1990s, there was a tremendous growth in the number of nonprofit organizations that either "replaced or complemented educational, welfare, and health services that the state previously provided."[104] If in 1980 fewer than 2,500 nonprofit organizations were registered in Israel, there were about 15,000 such organizations in 1990 and close to 35,000 by the end of 2001. Approximately three quarters of those registered at the turn of the twenty-first century were engaged in service provision in welfare, education and research, religion, and culture.[105]

Similar dynamics applied in PAI society as opportunity space was created for organized PAI activity to step in where the state was no longer present. As mentioned earlier, the number of registered PAI NGOs grew tremendously throughout the 1990s and 2000s. More than 80 percent of the PAI NGOs currently registered were established after 1988.[106] By 2001, over half of the associations that were registered dealt with service provisions in the realms of education, health, social services, development and housing, and religion. Of particular importance in this context is the space created for the Islamic movement as close to one-fifth of PAI NGOs were also religious.[107] Since many local PAI communities, particularly the smaller ones, were seriously affected by the shrinkage in the welfare state—whereas in Jewish towns there was an average of one primary healthcare clinic for 8,600 residents and one speciality clinic for 15,500 residents in 2003, the ratio in Arab towns was one primary healthcare clinic per 11,800 residents and one specialty clinic per 29,500 residents—the need and opportunities for NGOs to provide alternative services increased.[108]

The growing needs of the PAI population enabled the Islamists to replace the state in providing services. An extensive organizational framework that provides welfare services, healthcare facilities, educational services, and other welfare provisions has stepped in to replace the state. Being a political movement, the Islamic movement has developed a clientelistic approach whereby it expects political backing in exchange for the services it provides. Some have made the comparison with the Jewish Shas party, which hopes to reap the political reward for the social services that it provides to impoverished Jewish populations outside its parliamentary activity.[109] Yet perhaps more than Shas, the Islamists prefer extensive isolation from the state. Their aim has been to establish a public domain where they administer their own affairs. Providing a network of social services, including healthcare, education, sports clubs, an orphanage, a drug rehabilitation center, and religious services instead of the state, minimizes the need of the PAI population to interact with state agencies and provides the Islamists with opportunities to enhance the credibility of their message that "Islam is the solution". Their credibility is further bolstered because they maintain independent sources of funding, relying mostly on charitable Islamic foundations from inside and outside Israel and several revenue-generating enterprises of their own.

The hierarchical structure of the religious establishment has facilitated the clientelistic approach that the Islamists have taken toward politics. It should not come as a surprise, therefore, that the growth in the popularity and political strength of the Islamists, including the ability to win races for local councils, has followed the transformations in the social and economic structures. It is precisely because the state was limiting its presence in PAI locals that isolationist actors like the Islamists were provided with societal space for carving a distinct Islamic domain in which state presence is restricted.

Conclusion

The Israeli state has proven to be malleable in significant areas. The Israeli polity has been more fragmented than ever since the mid-1990s as multiple centers of authority and rival political and social forces are competing with each other and advancing rival norms. Furthermore, while the state is still relatively well institutionalized, its extensiveness has declined considerably. It is no longer present in as many social areas as it used to be. It has withdrawn from large portions of economic activity and social service provision, it no longer monopolizes the media, or controls public discourse, and its military no longer governs PAI areas. The ability of the central government to affect social group range of action has diminished considerably.

At the same time, the Israeli state has been relatively resilient when it comes to extending the boundaries of ownership beyond the nondominant Jewish majority. Despite some incremental changes on the margins, there has been resistance to renegotiating the structures of inclusion and exclusion. Thus, the response to increasing PAI ethnonational claims has been dual: rejection of minority demands, on the one hand, and greater political space for articulating these demands, on the other.

Conclusion

Israeli society remains deeply divided along ethnonational lines. The PAI minority has always had to face Jewish ownership of the state, yet only in recent decades has PAI politics widely confronted the lack of state neutrality by making ethnonational claims, challenging the state's foundational principles as a Jewish state, and demanding a distinct and expansive autonomous space. To some extent, Palestinian nationalism in Israel has completed a circle of sorts from the prestate period after transitioning through periods of quiescence and communist activism.

The ethnonational turn should not obscure the reality whereby the state still possesses sufficient capacity to enforce rules in which the rival ethnonational groups must operate. Despite the growing tensions between the majority and minority and the rise in popularity of ethnocentric political parties on both sides, the Jewish-PAI conflict has rarely manifested itself outside the established institutional framework. The events of October 2000, interethnic riots in Acre in October 2008, and rare involvement of PAI individuals in subversive activities are the exception to the rule. PAI patterns of political organization and mobilization mirror the general patterns in Israel at large. In this regard, at least, PAI political actors can be said to have accepted Israel's democracy as "the only game in town" and are "playing by the rules." This is a somewhat unexpected pattern of political behavior considering that important PAI leaders and intellectuals publicly reject Israel's categorization as a democracy.[1]

At the same time, the state is no longer able to control minority political organizations and demands as it did in the first decades. It has liberalized along many dimensions and is no longer as extensive and as penetrative into social space as it used to be. The military administration has long been removed from regions populated by Arabs; government control of the media has loosened considerably; the previously statist economy has been liberalized; the Histadrut's role in the economy has expired; government agencies have divested themselves of responsibility for providing many services; and independent civil society organizations that make demands on the state, scrutinize the central government, and offer alternative frameworks of social organization are abundant. Following in the footsteps of their Jewish counterparts, ethnically based PAI organizations that make demands on the state in the name of the ethnic-national minority carve an isolated sphere outside the reach of the state, and challenge central government policies have proliferated since the mid-1990s. They utilize the opportunity space that has been created by the contraction of state presence and outreach.

The decline in state extensiveness has been coupled with political and institutional fragmentation. Authority is no longer centralized in the hands of a relatively small group of elites as it once was. Nor is politics divided between two camps of relatively equal proportions. Whereas the Labor Party dominated politics for the first thirty years, controlled much of the state's resources, and co-opted the Arabs into clientelistic networks; and whereas the 1980s were characterized by polarization between Likud and its satellite parties, on one side, and Labor and its satellites, on the other side, the 1990s saw fragmentation of the political party scene. As a result, the central government has been weakened significantly. The popularity of the two main parties declined and the number and size of niche-clientele and single-issue parties grew considerably. PAI ethnically based political parties were strengthened like other parties with particularistic agendas, but the fragmented structure did not permit inclusion of PAI parties in coalition governments or accommodation of their demands. Jewish-centric parties that were vital for the survival of any coalition would not have tolerated that.

At the same time, competition among PAI parties vying for the PAI vote led to an outbidding dynamic whereby each party needed to enhance its credentials as the best representative of PAI interests. Thus, the electoral rules and the fragmented structure acted not only as conduits for expressing preferences, they also provided incentives for mobilizing ethnicity and hardening the ethnonational position.

The decline in the institutional cohesion of the state was also manifested in the changing judiciary-executive balance of power. As the judiciary was empowered by the "constitutional revolution," it could not only check the power of majoritarian institutions, such as the Knesset, but it also advanced, and operated according to, alternative norms that were less ethnocentric than those of the central government. Stated differently, different branches of the state were not synchronized in their preferences. The judicial branch became an avenue through which marginalized groups, including women, same-sex couples, reform and conservative Jews, and the Arab minority could pursue collective goals. The courts offered an alternative source of authority to the executive and Knesset, and as a result, litigation-activism in the name of a collective, including among the PAI, became a common form of mobilization.

Thus, changes in the domestic institutional setting have been central to this account. On the one hand, institutional change provided space for PAI political activism to challenge the foundational principles of the state and the ethnic order. In some instances, new institutions even provided incentives to accelerate the mobilization of ethnonationalism (most conspicuously the electoral and party systems). On this front, transitions in forms of PAI organization and mobilization mirrored changes in Israel at large. On the other hand, the boundaries of exclusion remained largely impermeable and even hardened on occasion (despite exceptions on the margins), in turn encouraging PAI adaptive preference formation. Representatives of the majority continue to counter PAI ethnonationalism using state instruments, most recently with bills setting imprisonment terms for those publicly calling to change Israel's definition as a Jewish and democratic state and plans by the Ministry of Education to ban the teaching of the Palestinian Nakba and enhance Zionist education in publicly funded schools.

Institutional changes, however, were not isolated from developments in the society scene. To a large extent, state institutions reflected intra-Jewish divides even as they also ended up reinforcing them. The left-right, religious-secular, orthodox-conservative and reform, liberal-conservative, Ashkenazi-Sepharadi, and have-have not divides were all connected to the loss of Labor hegemony, polarization and then fragmentation of politics, changes to election laws, empowerment of the courts, state retreat from economic activity, weakening power of the central government, and rise of organized social forces that check central state power. Conflicting societal pressures increasingly eroded regime capacity to regulate society.

Consequential social changes occurred among the Arabs as well. The modernization process that included urbanization, education, economic expansion, and occupational transition engendered new elites that established new political organizations and acted as mobilizing agents. Unlike their predecessors, these new elites were born into the state. They grew up experiencing both the period of control and subordination of their parents and the unsuccessful attempts at integration into Israeli society. The new elites were more familiar with the system, spoke Hebrew fluently, and were less susceptible to manipulation. It is true that hamula politics remained central at local level politics.[2] At the national level, however, the hamula largely gave way to new forms of organization that championed Palestinian nationalism in Israel. This is not to say that the Communists did not exhibit nationalist tendencies. But in the 1970s, the memory of how articulation of ethnonational sentiments was suppressed was still fresh while state attributes did not permit serious questioning of the state's foundational principles. Framing claims in socialist rather than ethnonationalist rhetoric was less risky before the institutional changes of the 1990s. Ultimately, without the new political organizations to take advantage of the new opportunities that emerged and translate grievances into political action, organized PAI ethnonationalist political activism would have been absent.

The implications of this argument extend beyond the Israeli case. Ethnic tensions between titular majorities and sizable homeland minorities with kin in the neighboring region characterize much of the post-Communist region in Central and Eastern Europe; Central, or Middle Asia; Turkey and Iraq and their Kurdish minorities; Malaysia and the Chinese minority; and many other regions. In many of these cases, the state seeks to promote the interests of ethnonational majorities over minorities. The analytical framework introduced in this book can be useful for anyone seeking to examine majority-minority tensions in similar contexts.

To briefly reiterate, much of the literature on minority mobilization, in general, and the PAI, in particular, not only fails to distinguish between minorities and organizations that claim to speak on their behalf, but also stresses the grievances that arise from inequalities and subordinate status. What grievance-based explanations are unable to account for is how grievances translate into political action. In the case of Israel and the PAI, objective inequalities and minority disaffection with subordination have remained relatively constant over a period of sixty years, while the forms of minority political organization, demands, and mobilization underwent significant transition. The increase in vociferous PAI ethnonational demands made by the burgeoning ethnically based organizations is a result of changes in the institutional structures of the Israeli state, which themselves resulted from transitions in intra-Jewish politics. Thus, the dynamic and ongoing interaction of state and ethnic groups and their reciprocal impact form the core of the explanation in this book.

Thoughts About Policy Implications

It is customary that authors end a book of this sort with some policy prescriptions, reasoning why they prefer some solutions over others. Indeed, a small number of academics have tried to propose ways for dealing with state-minority relations. Those with accommodationist inclinations have suggested solutions that range from institutional autonomy to the PAI to further liberalization of Israel's regime to reconstructing Israel as a civic state with a supranational identity.[3] Some take into consideration the broader context of the Palestinian-Israeli conflict and propose a single binational state in the whole of mandatory Palestine.[4]

Whichever policy prescription one finds most normatively appealing, however, real-life political constraints cannot be wished away from the debate. Israeli policymakers, on whom implementation of any relevant policy is dependent, have been far less giving than the accommodationist scholars. For the Israeli right and many on the Israeli left, Israel's Jewish identity is a nonnegotiable principle. In 2009, Prime Minister Binyamin Netanyahu introduced Palestinian recognition in Israel as a Jewish state as a precondition for the establishment of a Palestinian state in the West Bank and Gaza. In the 2009 elections, Yisrael Beytenu, the political party headed by Avigdor Lieberman, ran on a platform that made ethnic demands on the Arab minority and demanded that citizenship in Israel be conditioned on publicly swearing allegiance to the Jewish state. The party slogan "Rak Lieberman Medaber Aravit" (Only Lieberman Speaks Arabic) was meant to stress that this party knew best "the appropriate response" to PAI ethnonationalism. Lieberman's party won 11.7 percent of the vote, becoming the third largest faction in the Knesset. Subsequently, Lieberman became Israel's foreign minister.

On top of that, at the time of writing, the regional Palestinian-Israeli conflict appears to remain as intractable as ever and PAI ethnonational demands as well as their expressions of support toward their co-nationals in the West Bank are received with great suspicion by most Israeli Jews. Even on the center-left, there is little patience for Palestinian national demands in Israel. When serving as Israel's foreign minister, Tzipi Livni of the centrist Kadima

Party, who supports a two-state solution to the Palestinian-Israeli conflict, claimed that the national demands of all Palestinians should be satisfied with the creation of a Palestinian state in the West bank and Gaza. To the dismay of many PAI politicians and intellectuals, she reportedly stated that "it must be clear to everyone that the State of Israel is a national homeland of the Jewish people."[5] The response from PAI politicians and intellectual elites was incensed. And even Labor Prime Minister Ehud Barak chose to overlook the PAI in his policies during his short tenure as prime minister (1999–2001) so as not to alienate some of his coalition partners.[6]

Thus, while ideal solutions can be contemplated in abstraction, the reality of Israeli politics, and particularly the dynamics of intra-Jewish politics, makes accommodating the minority unlikely in the foreseeable future. Although nothing is inevitable, many of the causes behind the exacerbation of ethnic tensions in the first place are also responsible for reducing the prospects of future accommodation. The institutional framework provides incentives for hardening positions, not softening them. The Israeli polity is fragmented and the central government is usually too weak to impose a far-reaching solution. The Jewish majority is internally divided and the Israeli electoral system produces numerous parties. Israeli governments typically include six or more political parties, any one of which can bolt the coalition at any point and help bring down the government. The political institutions of the central government provide opportunities for small groups of interested parties to block concessions and significant policy change toward the minority such that even a willing prime minister would be hard pressed to pursue a policy of rapprochement. Hence, as long as the current overarching state-society framework persists, Jewish-Palestinian tensions in Israel (and beyond) are likely to remain intractable. Yet, as the conflict endures, PAI ethnonational political activism intensifies, and with it come increasing minority claims and demands.

Notes

Introduction

1. Lustick, *Arabs in the Jewish State.*

2. The Minorities at Risk Project (MAR) was founded by Ted Robert Gurr at the University of Maryland in 1986. The project produced the most extensive database available on more than 280 politically active minorities in the world, and categorizes them according to their status and political action. See http://www.cidcm.umd.edu/mar/data. asp, accessed 31 July 2010.

3. Different schools of thought offer diverse explanations. For an anthropological-primordialist perspective, see Geertz, *Old Societies and New States.* For a variety of constructivist perspectives, see Gurr, *Why Men Rebel*; D. Horowitz, *Ethnic Groups in Conflict*; Meadwell, "Cultural and Instrumental Approaches to Ethnic Nationalism"; Brass, *Ethnicity and Nationalism*; Gurr and Harff, *Ethnic Conflict in World Politics*; Fearon and Laitin, "Explaining Interethnic Cooperation"; Forbes, *Ethnic Conflict*; Hale, *The Foundations of Ethnic Politics.* For a sociobiological perspective, see Berghe, *The Ethnic Phenomenon.*

4. D. Horowitz, *Ethnic Groups in Conflict*, 291–332.

5. Adalah, *The Democratic Constitution*; National Committee for the Heads of the Arab Local Authorities in Israel, *The Future Vision of the Palestinian Arabs in Israel*; Y. Jabareen, *An Equal Constitution for All?*; Mada al-Carmel, *The Haifa Declaration.*

6. Stern, "Arab Rights Group Seeks 'Supranational Regime in All of Historic Palestine."

7. For example, Carmon, "Appeal to the Arabs of Israel"; Shamir, "An Open Letter to the Authors of the Future Vision"; Stern, "Council for Peace and Security Nixes Israeli Arab 'Vision' Document"; Sagi and Stern, "We Are Not Strangers in Our Homeland." Analyst Ze'ev Schiff denounced the proposals as "irredentist" in "Self-Inflicted Injury."

8. Yoaz and Khourie, "Shin Bet."

9. Among the most outspoken exceptions is minister of foreign affairs and former minister of strategic affairs Avigdor Lieberman, who proposed that Arab populated areas in Israel be transferred to the Palestinian Authority in exchange for Jewish settlements in the West Bank in any final agreement. See the Yisrael Beytenu party platform, http:// www.yisraelbeytenu.com, accessed 29 July 2010. Distinguished Israeli political scientist Shlomo Avineri, an Israel Prize laureate, suggested that a referendum take place in PAI

areas adjacent to the Green Line whereby the PAI inhabitants would be asked whether they want to be annexed to the Palestinian state; Shlomo Avineri, "Umm al-Fahm Tekhila." See also Biger, "The Only Solution That Will Work."

10. Rouhana and Ghanem, "The Crisis of Minorities in Ethnic States," 321–346.

11. Lustick, *Arabs in the Jewish State*, 47–51; Kimmerling and Migdal, *The Palestinian People*, 169–80; Rabinowitz and Abu Bakr, *Coffins on Our Shoulders*; al-Haj, *Education, Empowerment and Control*, 18–19; Ghanem, *The Palestinian Arab Minority in Israel*, 17–21.

12. Lustick, *Arabs in the Jewish State*.

13. Ghanem, *The Palestinian Arab Minority in Israel*, 18–19; Rouhana, *Palestinian Citizens in an Ethnic Jewish State*, 39–42; Peretz, *Israel and the Palestine Arabs*, 112–18.

14. For more on MAR, see note 2, also the project website, http://www.cidcm.umd.edu/mar, accessed 31 July 2010.

15. Rekhes, "The Evolvement of an Arab Palestinian Minority in Israel."

16. Rouhana, *Palestinian Citizens in an Ethnic Jewish State*, 113.

17. Haklai, "Palestinian NGOs in Israel"; Payes, *Palestinian NGOs in Israel*.

18. According to one prominent leader, the PAI situation resembles that of "native Americans or American Indians." See Amouyal, "We Are at a Crossroads," 280.

19. Farah, author interview; H. Jabareen, author interview.

20. Rouhana, *Palestinian Citizens in an Ethnic Jewish State*; Louër, *To Be an Arab in Israel*; Jamal, "The Counter-Hegemonic Role of Civil Society"; Jamal, *The Arab Public Sphere in Israel*.

21. Bob, *The Marketing of Rebellion*; Keating and McGarry, "Introduction"; Kymlicka, *Multicultural Odysseys*; Tarrow, *The New Transnational Activism*, 183–200; Tsutsui, "Global Civil Society and Ethnic Social Movements in the Contemporary World."

22. Brusis, "The European Union"; Kelley, *Ethnic Politics in Europe*.

23. Kymlicka, *Multicultural Odysseys*, 4.

24. Brusis, "The European Union"; H. Morris, "EU Enlargement and Latvian Citizenship Policies"; Csergo, *Talk of the Nation*, 3–5.

25. See, for example, Smooha, *Arabs and Jews in Israel*, 3–17; Kaufman, *Arab National Communism in the Jewish State*, 11–13.

26. Amouyal, "We Are at a Crossroads."

27. Rouhana, *Palestinian Citizens in an Ethnic Jewish State*, 113–14.

28. Brubaker, *Ethnicity Without Groups*.

29. Smooha, "Minority Status in an Ethnic Democracy"; Smooha, "Ethnic Democracy: Israel as an Archetype"; Peled, "Ethnic Democracy and Legal Construction of Citizenship."

30. Ghanem, Rouhana, and Yiftachel, "'Questioning 'Ethnic Democracy'"; Yiftachel, "'Ethnocracy' and its Discontents"; Yifchatel, *Ethnocracy*. See also Peled and Navot, "Ethnic Democracy Revisited."

31. Dowty, "Is Israel Democratic?"

32. Gavizon, "Jewish and Democratic? A Rejoinder."

33. Barnett, "The Politics of Uniqueness."

34. King, Keohane, and Verba, *Designing Social Inquiry*, 91–94.

35. Ibid., 227.

Chapter 1. Transitions in Minority Political Activism, Grievances, and Institutional Configurations

1. Peled, *Class and Ethnicity in the Pale*; Lynn, "The Creation and Recreation of Ethnicity"; Bonacich, "Class Approaches to Ethnicity and Race"; D. Horowitz, *Ethnic Groups in Conflict*, 141–228; Gurr, *Why Men Rebel*.

2. For example, Rouhana, *Palestinian Citizens in an Ethnic Jewish State*; Louër, *To Be an Arab in Israel*; Jamal, "The Counter-Hegemonic Role of Civil Society" and *The Arab Public Sphere in Israel*.

3. See Skocpol, "Bringing the State Back In"; Evans, Reuschemeyer, and Skocpol, eds., *Bringing the State Back In*.

4. Haklai, "Religious-Nationalist Mobilization and State Penetration."

5. For indicators of state autonomy from economic interests, see Johnson, "Political Institutions and Economic Performance," 138–39; Kohli, *The State and Poverty in India*, 9–10.

6. Brown, "Ethnic Revival: Perspectives on State and Society," 13.

7. Brubaker, *Nationalism Reframed*, 4–7.

8. Csergo, *Talk of the Nation*; Krasatkina and Beresneviciute, "Ethnic Structure, Inequality, and Governance of the Public Sector in Lithuania"; Galbreath and Rose, *Fair Treatment in a Divided Society*.

9. Csergo, *Talk of the Nation*.

10. Fearon and Laitin observe that even in regions that are especially rife with ethnic tensions, such as the post-Soviet world, cooperation is far more common than violence. See "Explaining Interethnic Cooperation."

11. See, for example, Yack, "The Myth of the Civic Nation," 104–5; Nielsen, "Cultural Nationalism, Neither Ethnic Nor Civil," 124–26.

12. D. Horowitz, "Irredentas and Secessions, 10–12; Roudometof, "The Consolidation of National Minorities in Southeastern Europe"; Saideman and Ayres, "Determining the Causes of Irredentism."

13. Kymlicka, *Multicultural Citizenship*, 36–37.

14. Breuilly, *Nationalism and the State*.

15. Brubaker, *Nationalism Reframed*, 5–6.

16. Kohli, "Can Democracies Accommodate Ethnic Nationalism?"

17. Haklai, "A Minority Rule over a Hostile Majority."

18. McGarry and O'Leary, *The Northern Ireland Conflict*.

19. For socioeconomic-based explanations, see, for example, Peled, *Class and Eth-*

nicity in the Pale; Lynn, "The Creation and Recreation of Ethnicity," 17–37; Bonacich, "Class Approaches to Ethnicity and Race"; Fox, Aull, and Cimino, "Ethnic Nationalism and the Welfare State." For social psychology approaches, see D. Horowitz, *Ethnic Groups in Conflict*, 141–228; Gurr, *Why Men Rebel*; Gurr and Harff, *Ethnic Conflict in World Politics*; Brass, *Ethnicity and Nationalism*.

20. Gurr, *Peoples Versus States*, 163.

21. Examples include al-Haj, *Arab Local Government in Israel*; Haidar, *On the Margins*; Peled, *Class and Ethnicity in the Pale*; Yiftachel, "'Ethnocracy' and Its Discontents."

22. Lichbach, "An Evaluation of 'Does Economic Inequality Breed Political Conflict?' Studies," 465.

23. Roeder, "Soviet Federalism and Ethnic Mobilization."

24. Ghanem, *The Palestinian Arab Minority in Israel*, 25.

25. Israel Central Bureau of Statistics, *The Arab Population in Israel*, 6–8.

26. In 1995, Ali Abed Yihyia was appointed the first Arab-Israeli ambassador; in 2005, Oscar Abu Razek was named first Arab director-general of the Interior Ministry; in 2004, Salim Jubran was selected as the first Arab judge to hold a permanent appointment in Israel's Supreme Court.

27. See D. Horowitz, *Ethnic Groups in Conflict*, 141–228.

28. For more on theories of the social psychology behind group comparisons, see Allport, *The Nature of Prejudice*; Brewer and Miller, *Intergroup Relations*; Runciman, *Relative Deprivation and Social Justice*; Tajfel and Turner, "The Social Identity Theory of Intergroup Behavior."

29. Rouhana, *Palestinian Citizens in an Ethnic Jewish State*; Ghanem, *The Palestinian Arab Minority in Israel*, 25–27.

30. Smooha, *The Orientation and Politicization of the Arab Minority in Israel*, 77–85; Ghanem and Lazar, *A Year After the October Events*, 30–36.

31. Peres, "Modernization and Nationalism of the Israeli Arab."

32. Smooha, *Arabs and Jews in Israel*, 156.

33. Smooha, *The Orientation and Politicization of the Arab Minority in Israel*, 27.

34. Ghanem and Ozacky-Lazar, *A Year After the October Events*, 34–36.

35. Israel Central Bureau of Statistics, *The Arab Population in Israel*, 6–8.

36. Tarrow, *Power in Movement*, 15.

37. McCarthy and Zald, "The Trends of Social Movements in America."

38. See, for example, Barth, *Ethnic Groups and Boundaries, and The Role of the Entrepreneur in Social Change in Northern Norway*; Brass, *Ethnicity and Nationalism*; Barreto, "Constructing Identities"; Snyder, *From Voting to Violence*.

39. Kaufman, *Arab National Communism in the Jewish State*; Jamal, "The Arab Leadership in Israel."

40. Migdal, *Through the Lens of Israel*, 6–15.

41. Lemarchand, *Burundi*.

42. Alford and Friedman, *Powers of Theory*, 275.

43. Skocpol, "Bringing the State Back In."

44. Some of the most influential works of New Institutionalism include North, *Institutions, Institutional Change and Economic Performance*; Hall, *Governing the Economy*; Pierson, *Dismantling the Welfare State*, and "Increasing Returns, Path Dependence and the Study of Politics"; Weaver and Rockman, eds., *Do Institutions Matter?*; Hall and Taylor, "Political Science and the Three New Institutionalisms."

45. Important works in the ethnic conflict literature to integrate institutionalist analysis include Bertrand, *Nationalism and Ethnic Conflict in Indonesia*; Brown, "Ethnic Revival: Perspectives on State and Society"; Brubaker, *Nationalism Reframed*; Esman, "The State and Language Policy"; Harty, "The Institutional Foundations of Substate National Movements"; S. Horowitz, "Explaining Post-Soviet Ethnic Conflicts."

46. Brubaker, *Nationalism Reframed*.

47. Smooha, *The Orientation and Politicization of the Arab Minority in Israel*, 47–50.

48. Ghanem and Ozacky-Lazar, *A Year After the October Events*, 34–45; Rouhana, *Palestinian Citizens in an Ethnic Jewish State*, 113.

49. Migdal, *Through the Lens of Israel*, 56–59.

50. Lecours, "Theorizing Cultural Identities." See also Harty, "The Institutional Foundations of Substate National Movements."

51. D. Horowitz, *Ethnic Groups in Conflict*, 291–440.

52. Migdal, *Strong Societies and Weak States*, and *State in Society*.

53. Enloe, *Police, Military and Ethnicity*; Tarrow, *Power in Movement*.

54. Cordesman and Hashim, Iraq, 44–56; Haklai, "A Minority Rule over a Hostile Majority"; Milne, *Politics in Ethnically Bipolar States*, 106–33.

55. North, *Institutions, Institutional Change and Economic Performance*.

56. Skocpol, *States and Social Revolutions*; Evans et al., eds., *Bringing the State Back In*.

57. For example, Skocpol and Crowley, "The Rush to Organize."

58. Migdal, Kohli, and Shue, eds., *State Power and Social Forces*. See also Migdal, *State in Society*.

59. Migdal, *State in Society*.

60. Bertrand, *Nationalism and Ethnic Conflict in Indonesia*, 10.

61. Mann, "The Autonomous Power of the State."

62. Migdal, *Strong Societies and Weak States*, and *State in Society*.

63. North, *Institutions, Institutional Change and Economic Performance*, 3–10.

64. Ibid.

65. Bertrand, *Nationalism and Ethnic Conflict in Indonesia*, 20–27.

66. For a discussion on the empowerment of the judiciary as a result of internal contestations, see Gad Barzilai, "Courts as Hegemonic Institutions"; Hirschl, *Towards Juristocracy*; Woods, *Judicial Power and National Politics*.

67. See, for example, Epp, *The Rights Revolution*; Posner, "The Political Salience of Cultural Difference," 535–37; Tarrow, *Power in Movement*, 123–24.

68. Wickham, *Mobilizing Islam*.

69. Migdal, *Through the Lens of Israel*, 6–15.

70. Elster, *Sour Grapes*, 109–40.

71. For a review of ethnic outbidding theories, see Chandra, "Ethnic Parties and Democratic Stability."

72. For a comprehensive discussion of Mapa'i's control of various aspects of Israel's society, economy, and political institutions, see Aharoni, "The Changing Political Economy of Israel"; Eisenstadt, *Israeli Society*; Kimmerling, *The Invention and Decline of Israeliness*; Shafir and Peled, *Being Israeli*, 37–73; Sternhell, *The Founding Myths of Israel*, 318–45. The characteristic of centralized control in the hands of Mapa'i is sometimes pushed too far in the literature. The ruling party had to strike several important compromises that produced sectoral authorities, particularly in the areas of education and family law where compromises with religious political forces were made.

73. Kaufman, *Arab National Communism in the Jewish State*, 28–32.

74. Annual surveys conducted by Mada al-Carmel: Arab Center for Applied Social Research reveal that the PAI are pessimistic about their future status in Israel. Available online at http://www.mada-research.org/sru/ann_survey.shtml, accessed 16 May 2009.

75. Harris and Doron, "Assessing the Electoral Reform of 1992."

76. Barzilai, "Courts as Hegemonic Institutions," 15–33; Hirschl, "The Political Origins of Judicial Empowerment Through Constitutionalization."

77. Aharoni, "The Changing Political Economy of Israel," 127–46.

78. Haklai, "Religious-Nationalist Mobilization and State Penetration."

Chapter 2. State Formation and the Creation of National Boundaries

1. One notable exception is Migdal, *Through the Lens of Israel*.

2. See Bertrand, *Nationalism and Ethnic Conflict in Indonesia*.

3. Shin, *The Making of the Chinese State*.

4. Haklai, "A Minority Rule over a Hostile Majority;" O'Leary and Salih, "The Denial, Resurrection, and Affirmation of Kurdistan"; Nakash, *The Shi'is of Iraq*.

5. Marx, "The Nation-State and Its Exclusions," 110.

6. Gellner, *Nations and Nationalism*; Greenfeld, *Nationalism*.

7. Kaufmann and Haklai, "Dominant Ethnicity."

8. Marx, "The Nation-State and Its Exclusions," 103; see also Marx, *Faith in Nation*.

9. Wilson, Address of the President of the United States.

10. O'Leary, "The Elements of Right-Sizing and Right-Peopling the State."

11. Shin, *The Making of the Chinese State*, 1.

12. Peleg, *Democratizing the Hegemonic State*.

13. Herzl, *The State of the Jews*.

14. Kedourie, *Nationalism*, 62–76; Shimoni, *The Zionist Ideology*, 5–56.

15. This objective is apparent in many of the writings of leading Zionists. See, for

example, Ben-Gurion, *From Class to Nation*, 209–11; Lileinblum, "Let Us Not Confuse the Issues," 170–73; Nardau, "Zionism," 242–45; Ginsberg, "Past and Future" and "The Spiritual Revival"; Dinaburg, *The Love of Zion*, 18; Cohen, *A Short History of Zionism*, 13–15; Avineri, *The Making of Modern Zionism*, 198–216.

16. See, for example, *Haolam* (6 January 1931): 13–14; (13 January 1931): 27.

17. The principle of "ownership by the people" is stipulated in "Covenant Between the State of Israel and Keren Kayemeth LeIsrael," 28 November 1961. The covenant can be found on the JNF Website: http://www.kkl.org.il.

18. See, for example, Sternhell, *Nation Building or a New Society?* 188–89.

19. See, for example, Ben-Gurion, *From Class to Nation*, 14; Dinaburg, *The Love of Zion*, 11. See also Sternhell, *The Founding Myths of Israel*, 15–16.

20. *Haolam* (13 January 1931), 26–27. See also Sternhell, *The Founding Myths of Israel*, 325, 335.

21. Horowitz and Lissak, *Origins of the Israeli Polity*, 23, 37–68.

22. Eisenstadt, *Israeli Society*, 24–26.

23. For an elaborate review of the Jewish Agency and its establishment, organizations, and functions in the prestate period, see Eilam, *The Jewish Agency*.

24. For relevant Zionist ideals, see Ginsburg, "The Spiritual Revival"; Ben-Yehuda, "A Letter of Ben Yehuda," 160–65; Ben-Gurion, *From Class to Nation*. For a discussion of the creation of a collective tradition, see Zerubavel, *Recovered Roots*.

25. For the 1880 ratio, see Arian, *Politics in Israel*, 19. For the number of Arabs residing in Palestine, see Gilbert, *The Arab-Israeli Conflict*, 3. For the proportion of Jews living in Israel in 1948, see Israel Central Bureau of Statistics, http://www.cbs.gov.il/hodaot, 2002/01, accessed April 2002.

26. Horowitz and Lissak, *Origins of the Israeli Polity*, 24.

27. Ibid., 44.

28. Dowty, *The Jewish State*, 45–46.

29. These election results were published in *Haolam* (13 January 1931); 33 (27 January 1931): 85.

30. Schiff, *A History of the Israeli Army*, 1–15; Haver and Schiff, *Lexicon for Israel Security*, 151–56.

31. Arian, *Politics in Israel*, 53–54.

32. Sternhell, *Nation Building*, 388.

33. Aharoni, "The Changing Political Economy of Israel," 131.

34. *Haolam* (13 January 1931), 33.

35. For the number of Histadrut members, see Sternhell, Nation Building, 387–88. For the number of Jews in Palestine, see American Jewish Committee, *American Jewish Year Book* 42 (1940–1941): 604.

36. Migdal, *Through the Lens of Israel*, 64–68.

37. Sternhell, *Nation Building*, 340.

38. Taking issue with what they perceived as an excessively reconciliatory policy by the mainstream organized Jewish community and advocating a firmer militant stance,

the Revisionists split away in the 1930s, and formed their separate paramilitary body, the Irgun Tzvai Leumi (National Military Organization).

39. The British and French declared that the purpose of their war against the Ottomans was to emancipate the indigenous populations and assist them in establishing national governments. The Balfour Declaration, a letter sent by British Foreign Secretary Lord Arthur James Balfour to Lord Rothschild, a leading figure in the Zionist movement, expressed commitment to a national Jewish home in Palestine. In the 1915–1916 McMahon-Husayn Correspondence, Sir Henry McMahon wrote on behalf of the British government, which was trying to enlist the support of Arab nationalists during World War I, to Sharif Husayn of Mecca, promising Arab control over the vast majority of the areas to be conquered from the Turks. The expectations of both sides and demands that the British fulfill the commitments made in these documents were reflected in the Palestine Royal Commission *Report*, 25.

40. Examples include, but are not limited to, Horowitz and Lissak, *Origins of the Israeli Polity*; Migdal, *Strong Societies and Weak States*, 142–73; B. Smith, *The Roots of Separatism in Palestine*; Kimmerling and Migdal, *The Palestinian People*, 76–131; B. Morris, *Righteous Victims*; Khalidi, *The Iron Cage*; Shlaim, *The Politics of Partition*.

41. Migdal, *Through the Lens of Israel*, 35. See also Horowitz and Lissak, *Origins of the Israeli Polity*, 19.

42. Horowitz and Lissak, *Origins of the Israeli Polity*, 33. See also B. Smith, *The Roots of Separatism in Palestine*, for the British economic policies that facilitated separation.

43. Kimmerling, "State Building, State Autonomy and the Identity of Society," 400.

44. Eisenstadt, *Israeli Society*, 24.

45. Muslih, *The Origins of Palestinian Nationalism*, 131–90; Talhami, *Syria and the Palestinians*, 1–13; Kimmerling and Migdal, *The Palestinian People*, 82. For a comprehensive account of the social make-up of the Palestine Arab nationalist elite, see Nashif, *The Palestine Arab and Jewish Political Leadership*, 25–58.

46. Kimmerling and Migdal, *The Palestinian People*, 76–86.

47. See Brass, *Ethnicity and Nationalism*; Smith, *The Ethnic Origins of Nations*.

48. Sulaiman, *Palestine and Modern Arab Poetry*, 17–41.

49. B. Smith, *The Roots of Separatism*, 14.

50. Government of Palestine, *Survey of Palestine*, 1945–1946, 1: 154. Cited in Horowitz and Lissak, *Origins of the Israeli Polity*, 20.

51. Salim Tamari, "Factionalism and Class Formation in Recent Palestinian History."

52. For more on hamula politics during the Ottoman period, see Hourani, "Ottoman Reform and the Politics of Notables."

53. Tamari, "Factionalism and Class Formation," 191.

54. Among the most important elite hamulas were al-Khatib, al-Khaldi, Nussiebeh, Nashashibi, and Husayni (all based in Jerusalem); al-Amr, al-Tamimi, al-Tahbub, and al-Ja'bari (al-Halil/Hebron); al-Shawa and al-Husayni (unrelated to the Jerusalem hamula; Gaza), al-Taji and al-Ghusayn (Ramle); Tukan and Abd al-Hadi (Nablus); al-Haj

Ibrahim (Tul Karem); Abd al-Hadi and 'Abushi (Jenin); al-Shuqayri and Khalifa (Acre); and al-Fahum, al-Dahr, and Bashara (Nazareth). Shimoni, *Arabs of Israel*, 211–39.

55. Kimmerling and Migdal, *The Palestinian People*, 82–86.

56. B. Smith, *The Roots of Separatism*, 13–16.

57. Between 1920 and 1938, the Jewish population increased by approximately 500 percent, the Arab population by only about 50 percent, roughly 90 percent due to natural growth. Palestine Royal Commission, *Report*, 125.

58. Swedenburg, "The Role of the Palestinian Peasantry in the Great Revolt (1936–1939)."

59. Porath, *The Emergence of the Palestinian-Arab National Movement*, and *The Palestinian Arab National Movement*.

60. Kimmerling and Migdal, *The Palestinian People*, 89–90.

61. See, for example, Tamari "Factionalism and Class Formation," 191–99; Swedenburg, "The Role of the Palestinian Peasantry in the Great Revolt (1936–1939)"; Kimmerling and Migdal, *The Palestinian People*, 97–131.

62. Kimmerling and Migdal, *The Palestinian People*, 111–27.

63. Arian, *Politics in Israel*, 27.

64. Palestine Royal Commission, *Report*, 359–60.

65. Ibid., 380–97.

66. Ben-Gurion's reasoning about partition and the constraints facing the aspirations of the Zionists can be found in Ben-Gurion, *Letters to Paula*, 118, 126–36. For an elaboration on Ben-Gurion's considerations, see also Bar-Zohar *Ben-Gurion*, 355–68.

67. Palestine Royal Commission, *Report*, 130–33, 143.

68. Ibid., 141.

69. For an extensive overview of the Supreme Muslim Council in Mandatory Palestine, see Kupferschmidt, *The Supreme Muslim Council*.

70. Gilbert, *The Arab-Israeli Conflict*, 50.

71. B. Morris, *The Birth of the Palestinian Refugee Problem*, 1947–1949, 2; Gilbert, *The Arab-Israeli Conflict*, 47.

72. Israel Central Bureau of Statistics, *The Arab Population in Israel*, 2

73. Sternhell, *The Founding Myths of Israel*, 319.

Chapter 3. State Autonomy, Marginalization, and Grievances

1. Eisenstadt, *Israeli Society*; Kimmerling, "State Building, State Autonomy and the Identity of Society."

2. Kimmerling, "State Building, State Autonomy and the Identity of Society," 406.

3. Dowty, *The Jewish State*, 62–73.

4. For the procedural criteria of a democracy and the inclusion of Israel in this category, see Dahl, *Polyarchy, Participation*, 3–9, 248. See also Lijphart, *Democracies*, 2–38, and "Democracies: Forms, Performance, and Constitutional Engineering."

5. Stock, *Chosen Instrument*, 13.

6. Arian, *Politics in Israel*, 51.

7. Aharoni, "The Changing Political Economy of Israel," 131. See also Peled and Navot, "Ethnic Democracy Revisited," 8.

8. Provisional Government of Israel, *Declaration of the Establishment of the State of Israel*.

9. Dowty, *The Jewish State*, 187.

10. Kretzmer, *The Legal Status of the Arabs in Israel*, 21.

11. Ben-Gurion, *Israel: A Personal History*, 348.

12. Picard, "Immigration, Health and Social Control."

13. American Jewish Committee, *American Jewish Year Book* 52 (1951), 195–96; 57 (1956), 291–95; 67 (1967), 471–74; 77 (1977), 515–18; 87 (1987), 418; 96 (1996), 518; 106 (2006), 559.

14. Robinson, "Occupied Citizens in a Liberal State," 39–182.

15. Peretz, *Israel and the Palestine Arabs*, 123.

16. Israel Government, *Government Yearbook*, 236.

17. Israel Central Bureau of Statistics, *Statistical Abstracts of Israel* 52 (2001), Table 1.1.

18. Arian, *Politics in Israel*, 31.

19. Israel Central Bureau of Statistics, *Statistical Abstracts of Israel* 52 (2001), Table 1.1.

20. The covenant can be read on the JNF website, http://www.kkl.org.il/kkl/english/main_subject/about_kkl/a_amana.htm. Initially under the Ministry of Agriculture, the ILA has been transferred several times to other ministries.

21. Basic Law: Israel Lands (1960). The complete text of the law is available on the Israeli Knesset website, http://www.knesset.gov.il/laws/special/eng/basic13_eng.htm

22. Lustick, *Arabs in the Jewish State*, 181–82; Kretzmer, *The Legal Status of Arabs in Israel*, 62.

23. Peretz, *Israel and the Palestine Arabs*, 90–91.

24. Benziman and Mansour, *Sub-Tenants—The Arabs of Israel*, 11–32.

25. Israel Central Bureau of Statistics, *The Arab Population in Israel*, 4.

26. This mode of reasoning can be identified in the writings of Israel's second prime minister, Levi Eshkol. See Eshkol, *The Enterprise of Settlement*, 200–206.

27. Ibid. See also Kimmerling and Migdal, *The Palestinian People*, 173.

28. Yiftachel, "The Internal Frontier."

29. Haidar, *On the Margins*, 44; Shafir and Peled, *Being Israeli*, 113; Kimmerling, *Zionism and Territory*, 140. While these are estimates only, there is general agreement among researchers that the PAI lost the vast majority of the land they held in 1948. See also Kretzmer, *The Legal Status*, 49–76; Lustick, *Arabs in the Jewish State*, 170–82; Zureik, *The Palestinians in Israel*.

30. Yiftachel, *Planning a Mixed Region in Israel*, 169.

31. Lustick, *Arabs in the Jewish State*, 99.

32. Yiftachel and Rumley, "On the Impact of Israel's Judaization Policy in the Galilee," 289.

33. Lustick, *Arabs in the Jewish State*, 179–80.

34. Mandelkern, "Water Allocation Policy in Israel"; Forman and Kedar, "From Arab Lands to 'Israel Lands.'"

35. Landau, *The Arabs in Israel*, 19.

36. Meir and Zivan, "Sociocultural Encounter on the Frontier."

37. Cohen and Susser, *Israel and the Politics of Jewish Identity*; Liebman, "Religion and Democracy in Israel."

38. Marx, *Faith in Nation*, 25–29.

39. The proportions were calculated on the basis of data taken from Israel Central Bureau of Statistics, *Statistical Abstracts of Israel* 56 (2005), 29, Table 2.1.

40. A. Peled, *Debating Islam in the Jewish State*, 3.

41. Peretz, *Israel and the Palestine Arabs*, 126.

42. A. Peled, *Debating Islam in the Jewish State*.

43. Aharoni, "The Changing Political Economy of Israel," 130.

44. Ben-Eliezer, "A Nation in Arms."

45. Levy, *From "People's Army" to "Army of the Peripheries."*

46. Ibid.; see also B. Morris, *The Birth of the Palestinian Refugee Problem, 1947–1949*, 237–53; Peri, *Generals in the Cabinet Room*.

47. Moshe Dayan provides an excellent example of how high-ranked military figures play a significant role in setting policy and how their role extends beyond the army and into the fields of diplomacy and public life. In 1949, while still in uniform, he participated in the armistice talks with the Jordanians in Rhodes Island, Greece. As chief of staff, he pushed in 1956 for Israel's invasion of the Sinai Peninsula. Having retired from the army in 1958, he joined Mapa'i and served as a cabinet minister in a number of ministerial posts, including Agriculture and Defense. Likewise, Yigal Alon served as a cabinet minister in a number of Mapa'i-led governments, in ministries such as Education and Immigration and Absorption.

48. Rosenhek describes the use of the welfare state to intensify Arab inferiority in "The Exclusionary Logic of the Welfare State." See also Haidar, *Needs and Welfare Services in the Arab Sector in Israel*.

49. al-Haj, *Education, Empowerment, and Control*; al-Haj and Rosenfeld, *Arab Local Government in Israel*.

50. Sikkuy, the Association for the Advancement of Civic Equality in Israel, *The Sikkuy Report 2002–2003*, 33.

51. Sikkuy, Press Release, 8 November 2000.

52. Jamal Zahalka, an outspoken PAI MK from Balad, reportedly labeled Arab volunteers to national service "lepers." Editorial, *Ha'aretz*, "Lepers?"

53. Ben-Eliezer, "Rethinking the Civil-Military Relations Paradigm."

54. Surveys conducted by the Tami Steinmetz Institute for Peace Research demon-

strate that of all of Israel's institutions, the Jewish public has the most faith in the army. Faith in the army is particularly high during periods of intense conflict. See, for example, the survey of February 2001. http://www.spirit.tau.ac.il/socant/peace/peaceindex/2001/data/february2001d.pdf, accessed August 2003.

55. Peri, *Generals in the Cabinet Room*, 77–90.

56. For a good comparison of civilian oversight over the armed forces in French Algeria and Israel, see Spruyt, *Ending Empire*, 88–116, 239–41.

57. Peri, *Generals in the Cabinet Room*, 77–90.

58. Smooha, "Minority Status in an Ethnic Democracy," 401.

59. Rates calculated using data published by National Insurance Institute of Israel, Department of Research and Planning, *The Trends in Poverty and Income Disparities in Israel in the Year 2000*, 12, 17, 19–21, 23.

60. This figure was taken from ILA online, http://www.mmi.gov.il, accessed 29 November 2002.

61. Yiftachel and Rumley, "On the Impact of Israel's Judaization Policy in the Galilee," 290.

62. Yiftachel, "The Internal Frontier"; See also, Rabinowitz, *Overlooking Nazareth*.

63. For comprehensive accounts of preference to Jewish neighborhoods in development and subtle transfers of land by the state, see Yiftachel, *Planning a Mixed Region in Israel*, and *Ethnocracy*.

64. Association of Forty website, http://www.assoc40.org/Unrecognized, accessed 18 August 2003.

65. Israel Central Bureau of Statistics, "Research on Characterization and Ranking of Local Authorities According to the Population's Socioeconomic Level."

66. The data are taken from American Jewish Committee, *American Jewish Year Book* 87 (1987), 418; 96 (1996), 518; 106 (2006), 559.

67. Bassok, "Israel at 61: Population Stands at 7.4 million, 75.5% Jewish."

68. *Ha'aretz*, 14 June 2002.

69. Rouhana, *Palestinian Citizens in an Ethnic Jewish State*, 66.

70. Alon, "Diskin."

71. Arian, *Politics in Israel*, 53.

72. Nitzan and Bichler, *The Global Political Economy of Israel*, 18–24.

73. Ettinger, "Number of Arab Directors Rises."

74. Sikkuy, *The Sikkuy Report 2002–2003*, Table 11, 33.

75. Sikkuy, *The Sikkuy Report 2004–2005*.

76. Ibid., 67.

77. The persistent gap in allocation of resources is well-documented in the Sikkuy annual reports; see the association's website, http://www.sikkuy.org.il/english/reports.html.

78. For a review of one version of this argument, see Peres, "Modernization and Nationalism of the Israeli Arab," 481.

79. Peretz, *Israel and the Palestine Arabs*, 131–35.

80. For 1955, see Israel Government, *Government Yearbook* (1955), 133–34; for 1948, see Peretz, *Israel and the Palestine Arabs*, 134.

81. Peretz, *Israel and the Palestine Arabs*, 121–39.

82. Peres, "Modernization and Nationalism of the Israeli Arab," 489.

83. Ibid., 491.

84. Lustick, *Arabs in the Jewish State*, 10–12.

85. Tibawi was a Palestinian born in Taibeh, which came under Israeli rule in 1948. He was in London at the time of the war; he remained there after the establishment of the state and considered himself a refugee.

86. Tibawi, "Visions of Return," 508–9.

87. Ibid., 509–11.

88. Darwish's personal experience is particularly relevant in this context. He fled to Lebanon during the 1947–1949 war; upon his return several years later, the state refused to grant him an identity card, questioning the legality of his presence in Israel.

89. The translation of this poem is taken from Nakhleh, "Wells of Bitterness," 33. This poem is also cited in Lustick, *Arabs in the Jewish State*, 11–12.

90. The translation of this poem is taken from Nakhleh, "Wells of Bitterness," 35–36.

91. Quoted in Kabha, "The Conspiracy and the Victim," 90–91.

92. For explanations focusing on the various ways in which the intelligentsia and intellectual elites are at the forefront of spreading national consciousness, see A. Smith, *The Ethnic Revival*; Elie Kedourie, *Nationalism*, 1–14. Benedict Anderson discusses how mass access to print matter and literature, which originated from the upper intellectual echelons of society, had an impact on national identity formation by providing masses with an image of themselves as a national community. See Anderson, *Imagined Communities*.

Chapter 4. From Quiescence to the Communist Party

1. Budeiri, *The Palestine Communist Party*, 3–13; Kaufman, *Arab National Communism in the Jewish State*, 24.

2. Budeiri, *The Palestine Communist Party*, 20, 41–68.

3. Ibid., 8; Nahas, *The Israeli Communist Party*, 18.

4. Budeiri, *The Palestine Communist Party*, 19–57.

5. Ibid., 27–34.

6. Nahas, *The Israeli Communist Party*, 25; see also Kaufman, *Arab National Communism in the Jewish State*, 23.

7. *Qol ha-Am* (4 September 1953), cited in Peretz, *Israel and the Palestine Arabs*, 107.

8. Knesset Israel, *Major Knesset Debates*, vol. 2, 622–23.

9. Peretz, *Israel and the Palestine Arabs*, 122–26.

10. Nahas, *The Israeli Communist Party*, 28, 42–48.

11. Ibid., 31.

12. Data available on the Israeli Knesset website, http://www.knesset.gov.il/faction/eng/FactionPage_eng.asp?PG=72

13. Following the 1967 War, the Jewish faction lost the sponsorship of the Soviets, who endorsed Rakah as the communist party in Israel.

14. This was an argument made by MK Twafik Toubi shortly prior to the split. For an elaboration on the debate leading to the split, see Nahas, *The Israeli Communist Party*, 55–72.

15. Kaufman, *Arab National Communism in the Jewish State*, 35–37.

16. Ghanem, *The Palestinian Arab Minority in Israel*, 84.

17. The MAR project classifies over 280 minority groups around the world, see http://www.cidcm.umd.edu/mar/. See also Introduction n 2.

18. Nahas, *The Israeli Communist Party*, 73.

19. Kaufman, *Arab National Communism in the Jewish State*, 54.

20. Stendel, *Arabs of Israel*, 215.

21. Ghanem, *The Palestinian Arab Minority*, 89–92.

22. The results of the 1965 elections are available on the Israel Knesset website, http://www.knesset.gov.il/description/eng/eng_mimshal_res6.htm.

23. Kaufman, *Arab National Communism in the Jewish State*, 92.

24. Rekhes, *The Arab Minority in Israel*, 52.

25. McCarthy and Zald, "Resource Mobilization and Social Movements: A Partial Theory"; McAdam, Tarrow, and Tilly, "Toward an Integrated Perspective on Social Movements and Revolutions," 147–48.

26. Kaufman, *Arab National Communism in the Jewish State*, 38–39.

27. Quoted in Kaufman, *Arab National Communism in the Jewish State*, 36.

28. Ibid., 47.

29. Ghanem, *The Palestinian Arab Minority*, 89–90.

30. Chetrit, *The Mizrahi Struggle in Israel*.

31. Knesset Israel, *Divrei HaKnesset*, vol. 84 (1978): 701–5.

32. Kaufman, *Arab National Communism in the Jewish State*, 39.

33. Ghanem, *The Palestinian Arab Minority*, 86–89.

34. Knesset Israel, *Major Knesset Debates*, Vol. 5, 2006–8.

35. Kaufman, *Arab National Communism in the Jewish State*, 102.

36. Rekhes, *The Arabs of the Galilee and the Land Expropriations*, 17; Payes, *Palestinian NGOs in Israel*, 75.

37. El-Taji, "Arab Local Authorities in Israel."

38. Kaufman, *Arab National Communism in the Jewish State*, 102–3.

39. Stendel, *Arabs of Israel*, 224.

40. Kaufman, *Arab National Communism in the Jewish State*, 51 and 98.

41. P. Smith, "Interview with Muhammad Kiwan."

42. Landau, *The Arab Minority in Israel 1967–1991*, 105–11.

43. Ibid., 106–7.

44. Haklai, "Palestinian NGOs in Israel."

45. Lustick, *Arabs in the Jewish State*.

46. Ibid., 79.

47. Ibid., 78.

48. Rouhana, *Palestinian Citizens in an Ethnic Jewish State*, 27.

49. See, for example, A. R. Peled, *Debating Islam in the Jewish State*; Robinson, "Occupied Citizens in a Liberal State."

50. Jiryis, *The Arabs in Israel*; Zureik, *The Palestinians in Israel*.

51. Lustick, *Arabs in the Jewish State*, 79.

52. Migdal, *Strong Societies and Weak States*, and *State in Society*.

53. Migdal, *State in Society*, 58–94.

54. Peri, "The Arab-Israeli Conflict and Israeli Democracy," 343–59.

55. Schwartz, *The Arabs in Israel*, 119.

56. *Ha'aretz* (26 October 1956), cited in Peretz, *Israel and the Palestine Arabs*, 138.

57. Peretz, *Israel and the Palestine Arabs*, 117.

58. Israel Central Bureau of Statistics, *Statistical Abstracts of Israel* 27 (1976): 279.

59. Landau, *The Arabs in Israel*, 92–95.

60. Ibid., 92–107; Jiryis, *The Arabs in Israel*.

61. Ben-Eliezer, *The Making of Israeli Militarism*, and "A Nation-in-Arms."

62. Lustick, *Arabs in the Jewish State*, 9.

63. Nasser and Nasser, "Textbooks as a Vehicle for Segregation and Domination: State Efforts to Shape Palestinian Israelis' Identities as Citizens."

64. al-Haj, *Education, Empowerment, and Control*, 153–71.

65. Ibid., 163.

66. See, for example, Medding, *The Founding of Israeli Democracy, 1948–1967*; Yanai, "Ben-Gurion's Concept of *Mamlachtyut* and the Forming Reality of the State of Israel"; Horowitz and Lissak, *Origins of the Israeli Polity*, 189–95.

67. Shafir and Peled, *Being Israeli*, 17–19, 53–73.

68. On the sociopolitical face of the military in the 1950s and 1960s, see Levy, *From "People's Army" to "Army of the Peripheries"*, 38–51; on economic elites, see Shafir and Peled, *Being Israeli*, 58.

69. The Civil Service Law, 1959, Clauses 1–3.

70. Kimmerling, "State Building, State Autonomy and the Identity of Society," 405.

71. For example, Ibid., 406; Arian, *Politics in Israel*, 48–49.

72. Shafir and Peled, *Being Israeli*, 58.

73. Aharoni, "The Changing Political Economy of Israel," 134.

74. Shafir and Peled, *Being Israeli*, 56.

75. Aharoni, "The Changing Political Economy," 132.

76. Ibid., 132–33.

77. Kimmerling, "State Building," 404–5; Shafir and Peled, *Being Israeli*, 56–66.

78. *Ha'aretz* (23 January 1955), quoted in Sternhell, *The Founding Myths of Israel*, 324.

79. Shafir and Peled, *Being Israeli*, 58.

80. Ben-Gurion, who served as prime minister from 1949 to 1954 and from 1955 to 1963, had a famous saying about his government coalitions, "Bli Herut ve-Maki" (with-

out the Revisionist Herut and the ICP). He ruled out the rightist Herut, the successor of the revisionists, because of their militancy and for breaking away from the organized Yishuv in the 1930s. The ICP was ruled out as a potential participant in coalition governments for its perceived support of Soviet-style communism.

81. For example, Cohen and Susser, *Israel and the Politics of Jewish Identity*, 21; Dowty, *The Jewish State*, 73–74.

82. B. Morris, *The Birth of the Palestinian Refugee Problem*, 50–51, 67, 70–110, 130.

83. Approximately 71 percent of those left were villagers. Tens of thousands had to relocate from one part of the country to another during the war. Peretz estimates the number of internally displaced people at 30,000, around 19 percent of the Arab population in Israel; *Israel and the Palestine Arabs*, 95.

84. Ibid., 128.

85. Peretz elaborates on the prevailing positive view in the Israeli press, Ibid., 128.

86. Stepan, *The State and Society*, 73–113.

87. Ibid., 79.

88. See, for example, Ibid; Ehteshami and Murphy, "The Transformation of the Corporatist State in the Middle East"; Hadiz, "State and Labor in the Early New Order."

89. Hourani, "Ottoman Reform and the Politics of Notables," 47–48; Miller, *Government and Society in Rural Palestine 1920–1948*, 32–89; Porath, "The Political Organization of the Palestinian Arabs Under the British Mandate," 2–3.

90. Lustick, *Arabs in the Jewish State*, 202–4.

91. Landau, *The Arabs in Israel*, 76–78, 137–40.

92. Lustick, *Arabs in the Jewish State*, 201–2.

93. Ibid., 205–6.

94. Peretz, *Israel and the Palestine Arabs*, 129.

95. al-Haj and Rosenfeld, *Arab Local Authorities in Israel*, 29–33.

96. El-Taji, "Arab Local Authorities in Israel," 115.

97. Ibid., 116.

98. Ibid., 132–33.

99. Ibid., 134.

100. See, for example, McAdam, McCarthy, and Zald, "Introduction."

101. The concept of international regimes is used here in conformity with Stephen Krasner's definition of "sets of implicit or explicit principles, norms, rules and decision-making procedures around which actors' expectations converge in a given area of international relations." Krasner, *International Regimes*, 2.

102. Examples include a letter dated 30 September 1965 from the permanent representative of the PLO in the UN through the permanent representative of Syria to the secretary general and a letter from Ellas Koussa, an Arab attorney from Haifa, dated November 1960, http://domino.un.org/UNISPAL.NSF, accessed January 2003. See also Jiryis, *The Arabs in Israel*, 319–22.

103. Knesset Israel, *Major Knesset Debates*, vol. 4, 1524.

104. Csergo, *Talk of the Nation*, 3–5.

105. Knesset Israel, *Major Knesset Debates*, vol. 4, 1524–26.

106. Knesset Israel, *Divrei HaKnesset*, vol. 33 (1962): 1321.

107. Knesset Israel, *Major Knesset Debates*, vol. 4, 1524.

108. *Ibid.*, 1523.

109. Caspi and Limor, *The Mediators*, 97.

110. Ibid., 99.

111. Ibid., 115–22.

112. Chetrit, *The Mizrahi Struggle in Israel*.

113. Development towns are small towns that were built mainly in the 1950s to settle the large wave of Jewish immigrants that fled from Arab countries following the 1948–1949 war. These towns were typically built in the periphery and did not provide sufficient employment opportunities for their inhabitants. The unemployment rates in these towns were generally higher than in the central urban areas. Lacking priority, the infrastructure in these places was often minimal and the state did not invest enough in education in these places to enable the youth to increase their access to opportunities.

114. Kimmerling, "State Building," 405.

115. Ibid., 407–8.

116. Arian, *The Second Republic*, 84.

117. Kimmerling, "State Building," 405.

118. These figures were taken from *Statistical Abstracts of Israel* 28 (1977), Table x/1, 234.

119. The data are taken from the Knesset website, http://www.knesset.gov.il/history.

120. For an extensive discussion of the dynamics of patron-client relations, see Clapham, "Clientelism and the State," 14–15.

121. Ibid., 7–8.

122. Arian, *Politics in Israel*, 56.

123. Aharoni, "The Changing Political Economy," 138–39.

124. Kimmerling, *The Invention and Decline of Israeliness*, 112–29, and *The End of the Ahusalim Rule*.

125. Martinussen, *State, Society and Market*, 194.

126. The Election Law, 1969, Clause 56; The Civil Service Law, 1959, Clauses 1–3.

127. Clapham, "Clientelism and the State," 12–13.

128. Stendel, *Arabs of Israel*, 290. The Likud reserved a slot on its candidate list for a Druze representative.

129. Smooha, *The Orientation and Politicization of the Arab Minority in Israel*, 30.

130. Ibid., 60.

131. Wallach and Lissak, *Carta's Atlas of Israel: The First Years*, 139.

132. The advantages for industries in Jewish populated regions would range from better access to transportation networks, allowing easier transfer of manufactured goods, to basic infrastructure, such as better hydro services.

133. Israel Central Bureau of Statistics, *Statistical Abstracts of Israel* 27 (1976): 299.

134. Wallach and Lissak, *Carta's Atlas of Israel: The Third Decade*, 22.

135. Israel Central Bureau of Statistics, *Statistical Abstracts of Israel* 52 (2001): 8–21.

136. Ibid., 8–25.

137. Wallach and Lissak, *Carta's Atlas of Israel: The Third Decade*, 20.

138. Ibid., 23.

139. Ibid.

140. Israel Central Bureau of Statistics, *Statistical Abstracts of Israel* 27 (1976): 279; Israel Central Bureau of Statistics, *Statistical Abstracts of Israel* 32 (1981): 311.

141. Tessler, "Israel's Arabs and the Palestinian Problem"; Smooha, *The Orientation and Politicization of the Arab Minority in Israel; Arabs and Jews in Israel*, vols. 1 and 2.

142. Smooha, *The Orientation and Politicization of the Arab Minority*, 49–50.

143. Ibid., 36.

144. Ibid., 87.

145. Ibid., 56–58.

146. Ibid., 49–71.

147. Ibid., 51.

148. Ibid., 57.

149. Ibid., 87.

150. McCarthy and Zald, "Resource Mobilization and Social Movements," 1212–41; McAdam, Tarrow, and Tilly, "Toward an Integrated Perspective on Social Movements and Revolutions," 147–48.

Chapter 5. The Ethnonational Turn

1. D. Horowitz, *The Deadly Ethnic Riot*, 1.

2. Jamal, "The Counter-Hegemonic Role of Civil Society," 288.

3. NCHALA, *The Future Vision of the Palestinian Arabs in Israel*; Mada al-Carmel, *The Haifa Declaration*; Adalah, *The Democratic Constitution*; Y. Jabareen, *An Equal Constitution for All?*

4. Yiftachel, "Take Slovakia For Example"; Rekhes, "No Balm in Galilee."

5. Mada al-Carmel, *Haifa Declaration*, 7–8.

6. Farah, "Preface," 6.

7. Y. Jabareen, *An Equal Constitution for All?* 18–19.

8. NCHALA, *The Future Vision*, 3.

9. Adalah, *Democratic Constitution*, 4.

10. See, for example, Y. Jabareen, *An Equal Constitution for All?* 71.

11. NCHALA, *The Future Vision*, 7; Y. Jabareen, *An Equal Constitution*, 71–72; Mada al-Carmel, *Haifa Declaration*, 16. The proposal embodied in *The Democratic Constitution* relies on such recognition.

12. See United Nations Declaration on the Rights of Indigenous Peoples (2007), http://www.un.org/esa/socdev/unpfii/documents/DRIPS_en.pdf; UN Declaration on the Rights of Persons Belonging to National or Ethnic, Religious and Linguistic Minori-

ties" (1992), http://www.ohchr.org/Documents/Publications/GuideMinoritiesDeclara-tionen.pdf; Council of Europe, Framework Convention for the Protection of National Minorities 1995), http://conventions.coe.int/Treaty/EN/Treaties/Html/157.htm

13. See, for example, Mada al-Carmel, *Haifa Declaration*, 14.

14. NCHALA, *The Future Vision*, 5.

15. Mada al-Carmel, *Haifa Declaration*, 11–12.

16. D.Horowitz, *Ethnic Groups in Conflict*, 207–9.

17. Ibid., 207–8.

18. For example, Mada-al Carmel's *Haifa Declaration* states: "We sympathize with the victims of the Holocaust. . . . We believe that exploiting this tragedy and its conse-quences in order to legitimize the right of Jews to establish a state at the expense of the Palestinian people serves to belittle universal, human, and moral lessons to be learned from this catastrophic event," 16–17. See also NCHALA, *The Future Vision*, 5, which describes the creation of Israel "in light of the results of the Second World War and the Holocaust."

19. Iyad Rabi, author interview.

20. Mada al-Carmel, *Haifa Declaration*, 12.

21. NCHALA, *The Future Vision*, 8. See also Adalah, *Democratic Constitution*, 5; Y. Jabareen, *An Equal Constitution for All?* 29–44, 61–67; Mada al-Carmel, *Haifa Declara-tion*, 16.

22. NCHALA, *The Future Vision*, 5.

23. Ibid., 6.

24. *The Future Vision* states that "Israel can not be defined as a democratic state. It can be defined as an ethnocratic state such as Turkey, Sri Lanka, Latvia, Lithuania, Esto-nia (and Canada forty years ago)," 5.

25. Y. Jabareen, *An Equal Constitution for All?* 71–78; NCHALA, *The Future Vision*, most visibly on pages 7 and 9; Mada al-Carmel, *Haifa Declaration*, 16; Adalah, *Demo-cratic Constitution*, 9–17.

26. Ghanem, Author Interview.

27. Mada al-Carmel, *Haifa Declaration*, 11–14.

28. Ibid., 7.

29. Ibid., 15.

30. Adalah, *Democratic Constitution*, 4.

31. Smooha, *Arabs and Jews in Israel*, Vol. 2, 228, and "Minority Status in an Ethnic Democracy," 398.

32. Smooha, *Arabs and Jews in Israel*, 137.

33. Or Commisson, "Official Summation."

34. Or Commission, "Official Summation," Section 1.

35. Ghanem and Ozacky-Lazar, *A Year After the October Riots*, 12.

36. Or Commission, *Report of the State Commission of Inquiry, Book 4*, chapter. 5.

37. Ibid.

38. Ibid., 6–15.

39. Ibid., 15–28.

40. Ibid., 4.

41. Ibid., 3–4.

42. D. Horowitz, *The Deadly Ethnic Riot*, 151.

43. Ibid., 74.

44. Or Commisson, "Official Summation."

45. Jamal, "Absention as Participation."

46. Survey conducted by Givat Haviva Institute for Peace Research: http://www.givathaviva.org, 28 February 2002, no longer available online.

47. Peled and Navot, "Ethnic Democracy Revisited," 15.

48. See Yisrael Beytenu party platform, http://www.yisraelbeytenu.com

49. Avineri, "Umm al-Fahm Tekhila."

50. Jamal, "The Arab Leadership in Israel."

51. For an elaboration of ethnic outbidding theory, see Chandra, "Ethnic Parties and Democratic Stability."

52. For a comparative perspective on the "reflective" and "causal" dimensions of ethnic parties, see D. Horowitz, *Ethnic Groups in Conflict*, 291–98.

53. Ghanem, *The Palestinian-Arab Minority in Israel*, 1948–2000, 102–5.

54. al-Haj, "The Political Behavior of the Arabs in Israel," 149.

55. Lustick, "The Changing Political Role of the Israeli Arabs," 115; Ghanem and Ozacky-Lazar, *Surveys of Israeli Arabs*, 11.

56. Interview by Sammy Smooha, 29 January 1987, cited in Ghanem, *The Palestinian Arab Minority in Israel*, 47.

57. Lustick, "The Changing Political Role," 119–20; Rouhana, *Palestinian Citizens in an Ethnic Jewish State*, 105; Ghanem, *The Palestinian Arab Minority in Israel*, 39, 44.

58. Ghanem, *The Palestinian Arab Minority in Israel*, 47–48.

59. Data on results of past elections, http://www.knesset.gov.il/description/eng/eng_mimshal_res.htm.

60. Rouhana, Saleh, and Sultany, "Voting Without Voice," 235.

61. Sarsur, author interview.

62. Rouhana, *Palestinian Citizens in an Ethnic Jewish State*, 212.

63. See testimony of Sheikh 'Abdallah Nimr Darwish before the Or Commission, as reported in *Ha'aretz*, 9 August 2002.

64. Amouyal, "We Are at a Crossroads."

65. Makhoul, author interview.

66. Amouyal, "We Are at a Crossroads," 281–83.

67. Editorial, *Ha'aretz* "Lepers?"

68. Bishara, "Interview: A Double Responsibility."

69. Ettinger, "Appealing to the Jewish Public."

70. Rosenfeld, "Israeli Parliamentarian Condemns Country's 'Apartheid.'"

71. Inbari, "International Protection to Arabs of Israel."

72. Stern and Ilan, "Bishara Suspected of Aiding Enemies During Second Lebanon

War"; Ze'ev Segal, "Legal Analysis/Maximum Penalty"; Lis and Harel, "Gag Lifted, Details of Bishara's Alleged Treason Emerge." See also Ali, "What Went Wrong with Azmi Bishara"; Rapaport, "Will He Come or Will He Go?"

73. D. Horowitz, *Ethnic Groups in Conflict*, 291.

74. For an elaboration of ethnic outbidding theory, see Chandra, "Ethnic Parties and Democratic Stability."

75. Jamal, "The Arab Leadership in Israel," 10.

76. Ghanem, *The Palestinian Arab Minority*, 74–75.

77. Rouhana, Saleh, and Sultany, "Voting Without Voice," 236.

78. DFPE, "Political and Social Platform for the Elections to the 17th Knesset" [Hebrew], see party website at: http://www.hadash.org.il/matzahadash.html.

79. Kaufman and Israeli, "The Odd Group Out," 95.

80. Reported in Stern, "MK Tibi."

81. Kaufman and Israeli, "The Odd Group Out," 89.

82. Rekhes, "The Arab Minority in Israel and the 17th Knesset Elections," 160–61.

83. Rekhes, *The Arab Minority in Israel*.

84. Reported in Yakobson, "Assad's Advocates."

85. Nachmias, "The Follow-up Committee."

86. Sartori, "The Party Effects of Electoral Systems."

87. Aronoff, "The 'Americanization' of Israeli Politics."

88. Gidron, Bar, and Katz, *The Israeli Third Sector*, 26.

89. Author interviews with civil society activists, Israel, July 2005.

90. Kaufman, *Arab National Communism in the Jewish State*, 101–2.

91. Haklai, "Palestinian NGOs in Israel,'?" and "State Mutability and Ethnic Civil Society."

92. Varshney, "Ethnic Conflict and Civil Society: India and Beyond," and *Ethnic Conflict and Civic Life*.

93. H. Jabareen, author interview. See also el-Taji, "Israeli-Arab Democracy."

94. See, for example, Gellner, *Conditions of Liberty*; Shils, *The Virtue of Civility*.

95. Carothers, "Civil Society," 21. See also Xavier de Souza Briggs, "Social Capital and the Cities."

96. Arab Center for Alternative Planning, *2003 Annual Report*, 3.

97. Y. Jabareen, "Ideas and Comments on the Legal Status of the Arab Citizens in a Future Constitution in Israel."

98. Haklai, "State Mutability and Ethnic Civil Society," 869.

99. H. Jabareen, author interview.

100. On the court's transformed standing and attitude toward subaltern groups, see Kimmerling, *The Invention and Decline of Israeliness*, 77; Shafir and Peled, *Being Israeli*, 260–77; Hirschl, *Towards Juristocracy*; Woods, *Judicial Power and National Politics*. Examples of court petitions include *Adalah, et al. v. Haifa Municipality* H.C. 1114/01, 2004; *Mohammed Sawa'ed, et al. v. Ministry of Interior, et al.* H.C. 3607/97; *Adalah, et al. v. Ministry of Health, et al.* H.C. 7115/97; *Dahlala Abu Ghardud, et al. v. Ramat HaNegev*

Regional Council, et al. H.C. 5211/00; *Regional Council of the Unrecognized Villages in the Negev, et al. v. Minister of Labor and Social Welfare et al.* H.C. 5838/99; *Adalah v. The Israel Lands Administration, et al.* H.C. 9205/04.

101. *The High Follow Up Committee for the Arab Citizens in Israel v. the Prime Minister of Israel.* H.C. 2773/98 and H.C. 11163/03. Cases related to unrecognized villages include *Adalah, et al. v. Ministry of Health, et al.* H.C. 7115/97; *Dahlala Abu Ghardud, et al. v. Ramat HaNegev Regional Council, et al.* H.C. 5211/00; *Mohammed Sawaʿed, et al. v. Ministry of Interior, et al.* H.C. 3607/97; *Regional Council of the Unrecognized Villages in the Negev, et al. v. Minister of Labor and Social Welfare, et al.* H.C. 5838/99.

102. *Adalah, et al. v. The Municipality of Tel Aviv-Jaffa, et al.* H.C. 4112/99, 2002. See also *Adalah, et al. v. The Ministry of Transportation, et al.* H.C. 4438/97, 1998.

103. Justice Mishal Cheshin in *Adalah, et al. v. The Municipality of Tel Aviv-Jaffa, et al.* H.C. 4112/99, 2002.

104. Stern, "Arab Rights Group Seeks 'Supranational Regime in All of Historic Palestine.'"

105. *Central Elections Committee v. Ahmed Tibi*, Election Confirmation 11280/02; *Central Elections Committee v. Azmi Bishara*, Election Confirmation 50/03; *Balad— The National Democratic Assembly v. the Central Elections Committee*, Election Appeal 131/03. See also *MK ʿIssam Makhoul v. The Knesset*, H.C. 12002/04; *MK Azmi Bishara, et al. v. Avner Erlich, et al.*, H.C. 2247/02.

106. Peleg, *Democratizing the Hegemonic State.*

107. Zeidan, author interview.

108. Haklai, "State Mutability and Ethnic Civil Society," 870.

109. Makhoul, author interview. On donations from Jewish Philanthropies to PAI NGOs see Haklai, "Helping the Enemy?"

110. Mayer, "'Young Muslims' in Israel."

111. Rouhana, *Palestinian Citizens in an Ethnic Jewish State*, 134–35.

112. Mayer, "'Young Muslims' in Israel."

113. Clarke, "Non-Governmental Organizations (NGOs) and Politics in the Developing World," 45.

114. Mayer, *The Awakening of the Muslims in Israel.*

115. Jamal, "The Counter-Hegemonic Role of Civil Society," 302.

116. Sorek, *Arab Soccer in a Jewish State.*

117. Ghanem, *The Palestinian Arab Minority in Israel*, 125.

118. Mayer, "'Young Muslims' in Israel," 15.

119. Ghanem, *The Palestinian Arab Minority in Israel*, 126.

120. Haklai, "Palestinian NGOs in Israel," 162.

121. Reported in Ettinger, "Northern Islamic Movement Leader Sentenced to Jail"; Stern, "Islamic Movement Leader Leaves Prison, Vows to Violate Parole."

122. Translated from Or Commission, *Report of the State Commission of Inquiry, Book 5*, 66; see also *Book 4*, chap. 5, 87–93.

123. Hanna Swaid, general director, Arab Centre for Alternative Planning (ACAP), author interview, 17 June 2005, Eilaboun.

124. Farah, author interview.

125. Quoted in Stern, "A Post-Prison Salah Is Stronger than Ever."

126. Yoaz and Khourie, "Shin Bet: Citizens Subverting Israel Key Values to Be Probed"; Melman, "The Shin Bet."

127. Yisrael Beytenu party platform, http://www.yisraelbeytenu.com.

Chapter 6. The Changing Israeli State-Society Relations

1. Y. Peled, "Ethnic Democracy and the Legal Construction of Citizenship."

2. Shafir and Peled, *Being Israeli*, 5.

3. Y. Peled, "Ethnic Democracy and the Legal Construction of Citizenship"; Smooha, "Minority Status in an Ethnic Democracy."

4. Ghanem, Rouhana, and Yiftachel, "'Questioning 'Ethnic Democracy'"; Yiftachel, "'Ethnocracy' and Its Discontents"; Yiftachel, *Ethnocracy*.

5. Peleg, *Democratizing the Hegemonic State*.

6. Basic Law: The Knesset, Clause 7A.

7. Kretzmer, *The Legal Status of the Arabs in Israel*, 29.

8. The Parties Law, Clause 5.

9. According to one survey conducted in 1988, as many as 95 percent of the Jewish majority held it important to maintain Israel as a Jewish Zionist state, Smooha, *Arabs and Jews in Israel*, vol. 1, 58; vol. 2, 55.

10. Shas, which joined the Labor-led coalition upon its formation, left the government after the Oslo Accord agreement was signed, although it abstained in the subsequent no-confidence vote.

11. Haklai, "Linking Ideas to Opportunities in Contentious Politics," 796–99.

12. Among the organized groups who share this belief were the National Religious Party, Gush Emunim, Zo Artzenu!, Mate Ma'amtz, Women in Green, Gamla, and several others. See Haklai, "Linking Ideas to Opportunities in Contentious Politics"; Lustick, *For the Land and the Lord*; Newman, *The Impact of Gush Emunim*.

13. The relationship between national identity in Israel and the Oslo peace process is explored in depth in Waxman, *The Pursuit of Peace and the Crisis of Israeli Identity*.

14. Elon, author interview.

15. Smooha, "Ethnic Democracy," 226.

16. Shafir and Peled, *Being Israeli*, 131.

17. Elster, *Sour Grapes*, 109–40.

18. Ibid.

19. Adalah, *Adalah Newsletter*, vol. 8, 6.

20. Survey summaries are available on the Mada al-Carmel website, http://www.mada-research.org/sru.shtml, accessed January 2009.

21. Whereas PAI voter turnout generally ranged around the low to mid-70 percent

in elections throughout the 1970s, 1980s, and 1990s, it declined to 62 percent in 2003, 56 percent in 2006, and 53.5 percent in the 2009 elections. The data were collected by the Israel Democracy Institute and can be found on the institute's website, http://www.idi. org.il/sites/english/ResearchAndPrograms/elections09/Pages/ArabVoterTurnout.aspx, published 22 April 2009, accessed April 2009.

22. Smooha's surveys of the 1970s and 1980s found that roughly half (sometimes slightly more) of the Arab minority in Israel felt that the term "Israeli" was appropriate for their collective identity, see Smooha, *The Orientation and Politicization of the Arab Minority*, 49; Smooha, *Arabs and Jews in Israel*, vol. 1, 86–90. In surveys conducted by Smooha with collaborators in 2001, only slightly more than one-third of PAI found "Israeli" suitable for their self-definition. The survey data appear in Ghanem and Ozacky-Lazar, *A Year from the October Riots*, 27; see also Rouhana, *Palestinian Citizens in an Ethnic Jewish State*, 8.

23. The data were published by Shiner, "How They Voted."

24. Brass, *Ethnicity and Nationalism*; Lemarchand, *Burundi*; Kohli, "Can Democracies Accommodate Ethnic Nationalism?; Snyder, *From Voting to Violence*; Posner, "The Political Salience of Cultural Difference"; Rothchild, "Liberalism, Democracy, and Conflict Management."

25. Ghanem, *The Palestinian Arab Minority in Israel*, 104.

26. National Democratic Assembly, Press Release. See also Barzilai, "The Case of Azmi Bishara."

27. See, for example, mission statements by Mossawa, http://www.mossawacenter. org/default.php?lng=3&pg=2&dp=1&fl=29; Mada al-Carmel, http://www.mada-research.org/about.shtml; and al-Ahali, http://www.ahalicenter.org/about.html.

28. Jamal, "The Arab Leadership in Israel."

29. Rabinowitz and Abu Bakr, *Coffins on Our Shoulders*.

30. Sarsur, author interview.

31. A. Makhoul, author interview.

32. Ibid.

33. Jamal, "The Arab Leadership in Israel," 10.

34. See, for example, Osamba, "The Dynamics of Ethnopolitical Conflcit and Violence in the Rift Valley Province of Kenya"; Cusack, "Nation-Builders at Work"; Hutchinson, "A Curse from God?"; Oberschall, "The Manipulation of Ethnicity."

35. Rouhana, *Palestinian Citizens in an Ethnic Jewish State*, 65–78.

36. Rouhana, "Palestinians in Israel."

37. Rouhana, *Palestinian Citizens in an Ethnic Jewish State*, 73–75; Ozacky-Lazar and Ghanem, "The Arabic Press in Israel and the Madrid Conference."

38. Rouhana, *Palestinian Citizens in an Ethnic Jewish State*, 75–78.

39. A. Makhoul, author interview.

40. Ibid.

41. The survey data appear in Ghanem and Ozacky-Lazar, *A Year from the October Riots*.

42. Smooha, *Jewish-Arab Relations in Israel Index 2003*, and *Jewish-Arab Relations in Israel Index 2004*.

43. Or Commission, Official Summation.

44. Or Commission, *Report, Book 4*, chap. 5.

45. Lustick, "The Political Road to Binationalism," 102–3.

46. Sartori, "The Party Effects of Electoral Systems."

47. Harris and Doron, "Assessing the Electoral Reform of 1992 and Its Impact on the Elections of 1996 and 1999."

48. Wilkinson, *Votes and Violence*.

49. Aronoff, "The 'Americanization' of Israeli Politics."

50. There were numerous cases of political parties running on a joint list in an attempt to increase their appeal. For example, Agudath Yisrael and Degel Hatora join forces in Yahadut Hatora; Likud run a joint list with Gesher and Tsomet in 1996; Labor, Gesher, and the religious dovish movement Meimad formed Yisrael Ahat in 1999; The National Religious Party and Ha'ihud Haleumi run on a joint list in 2006.

51. Ozacky-Lazar and Ghanem, "Arab Voting Patterns in the Fourteenth Knesset Elections"; "The Arab Vote to the 15th Knesset."

52. The United Arab list is counted as representing two parties when it is composed of the Islamists and the Arab Democratic Party, and three parties when Ta'al is added to the mix.

53. See, for example, Tachau, "Turkish Political Parties and Elections"; D.Horowitz, *Ethnic Groups in Conflict*, 291–364, and "Encouraging Electoral Accommodation in Divided Societies"; Wilkinson, *Votes and Violence*.

54. Chandra, "Ethnic Parties and Democratic Stability."

55. Rouhana, *Palestinian Citizens in an Ethnic Jewish State*, 106.

56. Lustick, "The Political Road to Binationalism"; "The Changing Political Role of the Israeli Arabs."

57. Lustick, "The Changing Political Role of the Israeli Arabs," 125.

58. Lustick, "The Political Road to Binationalism" and "The Changing Political Role of the Israeli Arabs," 123–28.

59. Haklai, "Religious-Nationalist Mobilization and State Penetration," 733–34.

60. For Jewish public opinion see, Smooha, *Index of Arab-Jewish Relations in Israel*, 2003; 2004; 2005; 2006; 2007. The indexes can be accessed at http://soc.haifa.ac.il/~s. smooha/frame_page.php?page=research. Kadima foreign minister Tzipi Livni justified the need for a Palestinian state alongside Israel as a means to sustain Israel as a Jewish and democratic state; Likud Prime Minister Binyamin Netanyahu made recognition of Israel as a Jewish state by the Palestinians a condition for achieving Israeli-Palestinian peace, see Ahren, "Livni," Eldar and Harel, "Netanyahu Demands Palestinian Recognize Jewish State," and Ha'aretz Service, "Netanyahu Backs Demilitarized Palestinian State."

61. Peled and Navot, "Ethnic Democracy Revisited," 14.

62. Kimmerling, *The Invention and Decline of Israeliness*, 112–29.

63. I have claimed elsewhere that organized Jewish settler mobilization has man-

aged to penetrate the state apparatus such that formal laws are not always enforced on settler violators, See Haklai, "Religious-Nationalist Mobilization and State Penetration."

64. Barzilai, "Courts as Hegemonic Institutions," 15–33; Woods, *Judicial Power and National Politics Courts*; Lahav, "Israel's Supreme Court."

65. Basic Law: The Judiciary, Chapter Three, Clause 15(d)(2) states that "the Supreme Court sitting as a High Court of Justice shall be competent" to "order State and local authorities and the officials and bodies thereof, and other persons carrying out public functions under law, to do or refrain from doing any act in the lawful exercise of their function."

66. Barak, "The Constitutional Revolution" and "Judicial Philosophy and Judicial Activism."

67. Hirschl, *Towards Juristocracy* and "The Political Origins of Judicial Empowerment Through Constitutionalization."

68. Kimmerling, *The End of the Ahusalim Rule*.

69. Barzilai, "Courts as Hegemonic Institutions," 15–33.

70. Woods, *Judicial Power and National Politics*.

71. Gidron, Bar, and Katz, *The Israeli Third Sector*, 24.

72. Dor and Hofnung, "Litigation as Political Participation."

73. Qa'adan v. Israel Land Administration, et al., H.C. 6698/95

74. Shafir and Peled, *Being Israeli*, 132.

75. Haklai, "Palestinian NGOs in Israel," 165.

76. Reported by Khoury, "ILA's 'Jews Only' Land Sales Challenged."

77. Yoaz and Barakat, "AG Mazuz Rules JNF Land Can Now Be Sold to Arabs."

78. Epp, *The Rights Revolution*.

79. Ibid., 3.

80. Nahhas-Daoud, author interview.

81. Gidron, Bar, and Katz, *The Israeli Third Sector*, 26–27.

82. See, for example, Harris and Doron, "Assessing the Electoral Reform," 25–27; Shafir and Peled, *Being Israeli*, 263.

83. Gidron, Bar, and Katz, *The Israeli Third Sector*, 102–15.

84. Haklai, "State Mutability and Ethnic Civil Society," 878.

85. Laskier, "Israeli Activism American Style."

86. Migdal, *Through the Lens of Israel*, 108–9.

87. Gidron, Bar, and Katz, *The Israeli Third Sector*, 26. See also Payes, *Palestinian NGOs in Israel*, 75–76.

88. Gidron, Bar, and Katz, *The Israeli Third Sector*, 27.

89. Tsutsui, "Global Civil Society and Ethnic Social Movements in the Contemporary World"; Kymlicka, *Multicultural Odysseys*, 31–55.

90. Haklai, "Helping the Enemy?" 585.

91. New Israel Fund, *Annual Report 2008*, Schedule 4, 24–33.

92. Haklai, "Helping the Enemy?" 581–99.

93. Shatil website, http://www.shatil.org.il/sites/english, accessed September 2008.

94. Haklai, "Helping the Enemy?" 589.

95. Nossak and Limor, "Military and Media in the 21st Century."

96. I'lam: Media Center for Arab Palestinians in Israel, http://www.ilamcenter.org, accessed 1 May 2007.

97. Arian, *Politics in Israel*, 59.

98. Aharoni, "The Changing Political Economy of Israel," 134–36.

99. Migdal, *Through the Lens of Israel*, 112.

100. Nitzan and Bichler, *The Global Political Economy of Israel*, 84–91.

101. Ibid, 88–91.

102. Arian, *Politics in Israel*, 55.

103. Martinussen, *State, Society and Market*, 211.

104. Gidron, Bar, and Katz, *The Israeli Third Sector*, 2.

105. Ibid., 22–24.

106. Ibid., 26–27.

107. Ibid., 26.

108. Sikkuy, *The Sikkuy Report 2003–2004*, 16.

109. Gidron, Bar, and Katz, *The Israeli Third Sector*, 110.

Conclusion

1. Ghanem, Rouhana, and Yiftachel. "Questioning 'Ethnic Democracy.'"

2. el-Taji, "Arab Local Authorities in Israel"; Jamal, "The Arab Leadership in Israel," 15.

3. Among those who have examined the idea of autonomy is Smooha, *Autonomy for the Arabs in Israel?* For a clear explanation of the civic state idea, see Rouhana, *Palestinian Citizens in an Ethnic Jewish State*, 225–31. Peleg proposes to further liberalize the ethnic state in *Democratizing the Hegemonic State*.

4. Ghanem, *The Palestinian Arab Minority in Israel*, 183–200.

5. Ravid and Stern, "Livni"; Stern, "Israeli Arab Leaders."

6. Peled and Navot, "Ethnic Democracy Revisited," 14.

Bibliography

Adalah: The Legal Center for Arab Minority Rights in Israel. *The Democratic Constitution*. Shafaʿamr: Adalah, 2007.

Aharoni, Yair. "The Changing Political Economy of Israel." *Annals of the American Academy of Political and Social Science* 555 (1998): 127–46.

Ahren, Raphael. "Livni: Israel Must Give Up Land to Remain Jewish and Democratic." *Haʾaretz*, 16 February 2009.

Alford, Robert and Roger Friedman. *Powers of Theory: Capitalism, the State and Democracy*. Cambridge: Cambridge University Press, 1985.

Ali, Riad. "What Went Wrong with Azmi Bishara." *Haʾaretz*, 12 April 2007.

Allport, Gordon W. *The Nature of Prejudice*. Cambridge, Mass.: Addison-Wesley, 1954.

Alon, Gideon. "Diskin: 11% of Palestinians Involved in Terror Entered Israel Through Family Unification." *Haʾaretz*, 20 July 2005.

American Jewish Committee. *American Jewish Year Book*. Vols. 42, 52, 57, 67, 77, 87, 96. New York: Jewish Publication Society of America, 1940–1941, 1951, 1956, 1967, 1977, 1987, 1996.

Amouyal, Ilan. "We Are at a Crossroads: Interview with Azmi Bishara." Rev. 1998 by Azmi Bishara in Carol Diament, ed., *Zionism: The Sequel*. New York: Hadassah, 1998. 279–86.

Anderson, Benedict. *Imagined Communities: Reflections on the Origins and Spread of Nationalism*. London: Verso, 1983.

Anderson, Christopher J. and Christine A. Guillory. "Political Institutions and Satisfaction with Democracy: A Cross-National Analysis of Consensus and Majoritarian Systems." *American Political Science Review* 91 (1997): 66–81.

Antoun, Richard T. and Donald Quataert, eds. *Syria: Society, Culture, and Polity*. Albany: State University of New York Press.

Arab Center for Alternative Planning. *2003 Annual Report*. Eilaboun: Arab Center of Alternative Planning, 2003.

Arian, Asher. *The Second Republic: Politics in Israel*. Chatham, N.J.: Chatham House, 1998.

———. *Politics in Israel: The Second Republic*. 2nd ed. Washington, D.C.: CQ Press, 2005.

Arian, Asher and Michal Shamir, eds. *The Elections in Israel: 1988*. Boulder, Colo.: Westview Press, 1990.

———. *The Elections in Israel: 1999*. Albany: State University of New York Press, 2002.

Aronoff, Myron. "The 'Americanization' of Israeli Politics: Political and Cultural Change." *Israel Studies* 5, 1 (2000): 92–107.

Avineri, Shlomo. *The Making of Modern Zionism: The Intellectual Origins of the Jewish State*. New York: Basic Books, 1981.

———. "Umm al-Fahm Tekhila." *Yediot Aharonoth*, 23 August 2002. [Hebrew]

Ayyad, Abdelaziz A. *Arab Nationalism and the Palestinians 1850–1939*. Jerusalem: Palestinian Academic Society for the Study of International Affairs, 1999.

Ayubi, Nazih N. *Over-Stating the Arab State*. London: I.B. Tauris, 1995.

Bangura, Yusuf, ed. *Ethnic Inequalities and Public Sector Governance*. New York: Palgrave Macmillan, 2006.

Bar-Mocha, Yossi. "The Disclosed Interest of Amiram Bogat." *Ha'aretz Weekend Supplement*, 12 January 2001. [Hebrew]

Barak, Aharon. "The Constitutional Revolution: Protected Fundamental Rights." *Mishpat u-Mishal* 1 (1992): 9–35. [Hebrew]

———. "Judicial Philosophy and Judicial Activism." *Tel Aviv University Law Review* 17 (1993): 475–501.

Barnett, Michael, ed. *Israel in Comparative Perspective: Challenging the Conventional Wisdom*. Albany: State University of New York Press, 1996.

———. "The Politics of Uniqueness: The Status of the Israeli Case." In Michael N. Barnett, ed., *Israel in Comparative Perspective*. Albany: State University of New York Press, 1996. 3–25.

Barreto, Amilcar Antonio. "Constructing Identities: Ethnic Boundaries and Elite Preferences in Puerto Rico." *Nationalism and Ethnic Politics* 7 (2001): 21–40.

Barry, Brian M. *Culture and Equality: An Egalitarian Critique of Multiculturalism*. Cambridge, Mass.: Harvard University Press, 2001.

Barth, Fredrik. *Ethnic Groups and Boundaries: The Social Organization of Cultural Differences*. Boston: Little, Brown, 1969.

———. *The Role of the Entrepreneur in Social Change in Northern Norway*. Oslo: Universiteforlaget, 1963.

Barzilai, Gad. "The Case of Azmi Bishara: Political Immunity and Freedom in Israel." *Middle East Report Online*, 9 January 2002, http://www.merip.org/mero/mero010902.html.

———. "Courts as Hegemonic Institutions: The Israeli Supreme Court in Comparative Perspective." *Israel Studies* 5 (1999): 15–33.

Bar-Zohar, Michael. *Ben-Gurion*. Tel-Aviv: Am Oved, 1975. [Hebrew]

Bassok, Motti. "Israel at 61: Population Stands at 7.4 million, 75.5% Jewish." *Ha'aretz*, 27 April 2009.

Beiner, Ronald, ed. *Theorizing Nationalism*. Albany: State University of New York Press, 1999.

Ben-Eliezer, Uri. *The Making of Israeli Militarism*. Bloomington: University of Indiana Press, 1998.

———. "A Nation-in-Arms: State, Nation and Militarism in Israel's First Years." *Comparative Studies in Society and History* 37 (1995): 264–85.

———. "Rethinking the Civil-Military Relations Paradigm: The Inverse Relation Between Militarism and Praetorianism Through the Example of Israel." *Comparative Political Studies* 30 (1997): 356–74.

Ben-Gurion, David. *From Class to Nation*. Tel Aviv: Am Oved, 1974. [Hebrew]

———. *Israel: A Personal History*. Tel Aviv: Sabra Books, 1972.

———. *Letters to Paula*. Trans. Aubrey Hodes. London: Valentine, 1968.

———. "On the Verge of Statehood." In L. Yaffe, ed., *The Congress Book: Marking the Fiftieth Anniversary of the First Jewish Congress*. Jerusalem: Jewish Agency, 1950. 209–11.

Ben-Yehuda, Eliezer. 1959. "A Letter of Ben-Yehuda." In Arthur Hertzberg, ed., *The Zionist Idea: A Historical Analysis and Reader*. New York: Atheneum, 1973. 160–65.

Benziman, Uzi, and Atallah Mansour. *Sub-Tenants—The Arabs of Israel: Their Status and the Policies Toward Them*. Jerusalem: Keter, 1992. [Hebrew]

Berghe, Pierre L. van den. *The Ethnic Phenomenon*. New York: Elsevier, 1981.

Berglund, Sten, Joakim Ekman, and Frank H. Aarebrot, eds. *The Handbook of Political Change in Eastern Europe*. 2nd ed. Cheltenham: Edward Elgar, 2004.

Bertrand, Jacques. *Nationalism and Ethnic Conflict in Indonesia*. Cambridge: Cambridge University Press, 2004.

Biger, Gideon. "The Only Solution That Will Work." *Haàretz*, 7 September 2007. [Hebrew]

Bishara, Azmi. "Interview: A Double Responsibility: Palestinian Citizens of Israel and the *Intifada*." *Middle East Report* 30 (2000): 26–29.

Blyth, Mark M. "Any More Bright Ideas? The Ideational Turn of Comparative Political Economy." *Comparative Politics* 29 (1997): 229–50.

Bob, Clifford. *The Marketing of Rebellion: Insurgents, Media, and International Activism*. Cambridge: Cambridge University Press, 2005.

Bonacich, Edna. "Class Approaches to Ethnicity and Race." *Critical Sociology* 25 (1999): 166–94.

Brass, Paul. *Ethnicity and Nationalism: Theory and Comparison*. Newbury Park, Calif.: Sage, 1991.

Breuilly, John. 1993. *Nationalism and the State*. Chicago: University of Chicago Press.

Brewer, Marilynn B. and Norman Miller. *Intergroup Relations*. Buckingham: Open University Press, 1996.

Briggs, Xavier de Souza. "Social Capital and the Cities: Advice to Change Agents." *National Civic Review* 86, 2 (1997): 111–17.

Brown, David. "Ethnic Revival: Perspectives on State and Society." *Third World Quarterly* 11 (1989): 1–16.

Brubaker, Rogers. *Ethnicity Without Groups*. Cambridge, Mass.: Harvard University Press, 2004.

———. *Nationalism Reframed: Nationhood and the National Question in the New Europe*. Cambridge: Cambridge University Press, 1997.

Brusis, Martin. "The European Union and Interethnic Power-Sharing Arrangements in Accession Countries." *JEMIE: Journal on Ethnopolitics and Minority Issues in Europe* 1 (2003).

Brynen, Rex, Bahgat Korany, and Paul Noble, eds. *Political Liberalization and Democratization in the Arab World.* Boulder, Colo.: Lynne Rienner, 1995.

Budeiri, Musa. *The Palestine Communist Party 1919–1948: Arab and Jew in the Struggle for Internationalism.* London: Ithaca Press, 1979.

Burke, Edmund and Ira M. Lapidus, eds. *Islam, Politics, and Social Movements.* Berkeley: University of California Press, 1988.

Carmon, Arye. "Appeal to the Arabs of Israel." *Yediot Aharonot,* 3 January 2007. [Hebrew]

Carothers, Thomas. "Civil Society." *Foreign Policy* 117 (Winter 1999–2000): 18–29.

Caspi, Dan and Yechiel Limor. *The Mediators: The Media in Israel 1948–1990.* Tel Aviv: Am Oved, 1993. [Hebrew]

Chabal, Patrick and Jean Pascal Daloz. *Africa Works: Disorder as a Political Instrument.* Bloomington: Indiana University Press, 1999.

Chandra, Kanchan. "Ethnic Parties and Democratic Stability." *Perspectives on Politics* 3 (2005): 235–52.

Chazan, Naomi, ed. *Irredentism and International Politics.* Boulder, Colo.: Lynne Rienner, 1991.

Chetrit, Sami Shalom. *The Mizrahi Struggle in Israel: Between Repression and Liberation, Between Identification and Alternative, 1948–2003.* Tel Aviv: Am Oved, 2004. [Hebrew]

Clapham, Christopher. "Clientelism and the State." In Christopher Clapham, ed., *Private Patronage and Public Power: Political Clientelism and the Modern State.* London: Frances Pinter, 1982. 1–36.

———. *Private Patronage and Public Power: Political Clientelism and the Modern State.* London: Frances Pinter, 1982.

Clark, Cal. "Democracy, Bureaucracy and State Capacity in Taiwan." *International Journal of Public Administration* 23 (2000): 1833–53.

Clarke, Gerard. "Non-Governmental Organizations (NGOs) and Politics in the Developing World." *Political Studies* 46, 1 (1998): 36–52.

Cohen, Asher and Bernard Susser. *Israel and the Politics of Jewish Identity.* Baltimore: Johns Hopkins University Press, 2000.

Cohen, Israel. *A Short History of Zionism.* London: Frederick Muller, 1951.

———. *Speeches on Zionism by the Right Hon. The Earl of Balfour.* London: Arrowsmith, 1928.

Connor, Walker. "Beyond Reason: The Nature of the Ethnonational Bond." *Ethnic and Racial Studies* 16 (1993): 373–89.

Council of Europe. "Framework Convention for the Protection of National Minorities." 1995. http://conventions.coe.int/Treaty/EN/Treaties/Html/157.htm

Cordesman, Anthony H. and Ahmed S. Hashim. *Iraq: Sanctions and Beyond.* Boulder, Colo.: Westview Press, 1997.

Csergo, Zsuzsa. *Talk of the Nation: Language and Conflict in Romania and Slovakia.* Ithaca, N.Y.: Cornell University Press, 2007.

Cusack, Igor. "Nation-Builders at Work: The Equatoguinean Myth of Bantu Unity." *Nationalism and Ethnic Politics* 7 (2001): 77–97.

Dahl, Robert A. *Polyarchy, Participation: Participation and Opposition.* New Haven, Conn.: Yale University Press, 1989.

Darwish, 'Abdallah Nimr. Testimony Before the State Commission of Inquiry into the Clashes Between Security Forces and Israeli Citizens. *Ha'aretz,* 9 August 2002.

Darwish, Mahmud. "A Lover from Palestine." *Arab World* 14 (1968): 13–14.

Deyo, Frederic C, ed. *Political Economy of East Asian Industrialism.* Ithaca, N.Y.: Cornell University Press, 1987.

Diament, Carol, ed. *Zionism: The Sequel.* New York: Hadassah, 1998.

Dinaburg, Benzion. *The Love of Zion.* Vol. 1. Tel-Aviv: Hevra, 1932. [Hebrew]

Diskin, Avraham. *The Elections to the 12th Knesset.* Jerusalem: Jerusalem Institute for Israel Studies, 1990.

———. *The Elections to the 13th Knesset.* Jerusalem: Jerusalem Institute for Israel Studies, 1993.

Dor, Gal and Menachem Hofnung. "Litigation as Political Participation." *Israel Studies* 11 (2006): 131–57.

Douglass, William A. "A Critique of Recent Trends in the Analysis of Ethnonationalism." *Ethnic and Racial Studies* 11 (1988): 192–206.

Dowty, Alan. "Is Israel Democratic? Substance and Semantics in the 'Ethnic Democracy' Debate." *Israel Studies* 4 (1999): 1–15.

———. *The Jewish State: A Century Later.* Berkeley: University of California Press, 1998.

Duvold, Kjetil and Mindaugas Jurkynas. "Lithuania." In Sten Berglund, Joakim Ekman, and Frank H. Aarebrot, eds., *The Handbook of Political Change in Eastern Europe.* 2nd ed. Cheltenham: Edward Elgar, 2004. 133–80.

Ehteshami, Anoushiravan and Emma C. Murphy. "The Transformation of the Corporatist State in the Middle East." *Third World Quarterly* 17 (1996): 753–72.

Eilam, Yigal. *The Jewish Agency: The First Years.* Jerusalem: Ahva, 1990. [Hebrew]

Eisenstadt, Shmuel N. *Israeli Society.* New York: Basic Books, 1967.

Elazar, Daniel J. and Shmuel Sandler, eds. *Israel at the Polls 1996.* London: Frank Cass, 1998.

Eldar, Akiva and Amos Harel. "Netanyahu Demands Palestinians Recognize 'Jewish State'." *Ha'aretz,* 16 April 2009.

Elster, Jon. *Sour Grapes: Studies in Subversion of Rationality.* Cambridge: Cambridge University Press, 1983.

Enloe, Cynthia H. *Police, Military, and Ethnicity: Foundations of State Power.* New Brunswick, N.J.: Transaction, 1980.

Epp, Charles R. *The Rights Revolution: Lawyers, Activists and Supreme Courts in Comparative Perspective.* Chicago: University of Chicago Press, 1998.

Eshkol, Levi. *The Enterprise of Settlement*. Tel-Aviv: Ayanoth, 1966. [Hebrew]

Esman, Milton J. "The State and Language Policy." *International Political Science Review* 13 (1992): 381–96.

Esteron, Yoel. "Who's in Favor of Annihilating Israel?" *Haʾaretz*, 28 November 2003.

Ettinger, Yair. "Appealing to the Jewish Public: An Interview with Dr. Jamal Zahalka." *Haʾaretz*, 22 November 2002. [Hebrew]

———. "Northern Islamic Movement Leader Sentenced to Jail." *Haʾaretz*, 12 January 2005.

———. "Number of Arab Directors Rises." *Haʾaretz*, 25 January 2005.

Evans, Peter. *States and Industrial Transformation*. Princeton, N.J.: Princeton University Press, 1995.

———. "Transferable Lessons? Re-Examining the Institutional Prerequisites of East Asian Economic Policies." *Journal of Development Studies* 34 (1998): 66–86.

Evans, Peter, Dietrich Rueschmeyer, and Theda Skocpol, eds. *Bringing the State Back In*. Cambridge: Cambridge University Press, 1985.

Falah, Ghazi. "Israeli 'Judaization' Policy in the Galilee." *Journal of Palestine Studies* 20 (1991): 69–85.

Farah, Jafar. "Preface." In Yousef Jabareen,. *An Equal Constitution for All? On a Constitution and Collective Rights for Arab Citizens in Israel*. Haifa: Mossawa Center, 2007.

Fearon, James D. and David D. Laitin. "Explaining Interethnic Cooperation." *American Political Science Review* 90 (1996): 715–35.

Forbes, H. D. *Ethnic Conflict: Commerce, Culture and the Contact Hypothesis*. New Haven, Conn.: Yale University Press, 1997.

Forman, Geremy and Alexander Kedar. "From Arab Lands to 'Israel Lands': The Legal Dispossession of the Palestinians Displaced by Israel in the Wake of 1948." *Environment and Planning D: Society and Space* 22 (December 2004): 809–30.

Fosse, John Leif. "Negotiating the Nation: Ethnicity, Nationalism and Nation-Building in Namibia." *Nations and Nationalism* 3 (1997): 427–50.

Fox, Richard G., Charlotte H. Aull, and Louis F. Cimino. "Ethnic Nationalism and the Welfare State." In Charles F. Keyes, ed., *Ethnic Change*. Seattle: University of Washington Press, 1981. 198–245.

Frisch, Hillel. "The Arab Vote: The Radicalization of Politicization?" In Daniel J. Elazar and Shmuel Sandler, eds., *Israel at the Polls 1996*. London: Frank Cass, 1998. 103–20.

Galbreath, David J. *Nation-Building and Minority Politics in Post-Socialist States*. Stuttgart: Ibidem, 2005.

Galbreath David J. and Richard Rose. *Fair Treatment in a Divided Society: A Bottom Up Assessment of Bureaucratic Encounters in Latvia*. Aberdeen: Centre for the Study of Public Policy, University of Aberdeen, 2006.

Gavizon, Ruth. "Jewish and Democratic? A Rejoinder to the 'Ethnic Democracy' Debate." *Israel Studies* 4 (1999): 45–72.

Gavison, Ruth and ʿIssam Abu-Ria. *The Jewish-Arab Divide in Israel: Characteristics and Challenges*. Jerusalem: Israel Democracy Institute, 1999. [Hebrew]

Geertz, Clifford. *Old Societies and New States: The Quest for Modernity in Asia and Africa*. London: Free Press of Glencoe, 1963.

Gellner, Ernest. *Conditions of Liberty: Civil Society and Its Rivals*. New York: Penguin, 1994.

———. *Nations and Nationalism*. Oxford: Blackwell, 1983.

Ghanem, As'ad. *The Palestinian Arab Minority in Israel: 1948–2000*. Albany: State University of New York Press, 2001.

Ghanem, As'ad and Sarah Ozacky-Lazar. "Israel as an Ethnic State: The Arab Vote." In Asher Arian and Michal Shamir, eds., *The Elections in Israel: 1999*. Albany: State University of New York Press, 2002. 121–40.

———. *Surveys of Israeli Arabs: Green Line, Red Lines, Israeli Arabs in the Intifadah*. Givat Haviva: Institute for Arab Studies, 1990. [Hebrew]

———. *A Year After the October Riots: What Has Changed?* Givat Haviva: Institute for Peace Research, 2001. [Hebrew]

Ghanem, As'ad, Nadim N. Rouhana, and Oren Yiftachel. "Questioning 'Ethnic Democracy': A Response to Sammy Smooha." *Israel Studies* 3 (1998): 253–67.

Gidron, Benjamin, Michal Bar and Hagai Katz. *The Israeli Third Sector: Between Welfare State and Civil Society*. New York: Kluwer Academic, 2004.

Gilbert, Martin. *The Arab-Israeli Conflict: Its History in Maps*. London: Weidenfeld and Nicolson, 1984.

Ginsberg, Asher (Ahad Ha-'am). "Past and Future" and "The Spiritual Revival." In *Selected Essays by Ahad Ha-'am*, trans. and ed. Leon Simon. New York: Atheneum, 1970. 80–90, 253–305.

Givat Haviva Institute for Peace Research. Public Opinion Survey, 2001. http://www.givathaviva.org, accessed 28 February 2002, no longer available online.

Government of Palestine. *Survey of Palestine, 1945–1946*. Jerusalem: Government Publisher, April 1946.

Greenfeld, Liah. *Nationalism: Five Roads to Modernity*. Cambridge, Mass.: Harvard University Press, 1992.

Gunter, Michael. *The Kurds of Iraq*. New York: St. Martin's Press, 1992.

Gurr, Ted Robert. *Peoples Versus States: Minorities at Risk in the New Century*. Washington, D.C.: U.S. Institute of Peace Press, 2000.

———. *Why Men Rebel*. Princeton, N.J.: Princeton University Press, 1970.

Gurr, Ted Robert and Barbara Harff. *Ethnic Conflict in World Politics*. Boulder, Colo.: Westview Press, 1994.

Ha'aretz Service. "Netanyahu Backs Demilitarized Palestinian State." *Ha'aretz*, 15 June 2009.

Hadiz, Vedi R. "State and Labor in the Early New Order." In Rob Lambert, ed., *State and Labor in New Order Indonesia*. Nedlands: University of Western Australia Press, 1996. 23–55.

Haidar, Aziz. *Needs and Welfare Services in the Arab Sector in Israel*. Tel Aviv: International Center for Middle East Peace, 1991.

———. *On the Margins: The Arab Population in the Israeli Economy*. London: Hurst, 1995.

al-Haj, Majid. *Education, Empowerment, and Control: The case of the Arabs in Israel*. Albany: State University of New York Press, 1995.

———. "The Political Behavior of the Arabs in Israel in the 1992 Elections: Integration Versus Segregation." In Asher Arian and Michal Shamir, eds., *The Elections in Israel: 1992*. Albany: State University of New York Press, 1995. 141–60.

al-Haj, Majid and Henry Rosenfeld. *Arab Local Government in Israel*. Boulder, Colo.: Westview Press, 1990.

———. *Arab Local Authorities in Israel*. Givat Haviva: Institute for Arab Studies, 1990. [Hebrew]

Haklai, Oded. "Helping the Enemy? Why Transnational Jewish Philanthropic Foundations Donate to Palestinian NGOs in Israel." *Nations and Nationalism* 14 (2008): 581–99.

———. "Linking Ideas to Opportunities in Contentious Politics: The Israeli Non-Parliamentary Opposition to the Peace Process." *Canadian Journal of Political Science* 36 (2003): 791–812.

———. "A Minority Rule over a Hostile Majority: The Case of Syria." *Nationalism and Ethnic Politics* 6 (2000): 19–50.

———. "Palestinian NGOs in Israel: A Campaign for Civic Equality or 'Ethnic Civic Society.'" *Israel Studies* 9 (2004): 157–68.

———. "Religious-Nationalist Mobilization and State Penetration: Lessons from Jewish Settler' Activism in Israel and the West Bank." *Comparative Political Studies* 40 (2007): 713–39.

———. "State Mutability and Ethnic Civil Society: The Palestinian Arab Minority in Israel." *Ethnic and Racial Studies* 32, 5 (2009): 864–82.

Hale, Henry E. *The Foundations of Ethnic Politics: Separatism of States and Nations in Eurasia and the World*. Cambridge: Cambridge University Press, 2008.

Hall, Peter A. *Governing the Economy: The Politics of State Intervention in Britain and France*. New York: Oxford University Press, 1986.

Hall, Peter A. and Rosemary C. R. Taylor. "Political Science and the Three New Institutionalisms." *Political Studies* 44 (1996): 936–57.

Harris, Michael and Gideon Doron. "Assessing the Electoral Reform of 1992 and Its Impact on the Elections of 1996 and 1999." *Israel Studies* 4 (1999): 16–39.

Harty, Siobhan. "The Institutional Foundations of Substate National Movements." *Comparative Politics* 33 (2001): 191–210.

Haver, Eitan and Ze'ev Schiff. *Lexicon for Israel Security*. Jerusalem: Zmora, Bitan, and Modan, 1976. [Hebrew]

Hertzberg, Arthur, ed. *The Zionist Idea: A Historical Analysis and Reader*. New York: Atheneum, 1973.

Herzl, Theodore. *The State of the Jews: An Attempt at a Modern Solution to the Jewish Question*. Trans. Henk Overbery. Northvale, N.J.: Jason Aronson, 1997.

Hirschl, Ran. "The Political Origins of Judicial Empowerment Through Constitutionalization: Lessons from Four Constitutional Revolutions." *Law and Social Inquiry* 25 (2000): 91–149.

———. *Towards Juristocracy: The Origins and Consequences of the New Constitutionalism*. Cambridge, Mass.: Harvard University Press, 2004.

Hobsbawm, Eric. *Nations and Nationalism Since 1780*. Cambridge: Cambridge University Press, 1990.

Holbrooke, Richard. *To End a War*. New York: Random House, 1988.

Horowitz, Dan and Moshe Lissak. *Origins of the Israeli Polity: Palestine Under the Mandate*. Chicago: University of Chicago University Press, 1978.

———. *Trouble in Utopia: The Overburdened Polity of Israel*. Albany: State University of New York Press, 1989.

Horowitz, Donald L. *The Deadly Ethnic Riot*. Berkeley: University of California Press, 2001.

———. "Encouraging Electoral Accommodation in Divided Societies." In Brij V. Lal and Peter Larmour, eds., *Electoral Systems in Divided Societies: The Fiji Constitution Review*. Canberra: National Center for Development Studies, 1997.

———. *Ethnic Groups in Conflict*. 2nd ed. Berkeley: University of California Press, 2000.

———. "Irredentas and Secessions: Adjacent Phenomena, Neglected Connections." In Naomi Chazan, ed., *Irredentism and International Politics*. Boulder, Colo.: Lynne Rienner, 1991. 9–22.

Horowitz, Shale. "Explaining Post-Soviet Ethnic Conflicts: Using Regime Type to Discern the Impact and Relative Importance of Objective Antecedents." *Nationalities Papers* 29 (2001): 633–60.

Hourani, Albert. "Ottoman Reforms and the Politics of Notables." In William R. Polk and Richard L. Chambers eds., *Beginnings of Modernization in the Middle East*. Chicago: University of Chicago Press, 1968. 41–68.

Human Rights Watch. *Second Class: Discrimination Against Palestinian Arab Children in Israel's Schools*. New York: Human Rights Watch, 2001.

Hutchinson, Sharon E. "A Curse from God? Religious and Political Dimensions of the Post-1991 Rise of Ethnic Violence in South Sudan." *Journal of Modern African Studies* 39 (2001): 307–31.

Inbari, Itamar. "International Protection to Arabs of Israel." *Ma'ariv*, 20 October 2007. [Hebrew]

Institute of Strategic Studies. Annual Reports, *The Military Balance*. London: Oxford University Press, various years.

Isaacs, Harold R. *Idols of the Tribe*. New York: Harper and Row, 1975.

Israel Central Bureau of Statistics. *The Arab Population in Israel*. Jerusalem: Prime Minister's Office, 2002. [Hebrew]

———. "Research on Characterization and Ranking of Local Authorities According to the Population's Socioeconomic Level." Jerusalem: Prime Minister's Office, 2001.

———. *Statistical Abstracts of Israel*. Vols. 27, 28, 32, 45, 51, 52. Jerusalem, 1976, 1977, 1981, 1994, 2001, 2002, 2005.

Israel Government. *Government YearBook*. Hakirya: Hamadpis Hamemshalti, 1955. [Hebrew]

Jabareen, Yousef. *An Equal Constitution for All? On a Constitution and Collective Rights for Arab Citizens in Israel*. Haifa: Mossawa Center, 2007.

———. "Ideas and Comments on the Legal Status of the Arab Citizens in a Future Constitution in Israel." Haifa: Mossawa Center, 2005.

Jamal, Amal. "Absention as Participation: The Labyrinth of Arab Politics in Israel." In *The Elections in Israel 2001*, ed. Asher Arian and Michal Shamir. Jerusalem: Israel Democracy Institute, 2002. 105–34.

———. "The Arab Leadership in Israel: Ascendance and Fragmentation." *Journal of Palestine Studies* 35 (2006): 6–22.

———. *The Arab Public Sphere in Israel: Media Space and Cultural Resistance*. Bloomington: Indiana University Press, 2009.

———. "The Counter-Hegemonic Role of Civil Society: Palestinian Arab NGOs in Israel." *Citizenship Studies* 12 (2008): 283–306.

Jewish National Fund. Covenant Between the State of Israel and Keren Kayemeth LeIsrael. 28 November 1961. http://www.kkl.org.il.

Jiryis, Sabri. *The Arabs in Israel*. Trans. Inea Bushnaq. New York: Monthly Review Press, 1969. Translated from *The Arabs in Israel 1948–1966*. Beirut: Institute for Palestine Studies, 1969. [Arabic]

Johnson, Chalmers. "Political Institutions and Economic Performance: The Government-Business Relationship in Japan, South Korea, and Taiwan." In Frederic C. Deyo, ed., *Political Economy of East Asian Industrialism*. Ithaca, N.Y.: Cornell University Press, 1987. 136–64.

Kabha, Mustafa. "The Conspiracy and the Victim." In Ruvik Rosenthal, ed., *Kafr Qasim: Events and Myths*. Tel-Aviv: Ha-Kibbutz ha-Me'uchad, 2000. 87–116. [Hebrew]

Kandeh, Jimmy. "Politicization of Ethnic Identities in Sierra Leone." *African Studies Review* 35 (1992): 81–99.

Kaufman, Ilana. *Arab National Communism in the Jewish State*. Gainesville: University Press of Florida, 1997.

Kaufman, Ilana and Rachel Israeli. "The Odd Group Out: The Arab-Palestinian Vote in the 1996 Elections." In Asher Arian and Michal Shamir, eds., *The Elections in Israel: 1996*. Albany: State University of New York Press, 1999. 85–115.

Kaufmann, Eric and Oded Haklai. "Dominant Ethnicity: From Minority to Majority." *Nations and Nationalism* 14 (2008): 743–67.

Keating, Michael and John McGarry. "Introduction: Minority Nationalism and the Changing International Order" In Michael Keating and John McGarry, eds., *Minority Nationalism and the Changing International Order*. Oxford: Oxford University Press, 2001. 1–15.

Kedourie, Elie. *Nationalism*. Oxford: Blackwell, 1993.

Kelley, Judith G. *Ethnic Politics in Europe*. Princeton, N.J.: Princeton University Press, 2004.

Kemp, Geoffrey and Janice Gross Stein, eds. *Powder Keg in the Middle East: The Struggle for Gulf Security.* Washington, D.C.: American Association for the Advancement of Science, 1995.

Khalidi, Rashid. *The Iron Cage: The Story of the Palestinian Struggle for Statehood.* Boston: Beacon Press, 2006.

al-Khatib, Yusuf. *Anthology of the Occupied Homeland.* Damascus: Dar Filistin, 1968. [Arabic]

Khoury, Jack. "ILA's 'Jews Only' Land Sales Challenged." *Ha'aretz*, 12 October 2004.

Khuri, Fuad I. "The Alawis of Syria: Religious Ideology and Organization." In Richard T. Antoun and Donald Quataert, eds., *Syria: Society Culture and Polity.* Albany: State University of New York Press, 1991. 49–61.

Kimmerling, Baruch. "Between Hegemony and Kulturkampf in Israel." *Israel Affairs* 4 (1998): 49–72.

———. *The End of the Ahusalim Rule.* Jerusalem: Keter, 2001. [Hebrew]

———. *The Invention and Decline of Israeliness: State, Society, and the Military.* Berkeley: University of California Press, 2001.

———. "State Building, State Autonomy and the Identity of Society: The Case of the Israeli State." *Journal of Historical Sociology* 6 (1993): 396–429.

———. *Zionism and Territory.* Berkeley: Institute of International Study, 1983.

Kimmerling, Baruch and Joel S. Migdal. *The Palestinian People: A History.* Cambridge, Mass.: Harvard University Press, 2003.

King, Gary, Robert O. Keohane, and Sidney Verba. *Designing Social Inquiry: Scientific Inference in Qualitative Research.* Princeton, N.J.: Princeton University Press, 1994.

Knesset Israel. *Divrei HaKnesset.* Vols. 33, 84. Jerusalem: Jerusalem Center for Public Affairs, 1962, 1978. [Hebrew]

———. (Netanel Lorch ed.) *Major Knesset Debates, 1948–1981.* Vols. 2, 4, 5. Jerusalem: Jerusalem Center for Public Affairs, 1993.

Kohli, Atul. "Can Democracies Accommodate Ethnic Nationalism? Rise and Decline of Self-Determination Movements in India." *Journal of Asian Studies* 56 (1997): 325–44.

———. *The State and Poverty in India: The Politics of Reform.* Cambridge: Cambridge University Press, 1987.

Kohli, Atul, Joel S. Migdal, and Vivienne Shue, eds. *State Power and Social Forces Domination and Transformation in the Third World.* Cambridge: Cambridge University Press, 1994.

Krasner, Stephen D. *Defending the National Interest.* Princeton, N.J.: Princeton University Press, 1980.

———. *International Regimes.* Ithaca, N.Y.: Cornell University Press, 1983.

Krasatkina, Natalija and Vida Beresneviciute. "Ethnic Structure, Inequality, and Governance of the Public Sector in Lithuania." In Yusuf Bangura, ed., *Ethnic Inequalities and Public Sector Governance.* New York: Palgrave Macmillan, 2006. 31–48.

Kretzmer, David. *The Legal Status of the Arabs in Israel.* Boulder, Colo.: Westview Press, 1990.

Kupferschmidt, Uri M. *The Supreme Muslim Council: Islam Under the British Mandate for Palestine.* Boston: Brill Academic, 1987.

Kymlicka, Will. *Multicultural Citizenship: A Liberal Theory of Minority Rights.* Oxford: Oxford University Press, 1995.

———. *Multicultural Odysseys: Navigating the New International Politics of Diversity.* Oxford: Oxford University Press, 2007.

Lahav, Pnina. "Israel's Supreme Court." In Robert O. Freedman, ed., *Contemporary Israel: Domestic Politics, Foreign Policy, and Security Challenges.* Boulder, Colo.: Westview Press, 2009. 135–58.

Lambert, Rob, ed. *State and Labor in New Order Indonesia.* Nedlands: University of Western Australia Press, 1996.

Landau, Jacob M. *The Arab Minority in Israel 1967–1991: Political Aspects.* Oxford: Clarendon Press, 1993.

———. *The Arabs in Israel: A Political Study.* London: Oxford University Press, 1969.

Laskier, Michael M. "Israeli Activism American Style: Civil Liberties, Environmental, and Peace Organizations as Pressure Groups for Social Change, 1970s–1990s." *Israel Studies* 5 (2000): 128–52.

Lecours, André. "Theorizing Cultural Identities: Historical Institutionalism as a Challenge to the Culturalists." *Canadian Journal of Political Science* 33 (2000): 499–522.

Lemarchand, René. *Burundi: Ethnocide as Discourse and Practice.* New York: Cambridge University Press, 1994.

"Lepers?" Editorial. *Ha'aretz*, 14 November 2007.

Levy, Yagil. *From "People's Army" to "Army of the Peripheries."* Jerusalem: Carmel, 2007. [Hebrew]

Lichbach, Mark Irving. "An Evaluation of 'Does Economic Inequality Breed Political Conflict?' Studies." *World Politics* 41 (1989): 431–70.

Liebman, Charles S. "Religion and Democracy in Israel." In Ehud Sprinzak and Larry Diamond, eds., *Israeli Democracy Under Stress*, Boulder: Lynne Rienner, 1993. 273–92.

Lileinblum, Moshe Leib. "Let Us Not Confuse the Issues." In Arthur Hertzberg, ed., *The Zionist Idea: A Historical Analysis and Reader.* New York: Atheneum, 1973. 170–73.

Lijphart, Arend. "Consociational Democracy." *World Politics* 21 (1969): 207–25.

———. *Democracies: Patterns of Majoritarian and Consensus Government in Twenty-One Countries.* New Haven, Conn.: Yale University Press, 1984.

———. "Democracies: Forms, Performance, and Constitutional Engineering." *European Journal of Political Research* 25 (1994): 1–17.

———. "The Evolution of Consociational Theory and Constitutional Practices, 1965–2000." *Acta Politica* 37 (2002): 11–22.

———. *Patterns of Democracy: Government Forms and Performance in Thirty Six Countries.* New Haven, Conn.: Yale University Press, 1999.

———. "The Power-Sharing Approach." In Joseph P. Montville, ed., *Conflict and Peacemaking in Multiethnic Societies.* Lexington, Mass.: Lexington Books, 1989.

Lis, Jonathan and Amos Harel. "Gag Lifted, Details of Bishara's Alleged Treason Emerge." *Ha'aretz*, 3 May 2007.

Louër, Laurence. *To Be an Arab in Israel*. New York: Columbia University Press, 2007.

Lustick, Ian. *Arabs in the Jewish State: Israel's Control of a National Minority*. Austin: University of Texas Press, 1980.

———. "The Changing Political Role of Israeli Arabs." In Asher Arian and Michal Shamir eds., *The Elections in Israel: 1988*. Boulder, Colo.: Westview Press, 1990. 115–31.

———. *For the Land and the Lord: Jewish Fundamentalism in Israel*. New York: Council on Foreign Relations, 1988.

———. "The Political Road to Binationalism: Arabs in Jewish Politics." In Ilan Peleg and Ofra Seliktar, eds., *The Emergence of Binational Israel: The Second Republic in the Making*. Boulder, Colo.: Westview Press, 1989. 97–123.

Lynn, Stephen. "The Creation and Recreation of Ethnicity: Lessons from the Zapotec and Mixtec of Oaxaca." *Latin American Perspectives* 23 (1996): 17–37.

Mada al-Carmel: The Center for Applied Social Research. Annual Surveys. http://www.mada-research.org/sru/ann_survey.shtml, accessed April 2007, January 2009, May 2009.

———. *The Haifa Declaration*. Haifa: Mada al-Carmel, 2007.

Malekafzali, Farhad and Robert G. Moser. "Primordial, Instrumental Identities and the Formation of Ethnic Collective Movements: The Case of Azeri Nationalism." *Canadian Review of Studies of Nationalism* 19 (1992): 31–41.

Mandel, Neville J. *The Arabs and Zionism Before World War I*. Berkeley: University of California Press, 1976.

Mandelkern, Ronen. "Water Allocation Policy in Israel: Ethno-Republicanism in Theory and Practice." Paper presented at the 21st Annual Conference of the Association for Israel Studies, Tucson, 29–31 May 2005.

Mann, Michael. "The Autonomous Power of the State: Its Origins, Mechanisms and Results." *Archives Européennes de Sociologie* 25 (1984): 185–213.

Ma'oz, Moshe, ed. *Palestinian Arab Politics*. Jerusalem: Jerusalem Academic Press, 1975.

Ma'oz, Moshe and Ilan Pappé, eds. *Middle Eastern Politics and Ideas: A History from Within*. London: I.B. Tauris, 1997.

Martinussen, John. *State, Society and Market*. London: Zed Books, 1997.

Marx, Anthony W. *Faith in Nation: Exclusionary Origins of Nationalism*. Oxford: Oxford University Press, 2002.

———. "The Nation-State and Its Exclusions." *Political Science Quarterly* 117 (2002): 103–26.

Mayer, Thomas. *The Awakening of the Muslims in Israel*. Givat Haviva: Institute of Arab Studies, 1988. [Hebrew]

———. "Young Muslims in Israel." *New East: Special Issue on the Arabs in Israel, Between Religion and National Awakening* 31 (1989): 10–21. [Hebrew]

McAdam, Doug, John D. McCarthy, and Mayer N. Zald. "Introduction: Opportunities, Mobilizing Structures, and Framing Processes." In Doug McAdam, John D. Mc-

Carthy, and Mayer N. Zald, eds., *Comparative Perspectives on Social Movements.* Cambridge: Cambridge University Press, 1996. 1–20.

———, eds. *Comparative Perspectives on Social Movements.* Cambridge: Cambridge University Press, 1996.

McAdam, Doug, Sidney Tarrow, and Charles Tilly. "Toward an Integrated Perspective on Social Movements and Revolutions." In Mark I. Lichbach and Alan S. Zuckerman, eds., *Comparative Politics: Rationality, Culture, and Structure.* Cambridge: Cambridge University Press, 1997. 142–73.

McCarthy, John D. and Mayer N. Zald. "Resource Mobilization and Social Movements: A Partial Theory." *American Journal of Sociology* 82 (1977): 1212–41.

———. "The Trends of Social Movements in America: Professionalization and Resource Mobilization." In John D. McCarthy and Mayer N. Zald, eds., *Social Movements in an Organizational Society.* New Brunswick, N.J.: Transaction, 1987. 337–92.

McGarry, John. *Northern Ireland and the Good Friday Agreement in a Comparative Perspective.* Oxford: Oxford University Press, 2001.

McGarry, John and Brendan O'Leary. *Explaining Northern Ireland: Broken Images.* Cambridge, Mass.: Blackwell, 1995.

———. *The Northern Ireland Conflict: Consociational Engagements.* Oxford: Oxford University Press, 2004.

Meadwell, Hudson. "Cultural and Instrumental Approaches to Ethnic Nationalism." *Ethnic and Racial Studies* 12 (1989): 309–28.

Medding, Peter Y. *The Founding of Israeli Democracy, 1948–1967.* Oxford: Oxford University Press, 1990.

Meir, Avinoam and Ze'ev Zivan. 1998. "Sociocultural Encounter on the Frontier: Jewish Settlers and Bedouin Nomads in the Negev." In Oren Yiftachel and Avinoam Meir, eds., *Ethnic Frontiers and Peripheries: Landscapes of Development and Inequality in Israel.* Boulder, Colo.: Westview Press, 1998. 241–67.

Melman, Yossi. "The Shin Bet: Guardian of Democracy?" *Ha'aretz*, 31 July 2008.

Migdal, Joel S. *State in Society: Studying How States and Societies Transform and Constitute One Another.* Cambridge: Cambridge University Press, 2001.

———. *Strong Societies and Weak States: State-Society Relations and State Capabilities in the Third World.* Princeton, N.J.: Princeton University Press, 1988.

———. *Through the Lens of Israel: Exploration in State and Society.* Albany: State University of New York Press, 2001.

Migdal, Joel S., Atul Kohli, and Vivienne Shue, eds. *State Power and Social Forces: Domination and Transformation in the Third World.* Cambridge: Cambridge University Press, 1994.

Miller, Ylana N. *Government and Society in Rural Palestine 1920–1948.* Austin: University of Texas Press, 1985.

Milne, Ralph S. *Politics in Ethnically Bipolar States.* Vancouver: University of British Columbia Press, 1981.

Montville, Joseph P., ed. *Conflict and Peacemaking in Multiethnic Societies*. Lexington, Mass.: Lexington Books, 1989.

Morris, Benny. *The Birth of the Palestinian Refugee Problem, 1947–1949*. Cambridge: Cambridge University Press, 1987.

———. *Righteous Victims: A History of the Zionist-Arab Conflict, 1881–1998*. New York: Knopf, 1999.

Morris, Helen M. "EU Enlargement and Latvian Citizenship Policies." *JEMIE: Journal on Ethnopolitics and Minority Issues in Europe* 1 (2003): 1–38.

Muslih, Muhammad Y. *The Origins of Palestinian Nationalism*. New York: Columbia University Press, 1988.

Nachmias, Roy. "The Follow-up Committee: No Recognition of Israel as a 'Jewish State.'" *Ynet*, November 2007. http://www.ynet.co.il/Ext/Comp/ArticleLayout/ CdaArticle-PrintPreview/1, 2506,L-3472417,00.html. [Hebrew]

Nahas, Dunia Habib. *The Israeli Communist Party*. London: Croom Helm, 1976.

Nakash, Yitzhak. *The Shi'is of Iraq*. Princeton, N.J.: Princeton University Press, 1994.

Nakhleh, Emile A. "Wells of Bitterness: A Survey of Israeli-Arab Political Poetry." *Arab World* 16 (1970): 30–36.

Nardau, Max. "Zionism." In Arthur Hertzberg, ed., *The Zionist Idea: A Historical Analysis and Reader*. New York: Atheneum, 1973. 242–45.

Nashif, Taysir N. *The Palestine Arab and Jewish Political Leadership: A Comparative Study*. New York: Asia Publishing House, 1979.

Nasser, Riad and Irene Nasser. "Textbooks as a Vehicle for Segregation and Domination: State Efforts to Shape Palestinian Israelis' Identities as Citizens." *Journal of Curriculum Studies* 40 (2008): 627–50.

National Committee for the Heads of the Arab Local Authorities in Israel (NCHALA). *The Future Vision of the Palestinian Arabs in Israel*. Nazareth: NCHALA, 2006.

National Democratic Assembly. Press Release, 8 September 2006, http://www.tajamoa.org/?mod=arch&ID=38.

National Insurance Institution of Israel, Department of Research and Planning. *The Trends in Poverty and Income Disparities in Israel in the Year 2000: Main Findings*. Jerusalem: National Insurance Institution, 2001. [Hebrew]

New Israel Fund. *Annual Report 2008*. Washington, D.C.: New Israel Fund.

Newman, David, ed. *The Impact of Gush Emunim: Politics and Settlement in the West Bank*. London: Croom Helm, 1985.

Nielsen, Kai. "Cultural Nationalism, Neither Ethnic Nor Civil." In Ronald Beiner, ed., *Theorizing Nationalism*. Albany: State University of New York Press, 1999. 119–30.

Nitzan, Jonathan and Shimshon Bichler. *The Global Political Economy of Israel*. London: Pluto Press, 2002.

North, Douglas C. *Institutions, Institutional Change and Economic Performance*. Cambridge: Cambridge University Press, 1990.

Nossak, Hillel and Yehiel Limor. "Military and Media in the 21st Century: Toward a

New Model of Relations." In Udi Libel, ed., *Security and Communication: The Dynamics of the Interrelationship*. Beer Sheva, 2005. 69–100. [Hebrew]

Oberschall, Anthony. "The Manipulation of Ethnicity: From Ethnic Cooperation to Violence and War in Yugoslavia." *Ethnic and Racial Studies* 23 (2000): 982–1001.

O'Duffy, Brendan. "Violence in Northern Ireland 1969–1994: Sectarian or Ethno-National?" *Ethnic and Racial Studies* 18 (1995): 740–72.

O'Leary, Brendan. "Debating Consociational Politics: Normative and Explanatory Arguments." Paper presented at the Annual Meeting of the American Political Science Association, Philadelphia, 27–30 August 2003.

———. "The Elements of Right-Sizing and Right-Peopling the State." In Brendan O'Leary, Ian S. Lustick, and Thomas Callaghy, eds., *Right-Sizing the State: The Politics of Moving Borders*. Oxford: Oxford University Press, 2001. 15–73.

O'Leary, Brendan and Khaled Salih. "The Denial, Resurrection, and Affirmation of Kurdistan." In Brendan O'Leary, John McGarry, and Khaled Salih, eds., *The Future of Kurdistan in Iraq*. Philadelphia: University of Pennsylvania Press, 2005.

Or Commission. "The Official Summation of the State Commission of Inquiry to Investigate the Clashes Between Security Forces and Israeli Citizens." *Ha'aretz Online*, September 2003, http:www.haaretz.com/hasen/pages/ShArt.jhtml?itemNo=335597&con trassID=2&subcontrass . . . , accessed 16 September 2003, no longer available online.

———. *Report of the State Commission of Inquiry into the Clashes Between Security Forces and Israeli Citizens in October 2000*. Jerusalem: Government Publisher, 2003. [Hebrew]

Osamba, Joshia. "The Dynamics of Ethnopolitical Conflcit and Violence in the Rift Valley Province of Kenya." *Nationalism and Ethnic Politics* 7 (2001): 87–112.

Osiel, Mark J. "Dialogue with Dictators: Judicial Resistence in Argentina and Brazil." *Law and Social Inquiry* 20 (1995): 481–560.

Owen, Roger, ed. *Studies in the Economic and Social History of Palestine in the Nineteenth and Twentieth Centuries*. Oxford: Macmillan, 1982.

Ozacky-Lazar, Sarah and As'ad Ghanem. "The Arabic Press in Israel and the Madrid Conference." Givat Haviva, Israel: Institute for the Study of Peace, 1991. Mimeograph.

———. "The Arab Vote to the 15th Knesset." *Studies of the Arabs in Israel* 24. Givat Haviva: Center for Peace Research, 1999. [Hebrew]

———. "Arab Voting Patterns in the Fourteenth Knesset Elections, 29 May, 1996." *Studies of the Arabs in Israel* 19. Givat Haviva: Center for Peace Research, 1996. [Hebrew]

Palestine Royal Commission. *Report. Presented by the Secretary of State for the Colonies to Parliament by Command of His Majesty*, July 1937. London: HMSO.

Payes, Shany. *Palestinian NGOs in Israel: The Politics of Civil Society*. London: Tauris Academic, 2004.

Pearson, Frederic S. "Dimensions of Conflict Resolution in Ethnopolitical Disputes." *Journal of Peace Research* 38 (2001): 275–87.

Peled, Alisa Rubin. *Debating Islam in the Jewish State: The Development of Policy Toward Islamic Institutions in Israel*. Albany: State University of New York Press, 2001.

Peled, Yoav. "Aliens in Utopia: The Civil Status of the Palestinians in Israel." *Theory and Criticism* 3 (1993): 21–35. [Hebrew]

———. *Class and Ethnicity in the Pale*. New York: St. Martin's Press, 1989.

———. "Ethnic Democracy and the Legal Construction of Citizenship: Arab Citizens of the Jewish State." *American Political Science Review* 86 (1992): 432–43.

Peled, Yoav and Doron Navot. "Ethnic Democracy Revisited: On the State of Democracy in the Jewish State." *Israel Studies Forum* 20 (2005): 3–27.

Peleg, Ilan. *Democratizing the Hegemonic State: Political Transformation in the Age of Identity*. Cambridge: Cambridge University Press, 2007.

Peleg, Ilan and Ofra Seliktar, eds. *The Emergence of Binational Israel: The Second Republic in the Making*. Boulder, Colo.: Westview Press, 1989.

Peres, Yochanan. "Modernization and Nationalism of the Israeli Arab." *Middle East Journal* 24 (1970): 479–92.

Peretz, Don. *Israel and the Palestine Arabs*. Washington, D.C.: Middle East Institute, 1958.

Peri, Yoram. "The Arab-Israeli Conflict and Israeli Democracy." In Ehud Sprinzak and Larry Diamond, eds., *Israeli Democracy Under Stress*. Boulder, Colo.: Lynne Rienner, 1993. 343–57.

———. *Generals in the Cabinet Room: How the Military Shapes Israeli Policy*. Washington, D.C.: United States Institute for Peace Press, 2006.

Picard, Avi. "Immigration, Health and Social Control: Medical Aspects of the Policy Governing *Aliyah* from Morocco and Tunisia, 1951–54." *Journal of Israeli History* 22, 2 (Autumn 2003): 32–60.

Pierson, Paul. *Dismantling the Welfare State: Reagan, Thatcher and the Politics of Retrenchment*. Cambridge: Cambridge University Press, 1994.

———. "Increasing Returns, Path Dependence and the Study of Politics." *American Political Science Review* 94 (2000): 251–68.

Pigenko, Vladimir and Cristina Novac. "Economic Reforms and Ethnic Nationalism in the Context of Transition to Democracy: The Case of Four Eastern European Nations." *Democratization* 9 (2002): 159–72.

Polk, William R. and Richard L. Chambers, eds. *Beginnings of Modernization in the Middle East*. Chicago: University of Chicago Press, 1968.

Porath, Yehoshua. *The Emergence of the Palestinian-Arab National Movement 1918–1929*. London: Frank Cass, 1974.

———. *The Palestinian Arab National Movement 1929–1939*. London: Frank Cass, 1977.

———. "The Political Organization of the Palestine Arabs under the British Mandate." In Moshe Ma'oz, ed., *Palestinian Arab Politics*. Jerusalem: Jerusalem Academic Press, 1975. 1–20.

Posner, Daniel N. "The Political Salience of Cultural Difference: Why Chewas and Tumbukas Are Allies in Zambia and Adversaries in Malawi." *American Political Science Review* 98 (2004): 529–45.

Provisional Government of Israel. *The Declaration of the Establishment of the State of Israel*. Tel Aviv, 14 May 1948.

Rabinowitz, Dan. *Overlooking Nazareth: The Ethnography of Exclusion in the Galilee.* Cambridge: Cambridge University Press, 1997.

Rabinowitz, Dan and Khawla Abu Bakr. *Coffins on Our Shoulders: The Experience of the Palestinian Citizens of Israel.* Berkeley: University of California Press, 2005.

Rapaport, Meron. "Will He Come or Will He Go?" *Ha'aretz,* 13 April 2007.

Ravid, Barak and Yoav Stern. "Livni: Palestinian State Will Benefit Israeli Arabs." *Ha'aretz,* 19 November 2007.

Rekhes, Eli. *The Arabs of the Galilee and the Land Expropriations.* Tel Aviv: Shiloah Center for Middle Eastern and African Research, 1977. [Hebrew]

———. *The Arab Minority in Israel: Between Communism and Arab Nationalism.* Tel Aviv: Kav Adom, 1993. [Hebrew]

———. "The Arab Minority in Israel and the 17th Knesset Elections." In Asher Arian and Michal Shamir, eds., *The Elections in Israel: 2006.* New Brunswick, N.J.: Transaction, 2008. 159–85.

———. "No Balm in Galilee." *Jerusalem Post,* 27 November 2007.

———. "The Evolvement of an Arab Palestinian Minority in Israel." *Israel Studies* 12, 3 (2007): 1–28.

Robinson, Shira Nomi. "Occupied Citizens in a Liberal State: Palestinians Under Military Rule and the Colonial Formation of Israeli Society, 1948–1966." Ph.D. dissertation, Stanford University, 2005.

Roeder, Philip G. "Soviet Federalism and Ethnic Mobilization." *World Politics* 43, 2 (1991): 196–232.

Rokeach, Milton. *The Nature of Human Values.* New York: Free Press, 1973.

Rosenburg, Gerald N. *The Hollow Hope: Can Courts Bring About Social Change?* Chicago: University of Chicago Press, 1991.

Rosenfeld, Jesse. "Israeli Parliamentarian Condemns Country's 'Apartheid': Jamal Zahalka Speaking in Montreal, Toronto." *Canadian University Press,* 16 February 2007.

Rosenhek, Zeev. "The Exclusionary Logic of the Welfare State: Palestinian Citizens in the Israeli Welfare State." *International Sociology* 14, 2 (1999): 195–215.

Rosenthal, Ruvik, ed. *Kafr Qasim: Events and Myths.* Tel-Aviv: Ha-Kibbutz ha-Me'uchad, 2000. [Hebrew]

Rothchild, Donald. "Liberalism, Democracy, and Conflict Management: The African Experience." In Andreas Wimmer, et al., eds., *Facing Ethnic Conflicts: Toward a New Realism.* Lanham, Md.: Rowman & Littlefield, 2004. 226–45.

Roudometof, Victor. "The Consolidation of National Minorities in Southeastern Europe." *Journal of Political and Military Sociology* 24 (1996): 189–207.

Rouhana, Nadim. *Palestinian Citizens in an Ethnic Jewish State: Identities in Conflict.* New Haven, Conn.: Yale University Press, 1997.

———. "Palestinians in Israel: Responses to the Uprising." In Rex Brynen, ed., *Echoes of the Intifada: Regional Repercussions of the Palestinian-Israeli Conflict.* Boulder, Colo.: Westview Press, 1991. 97–115.

Rouhana, Nadim and As'ad Ghanem. "The Crisis of Minorities in Ethnic States: The

Case of Palestinian Citizens in Israel." *International Journal of Middle East Studies* 30 (1998): 321–46.

Rouhana, Nadim, Nabil Saleh, and Nimer Sultany. "Voting Without Voice: About the Vote of the Palestinian Minority in the 16th Knesset Elections." In Asher Arian and Michal Shamir, eds., *The Elections in Israel: 2003*. New Brunswick, N.J.: Transaction, 2005.

Runciman, Walter G. *Relative Deprivation and Social Justice: A Study of Attitudes Toward Social Inequality in Twentieth-Century England*. Berkeley: University of California Press, 1996.

Sagi, Avi and Yedidia Stern. "We Are Not Strangers in Our Homeland." *Haaretz*, 23 March 2007.

Saideman, Stephen M. and William R. Ayres. "Determining the Causes of Irredentism: Logit Analysis of Minorities at Risk Data from the 1980s and 1990s." *Journal of Politics* 62 (2000): 1126–44.

Sartori, Giovanni. "The Party Effects of Electoral Systems." *Israel Affairs* 6, 2 (1999): 13–28.

Schiff, Ze'ev. *A History of the Israeli Army: 1874 to the Present*. New York: Macmillan, 1985.

———. "Self Inflicted Injury." *Ha'aretz*, 26 January 2007.

Schwartz, Walter. *The Arabs in Israel*. London: Faber & Faber, 1959.

Scott, James C. *Seeing like a State: How Certain Schemes to Improve the Human Condition Have Failed*. New Haven, Conn.: Yale University Press, 1998.

Segal, Ze'ev. "Legal Analysis/Maximum Penalty: Death, or Life Behind Bars." *Ha'aretz*, 26 April 2007.

Shafir, Gershon and Yoav Peled. *Being Israeli: The Dynamics of Multiple Citizenship*. Cambridge: Cambridge University Press, 2002.

Shamir, Shimon. "An Open Letter to the Authors of the Future Vision." *Al-Sinara*, 5 January 2007. [Arabic]

Shapiro, Yonathan. *The Formative Years of the Israeli Labor Party*. Beverly Hills, Calif.: Sage, 1976.

———. *Politicians as a Hegemonic Class: The Case of Israel*. Tel Aviv: Sifriat Hapoalim, 1996. [Hebrew]

Shils, Edward. *The Virtue of Civility*. Indianapolis: Liberty Fund, 1997.

Shin, Leo K. *The Making of the Chinese State: Ethnicity and Expansion on the Ming Borderlands*. Cambridge: Cambridge University Press, 2006.

Shiner, Doron. "How They Voted: See Israel Election Results by City/Sector." *Ha'aretz*, 11 February 2009.

Shlaim, Avi. The *Politics of Partition: King Abdullah, the Zionists, and Palestine, 1921–1951*. Oxford: Oxford University Press, 1990.

Sikkink, Kathryn. *Ideas and Institutions: Developmentalism in Argentina and Brazil*. Ithaca, N.Y.: Cornell University Press, 1991.

Sikkuy: The Association for the Advancement of Civic Equality in Israel. Press Release, 8 November 2000. [Hebrew]

———. *The Sikkuy Report: Monitoring Civic Equality Between Arab and Jewish Citizens of Israel, 2002–2003, 2003–2004, 2004–2005*. Jerusalem: Sikkuy, 2003, 2004, 2005. [Hebrew]

Shimoni, Gideon. *The Zionist Ideology*. Hanover, N.H.: University Press of New England for Brandeis University Press, 1995.

Shimoni, Ya'acov. *Arabs of Israel*. Tel Aviv: Am Oved, 1947. [Hebrew]

Shufani, Elias. "The Arab 'Citizens' of Israel." *Arab World* 15 (1969): 32–34.

Skocpol, Theda. "Bringing the State Back In." *Items* 36 (1982): 1–8.

———. *States and Social Revolutions: A Comparative Analysis of France, Russia and China*. Cambridge: Cambridge University Press, 1979.

Skocpol, Theda and Jocelyn Elise Crowley. "The Rush to Organize: Explaining Associational Formation in the United States, 1860s-1920s." *American Journal of Political Science* 45 (2001): 813–29.

Skocpol, Theda, Marshall Ganz, and Ziad Munson. "A Nation of Organizers: The Institutional Origins of Civic Voluntarism in the United States." *American Political Science Review* 94 (2000): 527–46.

Smith, Anthony D. *The Ethnic Origins of Nations*. Oxford: Blackwell, 1986.

———. *The Ethnic Revival*. Cambridge: Cambridge University Press, 1981.

Smith, Barbara J. *The Roots of Separatism in Palestine*. Syracuse, N.Y.: Syracuse University Press, 1993.

Smith, Pamela. "Interview with Muhammad Kiwan." *Journal of Palestine Studies* 8 (1978): 167–71.

Smooha, Sammy. *Arabs and Jews in Israel*. Vol. 1, *Conflicting and Shared Attitudes in a Divided Society*; Vol. 2, *Change and Continuity in Mutual Intolerance*. Boulder, Colo.: Westview Press, 1988, 1992.

———. *Autonomy for the Arabs in Israel?* Ra'anana: Institute for Israeli Arab Studies, 1999. [Hebrew]

———. "Ethnic Democracy: Israel as an Archetype." *Israel Studies* 2 (1997): 198–241.

———. *Jewish-Arab Relations in Israel Index 2003*. Haifa: Jewish-Arab Center, Citizens' Accord Forum in Israel, 2003.

———. *Jewish-Arab Relations in Israel Index 2004*. Haifa: Jewish-Arab Center, Citizens' Accord Forum in Israel, 2005.

———. "Minority Status in an Ethnic Democracy: The Status of the Arab Minority in Israel." *Ethnic and Racial Studies* 13 (1990): 389–413.

———. *The Orientation and Politicization of the Arab Minority in Israel*. Haifa: Institute of Middle East Studies, 1984.

Snyder, Jack. 2000. *From Voting to Violence: Democratization and Nationalist Conflict*. New York: Norton, 2000.

Sofer, Arnon. *The Demographic and Geographic Situation in Eretz Israel*. Haifa: Gastlist, 1988. [Hebrew]

Sorek, Tamir. *Arab Soccer in a Jewish State: The Integrative Enclave*. Cambridge: Cambridge University Press, 2007.

Spruyt, Hendrik. *Ending Empire: Contested Sovereignty and Territorial Partition*. Ithaca, N.Y.: Cornell University Press, 2005.

Stack, John F., Jr., ed. *The Primordial Challenge: Ethnicity in the Contemporary World.* Westport, Conn.: Greenwood, 1986.

Stendel, Ori. *Arabs of Israel: Between the Rock and the Hard Place.* Jerusalem: Academon, 1993. [Hebrew]

Stepan, Alfred C. *The State and Society: Peru in Comparative Perspective.* Princeton, N.J.: Princeton University Press, 1978.

Stern, Yoav. "Arab Rights Group Seeks 'Supranational Regime in All of Historic Palestine'." *Ha'aretz*, 20 December 2007.

———. "Council for Peace and Security Nixes Israeli Arab 'Vision' Document." *Ha'aretz*, 28 January 2007.

———. "Islamic Movement Leader Leaves Prison, Vows to Violate Parole." *Ha'aretz*, 18 July 2005.

———. "Israeli Arab Leaders: A Palestinian State Is Not a Solution for Us." *Ha'aretz*, 4 December 2007.

———. "MK Tibi: Israeli Arabs Should Get 20 Percent of State's Foreign Aid." *Ha'aretz*, 20 October 2005.

———. "A Post-Prison Salah Is Stronger Than Ever." *Ha'aretz*, 1 August 2005.

Stern, Yoav and Shahar Ilan. "Bishara Suspected of Aiding Enemies During Second Lebanon War." *Ha'aretz*, 25 April 2007.

Sternhell, Ze'ev. *The Founding Myths of Israel: Nationalism, Socialism, and the Making of the Jewish State.* Princeton, N.J.: Princeton University Press, 1998.

———. *Nation Building or a New Society?* Tel Aviv: Am Oved, 1995. [Hebrew]

Stock, Ernest. *Chosen Instrument: The Jewish Agency in the First Decade of the State of Israel.* New York: Herzl Press, 1988.

Sulaiman, Khalid A. *Palestine and Modern Arab Poetry.* London: Zed Books, 1984.

Swedenburg, Ted. "The Role of the Palestinian Peasantry in the Great Revolt." In Edmund Burke, III, and Ira M. Lapidus, eds., *Islam, Politics, and Social Movements.* Berkeley: University of California Press, 1988. 184–91.

Szeftel, Morris. "Clientelism, Corruption and Catastrophe (in Africa)." *Review of African Political Economy* 85 (2000): 427–41.

Tachau, Frank. 2000. "Turkish Political Parties and Elections: Half a Century of Multiparty Democracy." *Turkish Studies* 1 (2000): 128–48.

Tajfel, Henry and J. C. Turner. "The Social Identity Theory of Intergroup Behavior." In Stephen Worchel and William G. Austin, eds., *Psychology of Intergroup Relations.* Chicago: Nelson-Hall, 1986. 7–24.

El-Taji, Maha T. "Israeli-Arab Democracy: Clan Politics and the Ethnic State." Paper presented at the 22nd Annual Conference of the Association of Israel Studies, Banff, 29–31 May 2006.

———. "Arab Local Authorities in Israel: Hamulas, Nationalism and Dilemmas of Social Change." Ph.D. Dissertation, University of Washington, 2008.

Talhami, Ghada Hashem. *Syria and the Palestinians: The Clash of Nationalism.* Gaines-ville: University Press of Florida, 2001.

Tamari, Salim. "Factionalism and Class Formation in Recent Palestinian History." In Roger Owen, ed., *Studies in the Economic and Social History of Palestine in the Nine-teenth and Twentieth Centuries.* Oxford: Macmillan, 1982. 181–202.

Tarrow, Sidney. *The New Transnational Activism.* Cambridge: Cambridge University Press, 2005.

———. *Power in Movement: Social Movements and Contentious Politics.* Cambridge: Cambridge University Press, 1998.

Tessler, Mark. "Israel's Arabs and the Palestinian Problem." *Middle East Journal* 31, 3 (1977): 313–29.

Teveth, Shabtai. *Ben-Gurion: The Burning Ground, 1886–1948.* Boston: Houghton Mif-flin, 1987.

Thomas, Clive Y. *The Rise of the Authoritarian State in Peripheral Societies.* New York: Monthly Review Press, 1984.

Tibawi, A. L. "Visions of Return: The Palestine Arab Refugees in Arabic Poetry and Art." *Middle East Journal* 17 (1963): 507–26.

Tripp, Charles. "The Future of Iraq and of Regional Security." In Geoffrey Kemp and Janice Gross Stein, eds., *Powder Keg in the Middle East: The Struggle for Gulf Se-curity.* Washington, D.C.: American Association for the Advancement of Science, 1995. 133–59.

Tsutsui, Kiyoteru. "Global Civil Society and Ethnic Social Movements in the Contempo-rary World." *Sociological Forum* 19 (2004): 63–87.

Uvin, Peter. *Aiding Violence: The Development Enterprise in Rwanda.* West Hartford, Conn.: Kumarian Press, 1998.

Varshney, Ashutosh. *Ethnic Conflict and Civic Life: Hindus and Muslims in India.* New Haven, Conn.: Yale University Press, 2002.

———. "Ethnic Conflict and Civil Society: India and Beyond." *World Politics* 53 (2001): 362–98.

Villarreal, Andres. "Political Competition and Violence in Mexico: Hierarchical Societal Control and Local Patronage Structures." *American Sociological Review* 67 (2002): 477–98.

Wallach, Jehuda and Moshe Lissak, eds. *Carta's Atlas of Israel: The First Years 1948–1961; The Third Decade 1971–1981.* Jerusalem: Carta, 1983.

Waxman, Dov. *The Pursuit of Peace and the Crisis of Israeli Identity: Defending/Defining the Nation.* New York: Palgrave Macmillan, 2006.

Weaver, R. Kent and Bert A. Rockman, eds. *Do Institutions Matter? Government Capabili-ties in the United States and Abroad.* Washington, D.C.: Brookings Institution Press, 1993.

Wehner, Joachim. "Parliament and the Power of the Purse: The Nigerian Constitution of 1999 in Comparative Perspective." *Journal of African Law* 46 (2002): 216–31.

Wickham, Carrie Rosefsky. *Mobilizing Islam: Religion, Activism, and Political Change in Egypt*. New York: Columbia University Press, 2002.

Wilkinson, Steven I. *Votes and Violence: Electoral Competition and Ethnic Riots in India*. Cambridge: Cambridge University Press, 2004.

Wilson, Woodrow. Address of the President of the United States, delivered at a Joint Session of the Two Houses of Congress, Washington, D.C., 8 January 1918.

Woods, Patricia. *Judicial Power and National Politics: Courts and Gender in the Religious-Secular Conflict in Israel*. Albany: State University of New York Press, 2008.

Worchel, Stephen and William G. Austin. *Psychology of Intergroup Relations*. Chicago: Nelson-Hall, 1986.

Yack, Bernard. 1999. "The Myth of the Civic Nation." In Ronald Beiner, ed., *Theorizing Nationalism*. Albany: State University of New York Press, 1999. 103–18.

Yaffe, L. 1950. *The Congress Book: Marking the Fiftieth Anniversary of the First Jewish Congress*. Jerusalem: Jewish Agency, 1950.

Yakobson, Alexander. "Assad's Advocates." *Ha'aretz*, 31 January 2006.

Yanai, Nathan. "Ben-Gurion's Concept of *Mamlachtyut* and the Forming Reality of the State of Israel." *Jewish Political Studies Review* 1, 1&2 (Spring 1989): 151–77.

Yiftachel, Oren. 1992. "'Ethnocracy' and Its Discontents: Minorities, Protests and the Israeli Polity." *Critical Inquiry* 26 (2000): 725–56.

———. *Ethnocracy: Land and Identity in Israel/Palestine*. Philadelphia: University of Pennsylvania Press, 2006.

———. "The Internal Frontier: The Territorial Control of Ethnic Minorities." *Regional Studies* 30 (1996): 493–508.

———. *Planning a Mixed Region in Israel: The Political Geography of Arab-Jewish Relations in the Galilee*. Aldershot: Avebury, 1992.

———. "Take Slovakia for Example." *Ha'aretz*, 21 December 2006.

Yiftachel, Oren and Avinoam Meir, eds. *Ethnic Frontiers and Peripheries: Landscapes of Development and Inequality in Israel*. Boulder, Colo.: Westview Press, 1998.

Yiftachel, Oren and Dennis Rumley. "On the Impact of Israel's Judaization Policy in the Galilee." *Political Geography Quarterly* 10 (1991): 290.

Yoaz, Yuval and Amiram Barakat. "AG Mazuz Rules JNF Land Can Now Be Sold to Arabs." *Ha'aretz*, 27 January 2005.

Yoaz, Yuval and Jack Khourie. "Shin Bet: Citizens Subverting Israel key Values to Be Probed." *Ha'aretz*, 21 May 2007.

Zerubavel, Yael. *Recovered Roots: Collective Memory and the Making of Israeli National Tradition*. Chicago: University of Chicago Press, 1995.

Zimmerman, Warren. *Origins of a Catastrophe: Yugoslavia and Its Destroyers*. New York: Random House, 1997.

Zureik, Elia. *The Palestinians in Israel: A Study in Internal Colonialism*. Routledge & Kegan Paul, 1979.

Newspapers

Ha'aretz (Hebrew daily).
Haolam (official Hebrew weekly newspaper of the Jewish Agency in the pre-state period)
Al-Ittihad (official Arabic newspaper of the Communist Party).
Ma'ariv (Hebrew daily).
Al-Mithaq (official Arabic newspaper of the Islamic Movement, "southern branch").
Qol ha-Am (official Hebrew newspaper of the Communist Party).
Sawt al-Haqq Wal- Hurriya (official Arabic newspaper of the Islamic Movement, "northern branch").
Al-Sinara (unaffiliated Arabic daily).
Yediot Aharonot (Hebrew daily).

Websites

Adalah: The Legal Center for Arab Minority Rights in Israel, http://www.adalah.org/eng/index.php.
Ahali: Center for Community Development, http://www.ahalicenter.org/.
Arab Association for Human Rights (HRA), http://www.arabhra.org/HRA/Pages/Index.aspx.
Arab Center for Alternative Planning (ACAP), http://www.ac-ap.org/.
The Association of Forty online, http://www.assoc40.org.
Council of Europe, http://www.coe.int/.
Democratic Front for Peace and Equality (DFPE), http://www.hadash.org.il.
The Givat Haviva Institute for Peace Research, http:www.givathaviva.org.
Ha'aretz Online, http:www.haaretz.com
I'lam: Media Center for Arab Palestinians in Israel, http://www.ilamcenter.org.
Israel Central Bureau of Statistics, http://www.cbs.gov.il.
Israel Land Administration, http://www.mmi.gov.il.
Ittijah: The Union of Arab Community Based Organizations, http://www.ittijah.org/
Jewish National Fund, http://www.kkl.org.il.
Knesset. http://www.knesset.gov.il.
Mada al-Carmel: The Center for Applied Social Research, http://www.mada-research.org/.
Middle East Report, http://www.merip.org/mer/mer.html.
Minorities at Risk Project, http://www.cidcm.umd.edu/mar/.
Mossawa: The Advocacy Center for Arabs in Israel, http://www.mossawacenter.org.
National Democratic Assembly, http://www.tajamoa.org
Sikkuy: The Association for the Advancement of Equality, http://www.sikkuy.org.il/.
Tami Steinmetz Institute for Peace research, http://www.spirit.tau.ac.il/socant/peace
United Nations Documents on Israel-Palestine, http://domino.un.org/UNISPAL.NSF
Yisrael Beytenu, http://www.yisraelbeytenu.com.
Ynet, http://www.ynet.co.il.

Court Cases and Legal Proceedings

Adalah et al. v. The Municipality of Tel Aviv-Jaffa et al. H.C. 4112/99, 2002.

Adalah et al. v. The ministry of Transportation et al. H.C. 4438/97, 1998.

Mohammed Sawa'ed et al. v. Ministry of Interior et al. H.C. 3607/97.

Adalah et al. v. Ministry of Health et al. H.C. 7115/97.

Dahlala Abu Ghardud et al. v. Ramat HaNegev Regional Council et al. H.C. 5211/00.

Regional Council of the Unrecognized Villages in the Negev et al. v. Minister of Labor and Social Welfare et al. H.C. 5838/99.

Adalah et al. v. The Municipality of Tel Aviv-Jaffa et al. H.C. 4112/99, 2002.

Adalah e al. v. The ministry of Transportation et al. H.C. 4438/97, 1998.

Adalah et al. v. Yitzhak Eitan. IDF Major General, Central Command et al. HCJ3799/02.

Adalah et al. v. Haifa Municipality. H.C. 1114/01, 2004.

Adalah v. The Israel Lands Administration et al. H.C. 9205/04.

The High Follow Up Committee for the Arab Citizens in Israel v. the Prime Minister of Israel. H.C. 2773/98 and H.C. 11163/03.

Central Elections Committee v. Ahmed Tibi. Election Confirmation 11280/02.

Central Elections Committee v. Azmi Bishara. Election Confirmation 50/03.

Balad: The National Democratic Assembly v. the Central Elections Committee. Election Appeal 131/03.

MK Issam Makhoul v. The Knesset. H.C. 12002/04.

MK Azmi Bishara et al. v. Avner Erlich et al. H.C. 2247/02.

Author Interviews

Interviewees' titles and positions appear as they were at the time of the interview.

Elon, Benny, Member of Knesset. Jerusalem, 24 January 1997.

Essa, Jumanah, International Relations, Arab Center for Alternative Planning. Eilaboun, 17 June 2005.

Farah, Jafar, General Director, Mossawa Center. Haifa, 22 June 2005.

Ghanem, As'ad, Political Science Professor at Haifa University, Haifa, 23 December 2010.

Gonzalez, Maria, International Advocacy and Media Representative, Mossawa Center. Haifa, 22 June 2005.

Haider, Ali, Co-Executive Director, Sikkuy. Haifa, 19 June 2005.

Jabareen, Hassan, General Director, Adalah. Shafa'amr, 22 June 2005.

Jabareen, Yousef, Legal Advisor, Mossawa Center. Haifa, 22 June 2005.

Makhoul, Ameer, General Director, Ittijah: Union of Arab Community Based Organizations. Haifa, 28 June 2005.

Makhoul, Cameel, Director of Health Promotion and Education Department, The Galilee Society. Shafa'amr, 22 June 2005.

Nahhas-Daoud, Alhan, Legal Advisor, Mossawa Center. Haifa, 22 June 2005.

Nassar, Felice, Director of Resource Development, the Galilee Society. Shafa'amr, 22 June 2005.

Rabi, Iyad. General Director of al-Ahali: Center for Community Development. Haifa, 15 June 2005.

Sarsur, Ibrahim, Head of the Islamic Movement southern stream. Kafr Qasim, 26 June 2005.

Swaid, Hanna, General Director of Arab Centre for Alternative Planning. Eilaboun, 17 June 2005.

Zeidan, Mohammed, Executive Director of the Arab Association for Human Rights. Nazareth, 15 June 2005.

Index

Abd al-Nasser, Gamal, 74, 86, 130
Abna' al-balad (Sons of the Village), 81-82, 129, 153
Abraham Fund Initiatives, 167
Absentee Property Law, 59
Abu Razek, Oscar, 66, 182n26
Acre, 173
Adalah, 114–16, 118, 121, 136, 138–39, 150, 152, 164–65 167; *The Democratic Constitution*, 114–16, 120–21, 139, 165. *See also* Future Vision documents
Agranat Commission of Inquiry, 99
al-Ahali, 167–68
Albanians in Macedonia, 17–18
Alon, Yigal, 55, 63, 189n47
al-Aqsa Mosque, 123–24, 143
Arab Association for Human Rights (HRA), 139, 140, 144, 152, 167
Arab Center for Alternative Planning (ACAP), 137, 139, 144, 152, 164–65, 167–68, 199n96, 201n123
Arab Democratic Party (ADP), 6, 126, 127–29, 133–34, 138, 148, 150, 158, 160, 203n52
Arab Higher Committee (AHC), 50–51
Arab revolt, 48
Arafat, Yassir, 131
al-Ard (the Land), 86
Ariel, 142
Ashkenazim (Jews of European descent), 100, 154–55, 162, 175
Assefat Hanivcharim, 43
Association for Civil Rights in Israel (ACRI), 35, 136, 138, 145, 163–65

Association of Forty, 65, 167, 190n64
Avineri, Shlomo, 125, 179n9

Balad (National Democratic Assembly), 6, 123, 129–31, 133–34, 151, 153, 158, 189n52, 200n105, 202n26
Balfour Declaration, 46, 186n39
Baltic region, 39
Baluchis (Iran), 20
Banki, 80
Barak, Ehud, 64, 157, 160–61, 178
Barakeh, Mohammed, 132
Baransi, Salah, 86
Basic Laws: Freedom of Occupation, 162, 165; The Government, 156; Human Dignity and Liberty, 162, 165; Israel Lands, 58, 188n21; The Judiciary, 162, 204n65; The Knesset, 147, 201n6
Basques (Spain), 25, 40
Bedouins in the Negev, 58, 60, 65, 150. *See also* unrecognized villages
Begin, Menachem, 97
Ben-Gurion, David, 43, 45, 51, 54, 56, 87, 97, 187n66, 193n66
Binational: Arab demand for, 1, 4, 119, 129, 137; British and binationalism, 47; political parties, 12, 23, 71, 75, 132, 134; road to binationalism, 159
Bishara, Azmi, 123, 129–32, 151, 153
Biton, Charlie, 75, 78
Black Panthers, 75, 78, 99–100
Britain, 38, 46, 89. *See also* British Mandate
British Mandate for Palestine, 5, 12, 25, 42, 45, 46–48, 51, 52, 72, 81, 84, 177
Brubaker, Rogers, 16, 18, 24, 183n45

Acknowledgments

When I decided to write a book about the evolution of Arab political activism in Israel, I knew I would be dealing with highly sensitive issues. Indeed, one will be hard pressed to find studies of political issues that are as embroiled in normative controversies as those relating to Palestinian-Jewish relations. Several years ago, a leading Arab political figure, whose identity shall remain confidential, told me candidly, when we discussed the growing Palestinian ethnocentricity of Arab politics in Israel, "Your analysis of our politics is accurate, but I am worried that presenting it in such a direct way will be very damaging for us." I am not insensitive to the social and political environment in which Arabs in Israel operate. In recent years, suspicion and mistrust of Arabs in Israel have reached new peaks, and proposals to limit Arab participation in political and social life have gained popularity. However, I have always believed that the sensitive nature of the subject matter should not lead academics to sidestep serious questions or varnish findings that might cause discomfort. The role of academic analysts is to expose and analyze the reality they find, even if the conclusions they reach are not congruent with their expectations.

Throughout my work on this book, I have visited magnificent places and met many wonderful people whose contributions sadly I can only acknowledge in passing. I regret that I am bound to omit many who have aided and abetted the project, and hope they will accept my apology.

I am tremendously indebted to Emanuel Adler. I was extraordinarily fortunate to meet him when I began my research at the University of Toronto. Emanuel provided caring guidance and thoughtful suggestions. He read several very early versions, and his comments and criticism were always insightful and sound. I am also particularly grateful to Joel Migdal and Ian Lustick, two intellectual beacons. Joel's mentorship of junior scholars is second to none (he received the Distinguished Mentor Award at the University of Washington). His state-in-society approach has been incredibly illuminating and has provided intellectual direction to many students of politics. Ian's earlier work on Arabs in Israel provoked some of the questions asked in this book. I am grateful to both of them for numerous stimulating conversations. Both provided helpful comments on related papers at the early stages of the project.

Many other people provided feedback on earlier drafts, chapters, and related presentations at various institutions and conferences. I thank Richard Sandbrook and Joe Carens at the University of Toronto; my colleagues at the Ethnicity and Democratic Governance Project and the Research Group on Nationalism, Ethnicity, and Multiculturalism, Bruce Berman, Jacques Bertrand, Zsuzsa Csergo, Will Kymlicka, André Laliberté, John McGarry, and Margaret Moore; and my friends and colleagues at Queen's University and other institutions, Scott Matthews, Ilan Peleg, and Dov Waxman. We have held many intellectually stimulating discussions on state-minority relations, the politics of ethnicity and nationalism, and the Middle East conflict. The anonymous reviewers of the manuscript provided invaluable comments that turned this work into a much better book.

Research for this book required several field trips to Israel in the summers of 2003 and 2005–2007 and in 2010. Casual conversations and nonstructured interviews were held in 2005, 2006, and 2010. I wish to give special thanks to the many people who agreed to talk to me and expose some of the less visible, and often less pleasant, aspects of the internal dynamics of Arab politics in Israel. Many of them have asked not to be listed or mentioned by name, and their indispensable contribution will remain anonymous.

Part of this work was generously supported by the Social Science and Humanities Research Council of Canada. I am also grateful for the financial support I received from the Advisory Research Committee at Queen's University and institutional support at Queen's. In addition, I would like to acknowledge the Truman Institute for the Advancement of Peace at the Hebrew University of Jerusalem and the Moshe Dayan Center for Middle Eastern and African Studies at Tel Aviv University for their support during the final stages of this project.

I wish to thank Brendan O'Leary, editor of the series on National and Ethnic Conflict in the Twenty-First Century, Bill Finan, Developmental Editor, and all the editorial team at the University of Pennsylvania Press, for their support and belief in this project and for all the hard work they put into publishing this book.

My family has been extremely supportive. My parents, who live in Jeru-

salem, were always eager to have me reside in their home while doing fieldwork. They always made me feel that as far as they were concerned, the more
fieldwork the better. I am grateful to them. More than anyone, I am indebted
to Na'ama, Maya, and Tom. The support that my partner for life and children
have given me so that this book can be completed is beyond what anyone
should ever ask for. This book is dedicated to them.

Portions of the text appeared in an earlier form in "State Mutability and Ethnic Civil Society: The Palestinian Arab Minority in Israel," *Ethnic and Racial
Studies* 32, 5 (2009): 864–82. Reprinted by permission of Taylor and Francis.